# VALIANT
# WOMEN

# VALIANT WOMEN

The Extraordinary American Servicewomen
Who Helped Win World War II

## LENA ANDREWS

MARINER BOOKS
*New York   Boston*

HarperCollins books may be purchased for educational, business,
or sales promotional use. For information, please email the
Special Markets Department at SPsales@harpercollins.com.

FIRST EDITION

*Designed by Renata DiBiase*

Library of Congress Cataloging-in-Publication Data has been applied for.

ISBN 978-0-06-308833-7

23 24 25 26 27  LBC  5 4 3 2 1

*For the women who did their part*

Our debt to the heroic men and valiant women in the service of our country can never be repaid. They have earned our undying gratitude. America will never forget their sacrifices.

—President Harry Truman, April 16, 1945

# CONTENTS

---

\* Chapter titles are drawn from World War II military recruiting posters.

# Contents

## Part II: The Solution

# ORGANIZATIONAL CHART OF
# US MILITARY WOMEN'S PROGRAMS

## DEPARTMENT OF WAR
Secretary Henry Stimson

## UNITED STATES ARMY
General George Marshall, Chief of Staff

## UNITED STATES ARMY AIR FORCES
General Henry "Hap" Arnold,
Commander

### WOMEN'S AIRFORCE SERVICE PILOTS (WASP)
Jacqueline Cochran,
Director

### WOMEN'S ARMY CORPS (WAC)
Colonel Oveta Culp Hobby,
Director

## UNITED STATES MARINE CORPS
General Thomas Holcomb, Commandant (1936–1943)
General Alexander Vandegrift, Commandant (1944–1947)

## MARINE CORPS WOMEN'S RESERVE (MCWR)
Colonel Ruth Cheney Streeter, Director

President Franklin Roosevelt

DEPARTMENT OF THE NAVY

Secretary William Franklin "Frank" Knox (1940–1944)

Secretary James Forrestal (1944–1947)

UNITED STATES NAVY

Admiral Ernest King, Chief of Naval Operations

WOMEN ACCEPTED
FOR VOLUNTEER
EMERGENCY
SERVICE (WAVES)

Captain
Mildred McAfee,
Director

UNITED STATES COAST GUARD

Admiral Russell Waesche, Commandant

COAST GUARD WOMEN'S RESERVE (SPARS)

Captain Dorothy Stratton, Director

# VALIANT
# WOMEN

# "THANK YOU FOR EVEN THINKING OF ME"

The future of women in the military
seems assured. . . . What may be lost in
time is the story of how it happened.

—LIEUTENANT COLONEL CHARITY ADAMS EARLEY

"OH MY GOD, THERE ARE PEOPLE OUT THERE WHO still care about me?"

Merle Caples* and I had just spent almost an hour and a half on the phone, and were well over the allotted time for our interview. We were finishing up a lively discussion about the Marine Corps war hero John Basilone and his wife, Lena, whom Merle knew from her time at Camp Pendleton in California during World War II, and I was exhausted from trying to keep up.

But Merle showed no signs of tiring. At ninety-eight, her eyesight was deteriorating, as was some of her hearing, but her memory was sharp and she had the conversational stamina to match. Merle had shared many stories about her work during the war—she

---

* I use women's maiden names throughout the text, except in the prologue, acknowledgments, and notes. A reference list of women interviewed for the book, including both their maiden and married names, can be found in the sources section, under "Veteran and Family Interviews."

distributed supplies and equipment to men on their way to the front lines—but insisted that there was still more to tell. She urged me to be in touch with her daughter, Amy, to arrange another interview.

Merle was humble about nearly everything in her story, from the difficulty of her upbringing during the Depression to the importance of her service and even the state of her memory. Even so, I knew in the first five minutes of talking with her that she would be featured in this book. She had the type of story that grabs you instantly and was willing to be honest about the good and the bad of it all. Most important, she loved to talk about her experiences. She just needed someone to listen.

I found Merle the same way that I found many of the other living veterans whom I tracked down for this book, through a feature in a local newspaper. The women usually appeared in the personal-interest piece of the week, whether it was an announcement celebrating the veteran's 100th—or 108th—birthday, or a story about a veteran being honored at a professional sports game. In one very special case, it was an article featuring a veteran who had just gone skydiving for her 102nd birthday. Whenever I saw mention of a woman who served in World War II, I reached out to ask if they were willing to talk with me.

Like Merle, many of the women I interviewed were surprised by my interest, noting that until recently, few people outside the veterans' community cared much about their service. Though many of the women appreciated the sudden attention, they often wished it had come earlier, when their memories were sharper. "My memory's not very good now," warned one of the women I interviewed, adding, "I got old."

Their surprise was also a product of humility. Uniformly, the women I spoke with were modest about the contribution they made during their service, thinking it small in the grand scheme of things. "Thank you for even thinking of me," said another woman at the end of our first conversation.

In part, this humility is the product of generational attitudes about contributing to the war effort. Many men who served in World War II were also uneasy about celebrations of their service, believing firmly that they simply did their part and that doing the right thing

Merle [Selma] Caples on a military base in World War II (*top*). Caples celebrates her one hundredth birthday (*bottom*).
**Courtesy Caples Family.**

should not be deemed exceptional. Too often, however, the reservations of the women I interviewed were tinged with a troubling undercurrent, an unspoken sense that the work they did was too small, too peripheral, too feminine to count in a meaningful way.

How heartbreaking to learn that these incredible women feel this way.

Though I found this belief to be frustratingly commonplace among both the women veterans themselves and the American public, it is also groundless. The American women who donned military uniforms in World War II were, on the contrary, at the center of the Allied strategy for fighting and winning the war. These women were the critical link between the home front and the front lines that allowed the United States to defeat, near simultaneously and on opposite sides of the world, the German, Japanese, and Italian militaries. There is an indisputable line connecting the American victory in World War II to the contributions of women who served in the United States military, and it is time we acknowledged it.

This book is an attempt to correct the record. It begins with a simple set of facts. More than three hundred and fifty thousand American women served in uniform during World War II. They served in every service, in every combat theater, and in nearly two-thirds of the available military occupations at the time. Abroad, these women were sometimes mere miles away from the front lines, and they were directly involved in some of the most important moments of the war, caring for the wounded on the beaches of North Africa, following the front after the D-Day landings, and crash-landing in the Pacific. Many were injured or died for their country, and many received the nation's highest honors. Their stories are moving, shocking, and worthy of as many books as have been written on men's participation in this landmark conflict.

However, this book is more than just a recollection of note-worthy stories about the women who fought in World War II. It is also an invitation to look at this old war in a different way—to ask, What larger truths are revealed when we change our perspective?

That is where things get interesting. When we look at World War II from the standpoint of the hundreds of thousands of American women who served in it, we find that they can teach us a great deal about how the war was fought and why the Allies won.

This new perspective reveals that the requirements of total war in the modern era stretch the capacity of even the largest and best prepared combatants. It reveals that women were necessary in World War II because victory required an unprecedented supply and support infrastructure to sustain forces on the front lines, and, for the first time in American history, these demands could not be met by the male population alone. It reveals that although the United States won this war with men serving on the front lines, it also won the war with the contributions of women in uniform serving in unprecedentedly diverse roles, filling the gaps that those men left behind.

These gaps were everywhere. Not only did women work behind thousands of desks doing clerical and administrative tasks, but they also worked, often for the first time, in an extraordinarily diverse set of military occupations. They served as pilots, aircraft trainers, photo interpreters, gunnery instructors, radiomen, metal-smiths, machinist's mates, chemists, codebreakers, classification experts, lab technicians, translators, parachute riggers, ordnance experts, weather observers, control tower operators, mechanics, truck drivers, radarmen, quartermasters, pigeon trainers, and much more.

In these and many other roles, American women in uniform had a direct and outsize impact on the US war effort, especially in the support functions that underwrote the Allied victory. If we want to fully understand why the Allies won this war, then we must understand its women.

# "AMERICA WILL BE AS STRONG AS HER WOMEN"

ON A COOL SUMMER EVENING IN 1939, HUNDREDS of paper lanterns danced across the lawn of Paradise Pond in Northampton, Massachusetts, where the graduating women of Smith College's senior class had gathered near midnight. For weeks, the women had been looking forward to the evening— appropriately called Illumination Night—which was a revered tradition on campus and the high point of the graduation events.

Standing in locked arms among the neatly arranged lights, the graduates each held a small candle as they serenaded each other with songs from the campus songbook. Thousands of alumnae, who had returned to campus for the occasion, surrounded the women. Amid the buzz of commencement celebrations, the ritual provided an unusual moment of collective, peaceful reflection.

But for Ann Baumgartner, who stood in the crowd thinking hard about her future, the stillness of the night offered little reprieve from the nagging question that had been turning over in her mind for weeks: "Would I always be an observer of life?" she wondered.

Baumgartner had enjoyed her time at Smith. Forgoing her interest in art, she decided on a premed major, hoping that courses in advanced chemistry and zoology would satisfy her burgeoning interest in science. Baumgartner discovered, however, that while she liked science, she lacked the passion and focus necessary to make it a career. She often found herself daydreaming of different paths to pursue, "something with adventure and daring to it," as she put it in her memoir, but nothing stuck. By graduation, she had reluctantly settled on pursuing medicine, but the prospect of more school seemed daunting and dull. "Would I really want to, or be able to, spend four or more years inside dreary laboratories in old, however hallowed, buildings?"

Baumgartner felt unsettled about not having a firm grasp on the direction of her life in part because she had inherited high expectations for herself from the women in her family. Her mother, Margaret, was an artist, trained in New York at the Parsons School of Art and Design, and her aunt, Frances, was an opera singer. Her grandmother had been a dean of women at several colleges, as well as the hardworking wife of a Colorado rancher. Baumgartner's mother often reminded her of the storied family lineage, "a colorful, active lot," she remembered, that allegedly traced its roots back to Mary, Queen of Scots. With this in mind, when Baumgartner's parents saw her floundering after graduating from Smith, they booked her a ticket to visit her mother's family in England.

As frustrated as Baumgartner may have felt about her predicament, she, at least, had recourse to do something about it. Unlike Baumgartner, many American women in 1939 had no other option but to carry out the minutiae of their days, listless and bored, whether or not they found it particularly satisfying. Joy Lemmon, for instance, painted teacups at a factory in east Tennessee. Evelyn Zahn, having recently graduated from high school, looked for work as far away from her hometown as possible. Jessie Kontrabecki, also a recent high school graduate, started her new job at a shredded wheat plant in upstate New York. Charity Adams taught math and science at a junior high school in South Carolina. Mary

Sears, a Harvard-trained planktonologist, settled into her job at the Woods Hole Oceanographic Institution. And Baumgartner, feeling alone and adrift, boarded a ship to Europe.

Even by military standards, it was early for a phone call.

Just before four in the morning on September 1, 1939, military officers around Washington were being jolted awake by the shriek of a telephone. Only a few words were exchanged, but they were followed by a cascade of bedroom lights flickering on, uniforms being pulled from their hangers, front doors slamming shut, and polished shoes tapping down the sidewalk.

Early or not, it was time to get to work.

Any other summer, such a call would have been unusual. The final days of August in Washington are typically quiet, as its residents, especially the more distinguished among them, scatter in every direction to escape the oppressive humidity that coats the city. It is as if there is an implicit agreement with the rest of the world that crises can wait until after Labor Day weekend, when the city is a bit more bearable.

But the summer of 1939 was different. Washington had spent much of the previous three years watching warily as Adolf Hitler made evident his hostile designs on Europe. In that time, German military forces had fanned out in every direction with ruthless efficiency: marching west into Rhineland and reoccupying the territory sitting on the border of Germany and Belgium; annexing Austria to the south and Sudetenland, sitting astride the Czech and German border to the east; and, in an especially brazen move, occupying Czechoslovakia. The rest of the world watched on as European allies were mired in disputes about how best to respond and, for the most part, chose to do whatever was necessary to avert another world war, even if that meant conceding to Hitler's increasingly aggressive demands.

It was no surprise, then, that on that muggy September morning in Washington, the offices of the Munitions Building, the predecessor to the Pentagon that housed the Army's top brass, were uncharacteristically busy. The stunning news of Hitler's next move had broken hours earlier, proclaimed loudly and unequivocally by the *New York Times*: GERMAN ARMY ATTACKS POLAND.

That same morning, a man sporting a simple white suit and close-cropped silver hair walked up the steps of the Munitions Building and began his day.

General George Catlett Marshall Jr. had, literally, just been promoted. As of 11 a.m. on the day Germany invaded Poland, Marshall was officially appointed as Army chief of staff. His swearing-in had been a straightforward affair, repeating the oath of office that everyone in the Army chain of command takes when promoted to a new position. But as Marshall recited those familiar words, swearing "to support and defend the Constitution of the United States of America against all enemies, foreign and domestic," he could not possibly have known how difficult a task it would be.

Marshall, coming off a yearlong duty as deputy Army chief of staff, had a reputation for providing unvarnished, and sometimes unpopular, military advice, which made him one of the most highly regarded military commanders in Washington. Wherever Marshall went, accolades seemed to follow. Soon-to-be secretary of war Henry Stimson would later refer to Marshall as "the finest soldier I have ever known." He was a natural choice for the job.

Marshall would have been among the first to know of the Poland invasion. He quickly called his staff to ensure that they were closely monitoring developments as the day progressed, since Marshall himself was stuck in meetings for most of the morning. Almost immediately after his swearing-in, he was called over to the White House along with the rest of the Navy and War Department leadership to meet with President Franklin Roosevelt.

With his preternatural calm, Marshall walked into the Oval Office and delivered his first message as head of the United States Army:

The war—one that everyone in the room had desperately tried to avoid—had just begun.

In 1939, barely two decades after World War I, the reality was that many Americans were not interested in fighting another war. As Hitler and his forces charged through swaths of continental Europe and the Japanese military marched through similarly large expanses of Chinese territory, a significant portion of the American public expressed only a perfunctory concern about the developing conflict, remaining opposed to any involvement in the spreading violence. This was especially true in the Midwest, an electoral bloc critical to Roosevelt's political coalition, where there was loud opposition to any American participation in a struggle against enemies seen only as a distant threat. The world may have been at war but the United States, quite adamantly, was not.

Americans had good reasons for their disinterest in the approaching conflict. The public still carried vivid memories of the punishing combat of World War I in their minds: almost 5 million Americans had served in uniform; over 53,000 of them had died in combat; and over 200,000 had returned home wounded. Many Americans were shocked and angered by the physical and psychological toll of the injuries these men suffered defending far-flung European allies. When combined with a deep-seated popular distrust of profiteering government and business elites, who made fortunes from the war and then ran the American economy into the ground, the last thing that many Americans wanted to do was start preparing for another bruising global conflict.

This lack of concern, however, left President Roosevelt in a precarious position: from one direction, he saw the threat of global war darkening the horizon; and, from the other, he heard the rumbling of the antiwar contingent in his electoral coalition. Stuck squarely in the middle—and with his political future hanging in the balance—Roosevelt had to find a way to prepare for one storm without creating another.

This dynamic left the US military in particularly dire straits in the summer of 1939. The American public had spent most of the twenties and thirties insisting that the US military significantly curtail its size and spending, and, for the most part, the military had complied. They slashed budgets, slimmed rosters, and made do with outdated equipment. As a result, on the day Poland was invaded, the US Army "ranked approximately seventeenth in effectiveness among the armies of the world, just behind that of R[o]mania." Regular US Army strength totaled fewer than 200,000 soldiers and contained zero complete divisions. This was nowhere near enough to fight, let alone defeat, the forces making their way through Europe and Asia.

For the military elite, the solution was obvious: money and resources needed to be spent immediately if the United States was going to be prepared to fight a war. But, somehow, this would have to be done without raising the hackles of the still powerful antiwar contingent of Roosevelt's political coalition. It was a tricky balance, but one that had to be struck. Marshall would be the man responsible for pulling it off.

Even as Marshall and Roosevelt struggled to generate widespread popular support for undertaking war preparations, however, pockets of approval for increasing US involvement did exist among some Americans. On the day that Hitler ordered his forces into Poland, Baumgartner added herself to their ranks.

At the conclusion of her summer trip through Europe, Baumgartner arrived in Salisbury, England, to visit her extended family. The threat of war had stalked her travel throughout the voyage, but, with the German invasion of Poland, it had become a reality. On the morning of the attack, Baumgartner's two uncles—

one of whom was Vernon Kell, head of the British domestic security service, MI5—and a friend were huddled in the family home, exchanging hushed calls as the day's events unfolded. "The women walked the garden," remembered Baumgartner, and "played a desultory game of croquet."

As the day went on, Baumgartner recalled, it became clear that she and her mother would need to return to the United States as soon as possible. Relying on her uncle's connections, they secured tickets back to the United States on a Dutch steamer. The ship, with its close, damp quarters, dim lights, overflowing bathrooms, and blacked-out portholes, was nothing like the upscale steamboat that she arrived on. Just as the ship passed the Statue of Liberty and pulled into New York Harbor, it ran out of food and water.

But the onset of war, as dark as it seemed, was exactly the jolt Baumgartner needed to pull her out of her malaise. As she stepped off the steamer, she thought, "This was a time to settle down, at last . . . with the goal of helping in the war effort ahead."


Nine months after Baumgartner returned to New York, on the morning of May 13, 1940, Marshall found himself back on the couch of the Oval Office, again the bearer of bad news.

Three days prior, having received early reports of Germany's invasion of the Low Countries and France, Roosevelt had ordered Marshall—along with Secretary of the Treasury Henry Morgenthau Jr.—to present him with an overall sense of the military and monetary increases necessary to meet the growing German threat. "Get all of this together," Roosevelt demanded.

Roosevelt was right to be worried. On the morning of May 10, Hitler had directed his forces to undertake what would become known as one of the most significant tactical and operational surprises in the history of modern warfare. Flouting the expectations of most military observers at the time, the German forces had executed an invasion that was an unparalleled display of integrated, combined arms operations. The initial assault consisted of a three-pronged attack: first, a diversion in Holland and Belgium; then, the main attack into France through the densely wooded Ardennes Forest; and, finally, a screen in the south to prevent counterattack. It was a classic military feint, and it worked near perfectly.

The plan was executed so quickly and effectively that it even shocked German leadership, including Hitler himself. Though it would take six weeks for the German forces to overrun France, most observers predicted a sweeping defeat within days of the initial assault. France, with its seemingly impenetrable borders and huge land army, was falling.

Given the deteriorating circumstances on the European continent, Marshall expected to at least get a fair hearing at the White House, but he barely got a word in. Roosevelt kicked off the meeting by taking Morgenthau to task, rejecting his proposal to develop an advisory committee, and then cut him off when it came to discussions of military buildup. By the end of the meeting, Roosevelt was threatening to cut, rather than increase, the Army's allocated funding.

Recognizing that the Oval Office meeting was rapidly devolving and that Morgenthau was in danger of losing the critical funding that the military would need, Marshall made his move. "Recalling that a man has a great advantage, psychologically, when he stands looking down at a fellow," remembered Marshall, "I took advantage, in a sense, of the President's condition." Marshall walked over to the President's desk, where Roosevelt, confined to his wheelchair, was forced to look up at Marshall's six-foot frame towering above him.

In an unusual admission of his mood, Marshall raised his voice ever so slightly, and said, "I don't know quite how to express myself about this to the president of the United States, but

I will say this: you have got to do something, and you've got to do it today."


World War II was unprecedented in size and scale by almost every measure. The numbers speak for themselves. The United States alone required over 16 million personnel to fight the war, more combatants than any American war before or after, of which more than 400,000 died and 600,000 were wounded. The United States also produced an extraordinary amount of equipment to support these forces and its allies: over 2 million military trucks, 80,000 tanks, 300,000 aircraft, and 1,200 combatant vessels.

But what drove America's remarkable military heft is a less-well-known fact. World War II, while unparalleled in its scale, was equally exceptional in *how* it was fought. This war ushered in the use of innovative doctrines like amphibious assault, strategic bombing, and joint combined arms, among others, that would revolutionize warfare for generations to come. Moreover, advanced technologies like radar, aircraft, submarines, aircraft carriers, and the internal combustion engine were at the center of battlefield operations in World War II, and the conflict spurred the development of the jet engine, the long-range rocket, and, perhaps most significant, the atomic bomb. This war was cutting-edge.

During the interwar years, American military leaders, who had been monitoring these advancements closely, were trying to meet the anticipated challenges of the modern battlefield head-on. Trench warfare and pitched battles for meters-long strips of territory were relics of the past. Commanders knew the victors of tomorrow would need to levy massive armies, in integrated formations, loaded to the brim with modern, mechanized armaments, and send them charging into combat.

In principle, these commanders also understood that the noncombat demands of this type of warfare, and especially supply and support functions, could act as a firm brake on the pace, efficiency, and success of battlefield operations. Most of them, after all, had seen a preview of the staggering logistical challenges of modern warfare during World War I. The Great War, as it was known then, delivered a reckoning for American policymakers and commanders when it came to the logistics and support, and it was a harrowing one. During active US participation in the war, military commanders were often forced to rely on European suppliers to meet their needs, since American leaders had failed to anticipate the demands of sending two million uniformed personnel to Europe with all their military equipment in tow. As Marshall remembered it twenty years later, the US forces had arrived on World War I battlefields a ragtag group, "everything begged, borrowed, or stolen—certainly not manufactured in America."

The American performance in World War I had been particularly disappointing to US commanders because the importance of supply and support had been axiomatic for generations of senior military leaders. From Hannibal to Napoleon to Antoine-Henri Jomini, the military theorists studied by American commanders had argued that supply and support operations should be taken as seriously and planned as meticulously as the advance of their infantry. They argued that there should be a tight link between strategy and support and, specifically, that the limits of the latter should inform the scope and goals of the former. It was one thing to demand that your forces advance into battle, they pointed out, but it was quite another to ensure that those forces arrived fully equipped at the appointed time, with the tools, fuel, and food to sustain and enhance the effect of such a move. They knew militaries that lacked the equipment, or the *working* equipment; the troops, or the *trained* troops; and the food, or the *edible* food, in exactly the right place at exactly the right time, would lose. As military analyst James Dunnigan put it, "If you want to determine who is going to win a future war, examine the supply situation first."

While American commanders understood in theory that support functions would be important in the coming war, several reinforcing features of World War II made implementing this infrastructure especially difficult. First, the United States needed to produce highly mechanized equipment that was relatively technical and sophisticated for the time. Second, American commanders demanded extraordinary quantities of this equipment, and an unprecedented number of people and machines to build it and man it. Finally, this equipment needed to be transported across distances that, quite literally, spanned the globe. Together, these variables snowballed into a set of demands on support functions in World War II that were unmatched in the modern era. The American military would need to build, train, move, supply, and maintain a force of a size and sophistication that could wage multiple battles on multiple fronts in multiple parts of the world, near simultaneously, and with a mountain of new equipment in tow. It would be a colossal undertaking.

By 1940, even civilians and political leaders had begun to understand the magnitude of the challenge they would soon face. Most important, the president himself had caught on. In his May 1940 fireside chat, as France was falling, Roosevelt assured the American public that early investments in men and materiel had prepared the United States for the specter of war that was looming in Europe. "We have spent large sums of money on the national defense," he reported; "This money has been used to make our Army and Navy today the largest, the best equipped, and the best trained peace-time military establishment in the whole history of this country." Roosevelt then went into detail. In the preceding seven years, he stated, the Navy alone had laid down or commissioned over 200 ships, the Army Air Forces had purchased 6,000 planes, and the Army had undergone a massive transformation, including the purchase of 1,400 new antiaircraft guns, 1,500 modern infantry mortars, and 1,600 tanks and armored vehicles. He concluded by reassuring the American people that the US military was prepared for what was to come: "We are constantly improving and redesigning, testing new weapons, learning the lessons of the immediate war, and seeking to produce in accordance with the latest that the brains of science can conceive."

But even as Roosevelt assured the public of American preparedness, he and his commanders knew that production was just the first link in the complex support chain that moved equipment and men to battlefields around the world. Marshall and his colleagues needed to build the rest of that chain and, even for the most experienced commanders, the enormity of this undertaking was daunting.

Marshall, however, was a highly adept military planner, and he understood that there was, in fact, a straightforward solution to the problem they faced: people—and lots of them. "Personnel is our most serious deficiency," he testified in May 1940, "in light of the requirements that are being brought to bear on the War Department."

Marshall recognized that the requirements of the impending war necessitated simultaneously increasing manpower* in three places. First, the military needed people in the industrial sector to build the materiel on which Roosevelt's strategy depended; second, they needed people to do the actual fighting; and, third, the military needed people to connect the two—personnel who would ensure that soldiers, sailors, airmen, and Marines on the front lines received training and equipment when and how they needed it. People were the glue that would hold the US military's support infrastructure together and sustain the American strategy for winning the war—if only Marshall could find enough of them. Staring down this enormous undertaking, senior military commanders

---

* Although the US military has worked in recent years to update its lexicon to be more gender neutral, there are gendered terms still in use, such as "manpower," "airman," and "guardsman," that are intended to include both men and women in uniform. The original terms are used throughout the text for the purpose of accuracy.

reluctantly arrived at a conclusion that would alter the course of hundreds of thousands of lives: they would need women.

In 1940, most American women had little idea of just how much their lives were about to change, but Baumgartner certainly wished hers would. Having returned from Europe newly focused, she longed to find work supporting the Allies in Europe but had made few inroads. So far, all she had managed to do was get fired from her job testing fish oil on lab rats, for making an insulting remark about a German boss (fairly, she protested, since "he did wear his hair like Hitler").

On a hot summer evening in 1940, after an especially frustrating day at her job, Baumgartner stood on the roof of a New Jersey high-rise, looked up at the gray sky, and sighed. Then, just above the skyline, she saw the small black silhouette of a plane cutting through the clouds.

"I shall learn to fly," she thought.

Ann Baumgartner stands with an aircraft at Avenger Field, Sweetwater, Texas. **Courtesy of WASP Archive, Texas Woman's University, Denton, Texas.**

PART I

# THE PROBLEM

# 1

# "THE FIGHTING FILIPINOS"

## THE WAR ARRIVES

AS BAUMGARTNER SET A NEW COURSE IN LIFE, DOR-othy Still, a Navy nurse assigned to a base in the Philippines, was well into her own adventure. Still, a California native who had never even ventured out of state before joining the military, had been transferred to the Philippines about a year earlier. The posting had already been transformative.

Still was assigned to Cañacao Naval Hospital, just outside Manila. Although she found her work rather routine, mostly attending to sailors with various tropical diseases, she was enamored of the exotic setting. She became fascinated by the base's history and spent hours going through the hospital's archives, recording her observations on a newly purchased Underwood typewriter. On slower days, she watched the Navy's planes fly in formation over Cañacao Bay. "I loved to stand next to my special little lighthouse on the seawall, the farthest one down," she remembered in her memoir, adding "shivers ran up and down my spine when I watched Pat[rol] Wing 10's PBYs roar overhead in the V-formation, and I almost felt the spray of water when they touched down."

Between the dances, beaches, golf courses, and American movies shipped in from Hollywood, a posting to the Philippines before the war sometimes resembled a colonial vacation destination more than a military installation. The scene was vibrant, buzzing with energy and youthful vitality—"Formals and party dresses were an absolute must"—and most of the nurses were elated to be there. By 1941, Still, like many of the nurses stationed there, knew she had hit the professional jackpot, leaving behind a predictable civilian life on the mainland for the dreamy thrill of military life in the Pacific. So far, she had not been disappointed. "A delightful setting by day," wrote Still, the base "became a fantasyland in the colorful twilight hours, and pure magic under the thousands of stars in the night sky. . . . Who could have asked for anything more romantic than this in the moonlight?"

As the year came to a close, Still's only frustration with her posting proved to be her unreliable and arrogant boyfriend, a naval aviator. He had recently been promoted and, even as the prospect of war grew, no longer seemed to be taking their courtship seriously, outright laughing at the suggestion of marriage. Although Still had no intention of getting married, especially since it meant she would be sent home, her boyfriend's lack of interest still stung. After a particularly embarrassing evening, she sat down at her typewriter and penned a letter to him. She snapped out the date atop her stationery, "6 December 1941," but only got as far as the first line, "Dear Johnny," before she decided to go to bed.

What Still did not foresee as she fell asleep that night, fuming over Johnny's slight, was that two days later she would become part of the vanguard of military women in the United States.

General Douglas MacArthur, one of the most highly regarded American military officers of the time, was also enjoying his posting in the Philippines in late 1941. He had a long personal history with the country. Following in the footsteps of his father, who had served as military governor of the Philippines, MacArthur had

Navy Nurse Corps recruiting poster. **Courtesy National Archives, photo no. 516022.**

been posted there in the 1920s, and by the time he retired from the Army in the late thirties, he had accumulated two more tours in the country. When MacArthur's tour as chief of staff of the Army ended in 1934, the president-elect of the Philippines personally asked him to assist with developing the national defense forces of the newly liberated country. MacArthur agreed, and was happy to be back.

MacArthur's rationale for taking the posting was as much professional as it was personal. He felt a connection with and an obligation to the country and wanted to help ensure it could defend itself against the growing Japanese aggression in the region. At the end of 1935, he estimated that "it would take a full ten years and much help from the United States" to improve the island's defenses. "As it turned out," he added, "neither was forthcoming."

By 1941, it was impossible for MacArthur and his senior commanders to ignore the Japanese threat. Not only were the Japanese fully mobilized for war and making steady battlefield progress against the Chinese, whom they had been fighting for four years, but, in the fall of 1940, they had also captured French Indochina. The Japanese occupation of this key territory put them at the doorstep of American holdings in the Pacific. Then, on the heels of their successful offensive, the Japanese signed the Tripartite Pact with Germany and Italy, a bald statement of their strategic ambitions. Japanese revisionism in the region was now impossible to ignore.

Recognizing the Japanese designs for what they were, MacArthur was growing increasingly frustrated with the lack of American support in the region. He complained that "Washington had not, during this time, offered any meaningful assistance to Filipino defense plans," even as the Japanese steadily encroached on the island nation. Congress and the White House could see what was coming, he argued, but chose to do nothing about it.

Military leaders, however, did have one advantage in their favor: contingency planning. Then and now, the American military often planned for wars, even if they did not necessarily expect to fight them, in order to identify and resolve operational challenges before they arose in combat. In the 1930s, American military commanders had done just that, developing a series of plans for combat with a wide range of individual countries. Each of these plans was assigned its own color: red for war with the British, black for war with Germany, gold for war with France, and green for war with Mexico. "Plan Orange," the most relevant to commanders in the Philippines, envisioned an "offensive naval war in the Pacific with the Philippines as the main base." MacArthur and his team used its recommendations to implement as many preparatory measures as they could.

Adding to the insights of the individual color plans, the Army and Navy had also started to focus on more likely contingencies, including the possibility of a multifront war, and, in 1939, combined several of the individual color plans into the cleverly titled "Rainbow Plans." By late 1940, consensus was growing around a variant of these plans that envisioned fighting a two-front war—a primary effort focused on an offensive in Europe and a secondary element tasked with defensive operations in the Pacific—known as Rainbow 5.

In reality, however, the US military in the early 1940s was barely able to undertake one large-scale offensive, let alone simultaneous engagements in Europe *and* the Pacific. "We stand to lose everywhere and win nowhere," warned a concerned Marshall, for whom it had become clear that the United States would need to do more than plan for a military conflict in the abstract. By the summer of 1941, he knew it was time to concretely prepare for war in the Pacific.

To start, Marshall recalled MacArthur to active duty in July 1941 and appointed him as commander of the combined Philippine and American forces under the newly formed US Army Forces in the Far East (USAFFE). MacArthur accepted the appointment and "began an eleventh-hour struggle to build up enough force to repel an enemy."

Soon after, military leaders decided it was time to bolster the troops and equipment posted in the region. By December, over thirty thousand American and Filipino troops were added to the personnel stationed on the island, a fifty percent increase in just over three months. Along with this growth in personnel, over 100,000 ship tons of equipment was already on its way to the island by the end of 1941, including 130 light artillery pieces and 60 heavy guns, and 200,000 additional ship tons were ready for shipment, including several new 90 mm antiaircraft guns that had just finished testing stateside.

Moreover, the scope of reinforcement was soon expected to

grow. In early December 1941, Marshall had written a letter to MacArthur assuring him of his intention—by April 1942—to "meet to the fullest extent possible your recommendations for personnel and equipment necessary to defend the Philippines." In fact, on December 7, 1941, a convoy of American ships was on its way to the island, loaded with 52 dive bombers, 18 P-40 fighters, 9,000 drums of aviation fuel, 340 motor vehicles, 48 additional 75 mm guns, 2 light-field-artillery battalions, over 3 million rounds of ammunition, and 600 tons of bombs.

This, however, would prove to be too little, too late. The next day, just before dawn on December 8 in Manila—and December 7 in Hawaii—reports began to trickle into USAFFE headquarters that Japanese forces had attacked Pearl Harbor. By breakfast, Americans and Filipinos stationed at Camp John Hay, the northernmost base on the Philippines, looked up to see the rising red sun on the underside of Japanese planes flying low overhead.

In combat, darkness can be a tool. So when Dorothy Still was woken up in the dim predawn hours of December 8 from a fitful night of sleep, tossing and turning as she reviewed the case for breaking up with her insensitive and unserious boyfriend, Johnny, she had the presence of mind not to turn on a light. Doing so would have given up the building's position to the Japanese pilots presumed to be circling overhead, and Still, along with all of the nurses posted in the Philippines, had been trained to never, ever turn on lights during night drills. Rushing to get dressed, the nurses took in the shock of the situation and nervously whispered to each other. "You girls ready for a war?" asked one of Still's fellow nurses to no one in particular.

Once outfitted, Still placed blue cellophane over her flashlight and went directly to the place where she would be most needed: the hospital. When she and the other nurses arrived, however, they found nothing out of the ordinary. No blaring air raid sirens and no wounded men being rushed through the doors, just the silence of an empty hospital at dawn. Aside from the shuffle of their feet and hushed murmurs of confusion, it remained quiet in Manila.

As they waited anxiously, the nurses occupied themselves with a list of preplanned war preparations, focused mainly on discharging ambulatory patients and getting them back on duty. With test air raid sirens blasting in the background, Still and the other nurses also received boxes of their new uniforms. The crisp white outfits that had been a hallmark of American nurses around the world were put into storage, replaced by sailors' dungarees and work shirts. Outfitted in their less glamorous but far more functional attire, the nurses heard the low pulse of bombs in the distance.

By midday, Marie Adams, an Army nurse at Fort McKinley in Manila, reported that "there was almost no one left except the hospital staff and patients." American and Filipino ground forces had left the base and were already on the move as US commanders, having learned of the attacks in the north, wanted their ground forces dispersed and in fighting position before the Japanese made it to the city. The American B-17s, as well as the 20th, 17th, 3d, and 24th Pursuit Squadrons that had been circling overhead all morning, had just landed, and their pilots joined the relatively small group of hospital staff on their way to the dining hall for lunch.

But moments after the remaining nurses and pilots had gotten their lunch trays, air raid sirens pierced the silence. The aircraft warning service had spotted the brunt of the Japanese attack: 108 twin-engine bombers and 84 Zeros had flashed by.

On hearing the sirens, pilots scrambled out of the mess hall and sprinted to their planes, as commanders tried to get men into their cockpits and off the ground before the Japanese arrived. Their efforts were largely in vain. The enemy bombers were headed directly for Clark Field, just outside Manila, where the United States had just landed many of its aircraft.

The Japanese planes easily outran the American pilots. Surprised by the sheer number of aircraft sitting like ducks on the runway at Clark Field, the Japanese wasted no time bombarding the airfield. For over an hour, they picked off American planes on the ground, pausing only to strafe the barracks and score direct hits on the installations surrounding the runways. American anti-aircraft units—equipped with outdated munitions and manned by courageous yet unprepared crews—tried to return fire, while the few American pilots who managed to take off put up an equally brave but futile fight.

The Japanese succeeded in a brutal fashion. By the conclusion of the attack, 80 people had been killed and 150 wounded; and, critically for the war effort, the Far East Air Force, a linchpin of American fighting power in the Pacific, had been hollowed out. When combined with the devastatingly similar losses at Pearl Harbor hours earlier, the attacks in the Philippines shattered the façade of American military strength in the Pacific.

With this abrupt and unambiguous violence, the war had finally arrived on American territory. "The fact is that a shooting war is going on today in the Pacific," Roosevelt reported to a joint meeting of the congressional leadership on the evening of December 7, 1941, adding, "We are in it."

With the Japanese invasion, the Army and Navy nurses stationed in the Philippines and at Pearl Harbor became the first women in uniform engaged in World War II. The distinction was unsolicited but fitting, since nurses have been a near-constant presence on American battlefields since the revolution. But the idea of nursing as a profession, and especially military nursing, was still a novel concept well into the twentieth century. Although the nineteenth century had seen a burst of interest in professionalizing the field, there remained a widespread view in the United States that nursing was, by its very nature, indecent. As Evelyn Monahan and Rosemary Neidel-Greenlee state in their study of nurses on the front lines, the profession not only required young women to have knowledge of men's bodies—genitalia and venereal diseases included—but also necessitated physical work considered dirty and demeaning by the standards of the time. "Unmarried women with 'knowledge' of male anatomy, the sexual nature of marital relations, or venereal diseases were automatically suspect in an atmosphere that treated such topics with utmost secrecy and reluctance," they note, adding, "Knowing of these 'sinful' matters was itself proof of indecency."

Given that nursing in general still held some stigma, military nursing was doubly problematic. Both the Army and Navy had established their nurse corps at the turn of the century—the Army Nurse Corps in 1901 and the Navy Nurse Corps in 1908—and had been working to change the image of military nursing ever since. The difficulty was that the military itself had long been considered a bastion for moral indecency and questionable ethics. Hundreds of thousands of men had returned home with sexually transmitted diseases during and after World War I, and most Americans had heard the salacious stories of American troops cavorting with prostitutes and of drunken indecency at bases at home and abroad.

Indeed, military bases and the surrounding towns sometimes garnered deserved reputations for the unsavory behaviors they encouraged. According to one report on the circumstances in Leesville, Louisiana, home of Camp Polk, military and state authorities had worked diligently to "suppress prostitution by eliminating not only the professional prostitute but the sexually promiscuous woman attracted by the possibilities of entertainment and freedom of action in an area in which several hundred thousand soldiers were maneuvering." The public thought that putting a woman, nurse or otherwise, into that environment would be inviting trouble.

Even so, in the 1930s many women and their families, faced with crippling economic depression, reconsidered careers that might have once seemed unappealing. "In the face of staggering unemployment and concerns about a possible approaching war," Monahan and Neidel-Greenlee argue, "the military corps promised comparatively good salaries, a chance to serve one's country, travel to distant places, and gain contact with futures few civilian women would ever see." Or as Army nurse Edith Aynes put it, "I needed a job," and the "pay, considering the depression, was good."

Under the circumstances in the 1930s, many women found themselves responding to the Army and Navy advertisements for nurses. It was regular work, decent pay, and maybe even a little adventure.

By March 1942, the Japanese onslaught of the Philippines that began over the skies of Camp John Hay had left the American position badly deteriorated. In the face of the ill-equipped American and Filipino forces, the Japanese made quick work of their early objectives, and MacArthur had struggled to hold his ground. With the American position worsening, politicians at home became increasingly fearful that MacArthur would be captured and ordered him to leave the island. Despite his loud protestations, MacArthur was forced to transfer his command to Major General Jonathan Wainwright on March 11. MacArthur's final command on the island was a simple one: "Hold on till I come back for you."

By April, the American troops, now under Wainwright's command, were forced to surrender the Bataan peninsula, a key strip of territory west of Manila. Soon after, the remaining American forces pulled back onto Corregidor, a small island outpost just off the coast of Bataan, all but ensuring a surrender.

Even with the dire odds, however, the American and Filipino forces did not roll over in the face of the better-prepared Japanese. Instead, what these units lacked in equipment and training, they made up for in grit and skill, and they worked tirelessly to forestall their fate. Rations were cut in half, twice. Men bolted guns to fishing boats and took out Japanese sniper positions. The American and Filipino forces mounted a scrappy, desperate, and surprisingly entrenched defense, and, as a direct consequence, it took over five months for the Japanese to force a surrender.

Anticipating defeat, Wainwright ordered his commanders to prepare their personnel for the mental and physical ordeal of captivity. The American forces had heard of the notorious brutality that the Japanese inflicted on prisoners of war—only weeks earlier they had heard about the Bataan Death March, when tens of thousands of American and Filipino prisoners of war were forced to walk over sixty miles before being transferred into captivity—and many of the men remaining in the Philippines were girding themselves for a similar fate. With this in mind, American commanders were also deeply worried about the propensity of Japanese forces to commit violent acts of rape and murder against the women left behind, whether civilian or military.

It bears emphasizing that the assault of women during war is, and has always been, vicious, cowardly, and common. The Japanese were certainly not alone in their use of sexual violence against women to terrible effect in World War II, but, even by this standard, some of their attacks on women were especially gruesome. During the St. Stephen's College massacre, for instance, which occurred just weeks after Pearl Harbor, over one hundred Japanese soldiers overran an Allied hospital in Hong Kong and, after bayoneting patients in their beds, repeatedly raped the British, Canadian, and Chinese nurses stationed there. Later, the women were sexually mutilated and left for dead.

Having heard these and other stories—some true, some not—US commanders in the Philippines could not bear the prospect of their nurses suffering the same fate and feared how the American public would react to seeing these horrors splashed across the front page. If MacArthur had to be evacuated for fear

Allied forces in the Corregidor tunnel system during the Japanese advance.
Courtesy National Archives, photo no. 531336.

of how his capture would play in the US media, the same logic held true for the women on the island. The commanders moved to evacuate as many nurses as possible before the surrender.

Despite the risks they faced, however, the nurses were performing essential work. As the Japanese closed in during the early spring of 1942, the Corregidor hospital, squirreled away in a dark, damp tunnel and built to accommodate one thousand patients, was treating five thousand injured troops. These men needed to be cared for, and only a nurse could do the job. Moreover, the Japanese did not provide meaningful medical care for prisoners of war, which meant that captured American soldiers would have to rely on other prisoners to tend to their injuries. If some nurses were in captivity, they could provide that lifesaving care.

Many of the nurses, had they been given the choice, would not have left Corregidor. Alice Zwicker, an Army nurse from Brownville, Maine, put it best when she said, "Even all the rumors of what the Jap[anese] may do to us, and especially the women, mean little or nothing to me at present." She added, "Just end this awful destruction and find help for these patients who need the barest essentials so badly." Zwicker and her colleagues may have joined the nurse corps out of some vague sense of duty (or, just as likely, boredom), but in the five months since the Japanese attack they had irreversibly changed. The nurses knew they were on the first front line of the war, and many refused to leave their post.

Ann Mealor, the chief nurse in the Philippines, was among those who could not countenance abandoning the hospital. Even after receiving her orders to leave the island on the final escape submarine, Mealor insisted that she could not in good conscience abide by the directive, and refused to leave. As the USS *Spearfish* sailed away—her last opportunity to leave—Mealor watched from the coastline. "She knew," Wainwright remembered, "that she was signing her captivity warrant."

Soon after the last evacuations occurred on Corregidor, Wainwright surrendered the final American outpost to the Japanese, and the remaining forces, including Army and Navy nurses, were moved to prisoner camps. Dorothy Still, along with over sixty of her Army colleagues and a dozen Navy nurses, was transferred to the Santo Tomas internment camp. Once there, Still began doing the only thing she could: "waiting for the American forces to come back."

She would be waiting for almost three years.

## 2

# "THEY CAN'T DO ANY MORE, BUT YOU CAN"

## THE ARSENAL OF DEMOCRACY

THE SIX MONTHS FOLLOWING THE ATTACK ON THE Philippines did not go well for the US military. The onslaught that began in December 1941 continued, virtually unabated, until the Japanese controlled Guam, Wake Island, Malaya, Singapore, Hong Kong, Burma, the Dutch East Indies, New Guinea, the Solomon Islands, Bali, and Timor. Dorothy Still, adjusting to her new life imprisoned at Santo Tomas, read about the advance in the *Manila Tribune,* recently taken over by the Japanese. Each day's headlines seemed somehow worse than the last—BOMBS DEMOL-ISH CORREGIDOR GUNS, on April 15; CORREGIDOR FALLS, on May 8; JAPAN SET FOR NEW DRIVE IN NEW GUINEA, months later—and it was difficult not to feel hopeless.

As the Japanese advance steadily continued, leaving hundreds of American nurses like Still reconciling themselves to continued imprisonment, the Allies were not faring much better in Europe. Germany continued its march across the continent, barely re-buffed by the combined efforts of the British and Russians. At the same time, the Italians continued their occupation of the Balkans and offensives in North Africa.

At home, the American military fared just as poorly. The surge of enlistments after Pearl Harbor had been met by bottlenecks in the training apparatus, and quickly exposed major holes in the American ability to prepare men for combat. A chronic shortage of battle-hardened soldiers hampered the training of green troops, and equipment shortages led to embarrassing choke points. In the earliest days of the war, for instance, men arrived at field exercises forced to take turns training with M1 rifles since there were not enough to go around.

Even with the bad news coming from Europe, the Pacific, and training centers around the country, however, the United States had given itself a head start in two critical ways. First, the US was beginning to see the gains of incremental federal investment in expanding military manufacturing capacity; and, second, the United States was getting a clearer picture of its manpower demands— and how to go about meeting them. Both would prove decisive.

In the final accounting, the American manufacturing industry, and the millions of women who entered the workforce to keep it humming, rose to the occasion. The production feats of World War II remain, to this day, among the greatest manufacturing achievements in American history. By metrics big and small, the United States' productive capacity became unstoppable within a matter of years. For instance, in 1941, the United States had produced under twenty thousand military aircraft; by 1944, it would produce almost one hundred thousand. In almost the same period, the United States went from spending about one billion dollars on defense to spending more than eighty-two billion dollars on the military—an 8,000 percent increase. Though American production had more than its fair share of problems, including shortages of equipment and manpower, open fighting within labor organizations, standoffs between workers and managers, and heated

disputes between government and industry, the American manufacturing giant had awakened.

Part of the success of American industry came from making
investments in key projects well before Pearl Harbor. American
commanders understood that militaries—and especially those
composed of significant amounts of technical equipment and
trained personnel—do not simply appear from thin air when
needed. Creating this type of force was, and remains, a complex, lengthy process. It requires time to generate the massive
resources necessary for manufacturing, time to find and then
spend astonishing amounts of money, time to test equipment
and train personnel, time to organize and outfit forces for deployment, and time to revise and fix problems. As Marshall put
it in July 1940, "Time is the dominant factor in all this business,"
adding, "Once the dilemma has arisen, it is too late; we have to
take our preliminary measures in time to reach some degree of
preparation."

Given their awareness of these constraints, military planners
had placed an early emphasis on the projects of long duration, especially capital ships and aircraft, in the mid-1930s. As a result of
their foresight, American shipbuilding and aircraft production was
steadily ramping up as Hitler began his advance across Europe. By
one estimate, in the spring of 1940, "American shipyards were in
the midst of building two new aircraft carriers, eight battleships,
five cruisers, and three dozen destroyers," and the US aircraft industry was already working on "nearly six thousand planes and
more than fourteen thousand engines, at a cost of $573 million."
Though, in the war's earliest days, American leaders had gone to
great lengths to avoid fighting it, they had managed to establish
the industrial foundation necessary to win it.

In this mammoth industrial undertaking, women played a vital
role. As has been well documented, women were at the very center
of American industrial mobilization for World War II, steadily filling the ranks of factories, offices, and depots around the country.

The estimates of American women's participation in the war economy are staggering. By one account, women composed nearly forty percent of the workers in war industries by 1944 and, at their peak, made up thirty-five percent of the overall labor force, a ten percent increase from before the war. Women participated at even higher rates in specific sectors, especially in heavy manufacturing. In 1942, for example, the nation's largest aircraft-manufacturing plant employed twenty-eight women; the next year they employed over forty thousand. Ultimately, women made up nearly a third of the total aircraft-production workforce. In doing all this, American women were propelled into the twentieth-century economy at unprecedented rates and created an inspirational mythology around their contributions.

But the manufacturing behemoth of which these women were a part was just the first part of the long supply chain that outfitted

Lineup of women welders of Ingalls Shipbuilding Company. **Courtesy National Archives, photo no. 522890.**

American troops at the front lines. In between the plant and the battlefield were military support functions that were equally, if not more, expansive.

When broadly conceived, support functions consist of the forces and organizations that generate, transport, sustain, and allocate materiel and men. For each phase of this chain to run smoothly, personnel—behind the front lines but still in uniform— are essential. In 1942, this meant that from the factory floor to the front lines there needed to be people in uniform: people to do the maintenance, people to train troops, people to keep track of parts, people to classify memos, people to send cables, people to build facilities, people to serve food, people to pay personnel, and, perhaps most important, people to do the paperwork.

In the military of World War II, the people responsible for these tasks generally fell into the category of noncombat forces, also referred to as combat support forces. Although these types of military personnel were not usually on the front lines, they enabled and enhanced combat effects with their niche specialties and capabilities. Combat support forces, such as signals units, transport units, medical units, maintenance units, supply units, military police, ordnance units, quartermaster units, and even headquarters units, were a critical, though often unseen and underappreciated, element of battlefield operations.

In previous wars, finding men to staff the support elements of the military without undermining the equally important tasks of manning the front lines and the production facilities at home was not an insurmountable problem. But as the scale of World War II's demands became apparent, military planners realized it was going to necessitate particularly large numbers of production, combat, and support personnel, and especially the latter. This left them wrestling with the nagging question of where to find all these people.

\* \* \*

At first glance, the wartime manpower considerations for a country the size of the United States might seem trivial: 16 million military personnel served in World War II, from a population of over 133 million people. What could be so difficult about that?

In fact, the math was less straightforward than it seems. The main challenge resided at the intersection of how many people were needed to serve in uniform, how many people were needed in American manufacturing, and who both industries actually *wanted* to employ. At the outset of World War II, the answers to those questions were starkly at odds.

The plain fact is that, traditionally, militaries have not allowed everyone in the population to serve. This was even more the case in the early 1940s than it is now. The military largely prohibited or actively discouraged young or old men, Black men, and, of course, women from serving. So when military leaders in the 1940s talked about manpower, they actually meant something narrower: White men between twenty and forty-five years old.

This made the math considerably more difficult. According to the 1940 census, simply limiting military service to men immediately reduced the eligible population to about 66 million people. Further placing age restrictions on that population brought the number down to about 25 million. Subtracting further over 5 million Black men, who were eligible for military service but significantly constrained in how they were permitted to serve, shrank the number to 20 million.

Complicating the manpower challenges even more was the fact that the population most coveted by the military—White men in their twenties and thirties—was the same population that, at least initially, was most prized by the manufacturing sector that needed to churn out essential military equipment. This meant that the military could not draft every single eligible man for service without draining the American economy of working-age men, and that it would need to be careful not to rob Peter to pay Paul.

Initially, the solution to this problem was to allow men in critical industrial positions to defer their military service. Early on, it seemed, the United States could support both the military and industrial demands with the men available. But this strategy proved short-sighted. The droves of men claiming occupational deferments for their work in essential industries or medical deferments for treatable physical conditions whittled down considerably the twenty million or so White men between twenty and forty-five eligible for military service. Indeed, by the Army's own estimate, less than eight percent of the American population—about ten million men—were eligible to serve at the start of World War II, after accounting for the wartime demands on American industry and physical fitness requirements.

The math, then, did not look good. With the steadily growing pressure of feeding the manpower demands of the front lines, of the factories, and of the growing military support infrastructure connecting the two, the US military had to start finding ways to fill the gaps.

It did not take long for senior commanders to realize that the same women who were starting to man the conveyor belts and riveting guns of American manufacturing plants could also be used in the military, filling the desks left behind by the men now needed for combat tasks. "There are a great many jobs connected with the Army's war program which women can handle better than men," wrote Marshall, concluding, "The demands on manpower would be so great that a large number of women should be incorporated in the Army's effort."

# 3

# "I'M IN THIS WAR TOO!"

## WOMEN'S ARMY AUXILIARY CORPS

"WOMEN," WROTE ELEANOR ROOSEVELT IN 1942, "are a weapon waiting to be used."

Ann Baumgartner, having achieved her dream of becoming a pilot, agreed. From the moment in 1941 when she stepped into a plane on a small airfield twenty-five miles outside Newark, New Jersey, she knew in her bones that flying would allow her to make a difference in the war. "I was eager to be off to try to do my part in the war," she remembered.

Although there was little public discussion of women joining the armed services when Baumgartner started flying, she reasoned that she should be prepared for the eventuality. Her first step was to get a pilot's license. This was no small feat. A license required two hundred hours of flying time, which was difficult to come by under normal circumstances and near impossible in 1941 with so many men being trained for the Air Force at civilian airfields. But Baumgartner would not be dissuaded from her calling. "This is what I was made for," she thought to herself. Imagining the adventures she might one day have, she recalled, "I could not sit still. I circled round and round the room, imagining dangerous wartime rescues."

While the idea of women pilots remained at the extreme end of the American imagination, by the time the United States entered World War II, the notion of women serving in uniform was hardly unprecedented. Thousands of women had served in the military, primarily as nurses, since at least the American Revolution, and, by the end of World War I, the Army was actively considering a proposal to formally integrate women in a wider range of positions. The notion even garnered the support of World War I general John J. Pershing—notorious for his strict discipline, demanding standards, and ability to inspire fear and loyalty in equal measure—who himself had requested a detachment of women to join his command as translators and telephone operators. The Navy had been equally supportive of women in uniform during World War I, authorizing a small corps of several thousand "Yeomanettes" to provide clerical assistance at naval bases across the country.

Since the military had come so close to fully integrating women into its ranks during World War I, several proposals for women's service in future conflicts were considered during the interwar period. The Army, in particular, devoted much study to the idea. The detailed and comprehensive reports they produced proved to be instantly controversial. As one of the primary authors pointed out, "Nothing but fruitless conflict had resulted from previous arguments between extreme feminists on the one side and male diehards on the other, all disagreeing endlessly over minor details."

Though War Department studies of the subject would prove prophetic on several issues related to women's service in the military, the noise coming from both ends of the spectrum drowned out most of their insights. Consequently, the studies faced the same fate as most other well-considered government reports on contentious issues: they were filed in a drawer and forgotten for over a decade. Peacetime consideration of a women's program was suspended in 1931 since, as one memo put it, "no one seems willing to do anything about it."

Nevertheless, much had changed in the decade since the reports were unceremoniously tossed in a file cabinet. Not only were American commanders facing unparalleled manpower demands, but a growing number of American women were showing interest in signing up. When the War Department offered no officially sanctioned way to contribute, many women took matters into their own hands. The Chicago Women's Defense League started enrolling and classifying women ready to volunteer in the event of a war, and the Los Angeles Women's Ambulance and Defense Corps created a military training program and pleaded for official Army recognition. "Women must play their part in building of a greater US national defense," remarked Marie Reed, organizer of the California group. Even movie stars got involved with the ad hoc effort. According to the *Lancaster New Era,* Hollywood starlet Ida Lupino had signed up for an ambulance unit: "Knitting would drive her crazy," they reported, "but two nights a week she attends a first aid class for the women's ambulance defense corps."

Facing this surge of interest, General Marshall had little choice but to embrace the enthusiasm and find a way to channel it for the Army's benefit. By March 1941, he had conceded it was time for the War Department to "provide some outlet for the patriotic desires of our women."

Marshall's support, however, was just the first of many hurdles legislation authorizing a women's program needed to clear. Convincing Congress, the rest of the military, and the American public to allow women into the Army proved more challenging. For starters, both sides of the social milieu largely opposed the idea. On one side, vocal pacifists and isolationists, with many women among them, had become a powerful brake on efforts to maintain a standing military and equally opposed any suggestion that women be included in whatever Army remained. On the other side, traditionalists and conservatives loudly proclaimed the view that a woman belonged in the home. Many congressmen on the powerful Senate and House Armed Services Committees fell into that camp and were nearly apoplectic about the prospect of women serving in the Army. "Take the women into the armed service," one congressman protested, and "who then will do the cooking, the washing, the mending, the humble homey tasks to which every woman has devoted herself? Think of the humiliation! What has become of the manhood of America?"

But the program's long odds did not deter the staunchest defenders of women's military service and, in this respect, no one surpassed congresswoman Edith Nourse Rogers. A Republican from Massachusetts, Rogers had won her late husband's former seat with a seventy-two percent majority in 1925. She had a biting sense of humor and was well liked by her colleagues and constituents. "I hope," she noted early in her tenure, "that everyone will forget that I am a woman as soon as possible."

Rogers was also a savvy political animal with a knack for foreign policy. Within a decade of her initial term, she had won several of the prestigious committee assignments—including a seat on the coveted House Foreign Affairs Committee—that had been held by her husband before his death. Once on these committees, she routinely broke with her party on several key foreign policy decisions, including a vote against the Neutrality Act and a vote for the Selective Service Act, always following her conscience over her party. Rogers's constituents rewarded her backbone and routinely reelected her by increasingly large margins.

From the start, Rogers was also one of the most vocal advocates for American veterans in Congress, including and especially women veterans. In the wake of World War I, Rogers had been motivated by the mistreatment of servicewomen in the conflict: "I saw the women in France, and how they had no suitable quarters and no Army discipline," she remembered, adding, "I was resolved that our women would not again serve with the Army without the protection men got."

As another war approached, Rogers's interest in women's service broadened, and she soon became the most ardent supporter in Congress of formalizing women's military service in the Army.

By early 1941, she was hard at work drafting legislation that would protect women in uniform from mistreatment during the next war. The only ironclad way to ensure they would be treated fairly, Rogers reasoned, was to integrate them fully into the Army.

By the spring of 1941, Rogers felt she had waited long enough for the Army to act on the question of women joining their ranks. After resolving that it was time for her to introduce her draft legislation, she picked up the phone to warn Marshall it was coming. Marshall, realizing that Rogers had decided to introduce the legislation with or without the Army's approval, rushed to develop a counteroffer. He asked for a week to consider Rogers's proposal—then extended his review to a month—and promised that the Army was studying the best way forward on the issue. Soon after, he presented Rogers with an initial plan for the incorporation of women: a civilian auxiliary corps that would be affiliated with, administered by, and under the authority of the Army—but technically not a part of it.

Rogers was disappointed that the Army's counterproposal had not made the women's program a part of the Army itself, since it meant that women would not be entitled to the same pay, pension, and benefits of service. But she was also a politician. Rogers knew that compromise was necessary, not just because of opposition within the Army to fully integrating women but also given the heated discord brewing in Congress on the issue. She recognized that even if she secured the needed support within the War Department, full integration into the regular Army could also poison the bill in Congress. She and Army leadership decided it was not worth the risk to force the issue of fully integrating the women. "The desire is that there be created a Women's Army Auxiliary Corps," reported Major General John Hilldring, assistant chief of staff for the Army, adding that "whether such a corps be in or with the Army is of secondary importance."

As expected, congressional approval was a formidable obstacle. The legislation sat, virtually untouched, for the better part of 1941 and 1942, languishing in bureaucratic no-man's-land. The biggest obstacle, however, did not come from the conservative members of the Senate and House Armed Services Committees or Army bureaucrats. Rather, it emerged on the House floor, where Rogers's colleagues took the opportunity to assail not just the proposal, but also war, women, and nearly everything in between. "Representative Somers of New York," reported the *New York Times*, "called the bill 'the silliest piece of legislation I have ever seen come into this house,'" with Representative Fulmer of South Carolina adding that it was the most ridiculous piece of legislation he, too, could remember seeing on the floor. His colleague, Representative Hare, wondered what it said about the men of the Army that they would let the women of America do their fighting for them.

In the end, it took the personal intervention of both Marshall and Secretary of War Henry Stimson to get the bill over the finish line. They assured reluctant congressmen that the legislation had enough constraints in it to allay their worst fears. Not only was the program an auxiliary, they argued, but the legislation limited the size of the Corps. Further, it capped the rank of its director to the equivalent of a lieutenant colonel, which ensured that "little women generals" and their hordes of subordinates would not be found running around Washington. Convinced by these restrictions and the emphatic support of Marshall and Stimson, Congress passed Rogers's proposal in the spring of 1942.

On May 15, 1942, over a year after Rogers had first introduced the legislation for a women's program, President Roosevelt authorized women "for noncombatant service with the Army of the United States for the purpose of making available to the national defense when needed the knowledge, skill, and special training of the women of this Nation." The new organization would be called the Women's Army Auxiliary Corps, the WAAC for short.

The following day, at a ceremony announcing the program, the War Department leadership hinted at what was in store for American women. "For the first time in the history of our nation, women may volunteer for direct service to a national war effort with the army of the United States. . . . Some of these jobs will be dramatic; many will be monotonous. All will be important."

Women's Army Auxiliary Corps Recruiting Poster.
**Courtesy National Archives, photo no. 515988.**

# 4

# "RELEASE A MAN TO FIGHT!"

## BUILDING THE WAAC

OVETA CULP HOBBY LOVED HATS.

Before the summer of 1942, Hobby's affection for the accessory mattered appropriately little, as very few people outside Texas had ever heard of her, let alone her hats. However, the moment that Hobby was appointed director of the new Army women's program, her choice of headwear became an instant flashpoint. "Her enemies, who have been poking fun at the appointment," wrote a *Vogue* profiler, "say that she wears absurd hats." The author playfully agreed, but with an approving qualifier, "She wears absurd and charming hats."

On the day of her swearing-in as the first director of an American women's military program, Hobby arrived, true to form, in an elegant and extremely large hat. The outfit looked stunning, but it did not photograph well. Every angle caused the hat to produce a shadow over her face, and Hobby was forced to repeat her oath of office several times before the photographer succeeded in capturing the perfect shot.

In the end, however, most of the observers forgot about the hat. The press, rapturous about Hobby's appointment, covered the event glowingly. "Slim and gracious in a dark tailored suit, perfectly poised, with a flashing smile," wrote one profiler, "Mrs. Hobby was variously reported as magnetic, brilliant, able, glamorous, dynamic, beautiful."

Born in the railroad town of Killeen, Texas, Hobby was an exceptional woman. Her raw intellect stood out from the start: at ten, she had read all of the Texas Congressional Record, and by seventeen she had acquired a personal library of 750 books.

From a young age, Hobby also liked rules. Her early exposure to Texas state politics had made her a keen student of parliamentary law, and in the late 1930s she had written an entire book on

Oveta Culp Hobby sworn in as director, Women's Army Auxiliary Corps. *Left to right*: Maj. Gen. Myron Cramer, Gen. George Marshall, Oveta Culp Hobby, and Secretary of War Henry Stimson. **Courtesy National Archives, Eisenhower Presidential Library, Abilene, Kansas.**

the subject, aptly titled *Mr. Chairman*. "Almost every phase of life is organized," she wrote, adding, "Those who participate in organizational affairs must know certain fundamentals such as: how and when to obtain recognition from the chair; which motions are debatable, and which are undebatable; what a member's remedy is if his rights are abused; and the principles which ensure protection to the minority against the majority." Rules, she argued, were essential to the proper functioning of communities around the country, no matter how large or small.

By the late thirties, Hobby had become well known in Texas politics. Though she had started her career with a failed bid for the Texas legislature in 1930, after marrying her husband—one of Texas's most famous politicians, William "Governor" Hobby—she became the editor and publisher of the *Houston Post* and cemented her position as an influential figure in Texas's political scene.

Hobby's engagement in politics reflected her belief that women had a rightful place in the public sphere, if only they would claim it. Over and over again, she would exhort the women of America to participate in the governance of their communities. "How many of us rear our daughters—as we rear our sons—to expect to serve their country wherever needed in peacetime as well as in war?" she asked a group of women assembled at the City Club of Cleveland, continuing, "And to bring it down to less heroic terms, how many of us—each one of us here today—bears her own responsibility of government: that basic vital responsibility of voting intelligently[?]"

In Hobby's estimation, women had a role to play in their own futures, but they would have to seize it. A woman, she remarked, "is a citizen by constitutional authority, she is an office holder by courage and merit."

When the Japanese bombed Pearl Harbor and invaded the Philippines in late 1941, Hobby was acting as the head of the Women's

Interest Section of the War Department's Bureau of Public Relations. There, she had been charged with overseeing the War Department's efforts to communicate with women about the day-to-day life and well-being of the men in the armed services. As an Ohio newspaper reported it, "The Army has selected a woman editor to interpret the activities of Mars to the wives, sweethearts, and mothers."

The idea for the Women's Interest Section had emerged from Army leadership as more and more men were signing up to join the rapidly growing military forces and disappearing from their communities into the training camps around the country. The office was tasked with using newspapers, radio programs, and speakers to provide information on "how the men are being fed, how their health is protected, and what provisions are made for their recreation and spiritual welfare," presuming, of course, that "all women—whether their concern is personal or general—are interested in the gigantic housekeeping problem of the Army and the care given men who are training for the defense of this country." Hobby had endorsed the idea in its early days and helped draft a plan for the establishment of the organization. She knew that the government would need all the help it could get in convincing women, some of the war's greatest skeptics, to support the effort and assure them that the men they cared for would be well taken care of.

When Hobby was offered a job directing the office, however, she demurred. Her primary concern was logistical. She worried that she could not sustain the long commute from Houston to Washington, as well as her obligations to the *Houston Post*, with two young children at home. Given the stakes, however, she reluctantly agreed to run the Women's Interest Section for four months.

But by February 1942, when the War Department began its search for the director of the WAAC, one name repeatedly emerged from the military officials solicited for recommendations: Oveta Culp Hobby. In her short time in Washington, Hobby had impressed nearly every person she had encountered, including both Marshall and First Lady Eleanor Roosevelt, two of her earliest supporters. They quickly recognized that Hobby was endowed with precisely the balance of tenacity, patience, and, above all else, charisma that would be required for the director post. On the day of her appointment, Secretary Stimson put it simply: "The war department considers itself very fortunate to have a woman of your ability to lead the women's auxiliary army corps," he stated, adding, "We have every confidence in you."

What all of them underestimated, however, was just how many disadvantages Hobby would face from the moment she arrived on the job in the summer of 1942. First among them was the simple fact that Hobby was a woman operating in an overwhelmingly male institution. Not only was she one of the first women to set foot in the War Department in a nonclerical role, but she became responsible for an undertaking that frequently put her at odds with two- and three-star generals. Many of these men were neither used to nor generous toward a thirty-seven-year-old woman sitting across from them at the decision-making table.

Even more problematic than her gender, however, was Hobby's lack of status in the military hierarchy. Since the WAAC had been authorized as an auxiliary corps, Hobby's appointment as director came with no official military rank. Instead, she was a civilian appointee in a small planning office. Though she was technically the rank equivalent of a lieutenant colonel, Hobby was outside the military hierarchy, and "the actual and legal responsibility of the Director," she remembered, "was clearly defined by law—and clearly limited." As she put it, "I could scarcely feel like a powerful person in position of command."

Finally, in addition to her lack of authority, Hobby knew little about the written and unwritten rules of the military institution of which she was suddenly a part. Within the course of six months, she had gone from being a civilian observer of the war, tasked with reassuring wives and sweethearts, to overseeing a command that would have thousands of Army personnel. With little warning, Hobby needed to ascertain the equivalent of twenty-five years of military experience seemingly overnight. Hobby and her senior staff, which at first numbered two prominent society women, two retired Army officers, and two reserve officers with little Army experience, were far out of their depth.

The early odds had not fallen in Hobby's favor. She was a woman with limited authority and virtually no background in military affairs who was now expected to organize one of the most controversial programs of the war, within one of the most conservative institutions in the US government. It seemed like an impossible task, and certainly one that no ordinary person—man or woman—could be expected to perform well.

But Hobby was not easily rattled. This was the same woman who, while she was two months pregnant, survived a plane crash and rescued her husband from the burning wreckage. Even Eleanor Roosevelt had been impressed with her nerve, writing to Hobby after the accident that "it must have been a terrifying experience." She was a woman of steely resolve, and in the years ahead she would face this new challenge with her characteristic backbone.

Hobby, right from the start, decided to overcome what she lacked in experience and status with tenacity. The day before her first press conference, she stayed up all night, practicing answers to all the questions she anticipated the press would ask about the program. The next day, reporters peppered her with inquiries about the women's program, all of which she anticipated, but few of which had much to do with women's fitness for service:

**Q.** How about girdles?

**A.** *If you mean, will they be issued, I can't tell you yet. If they are required, they will be supplied.*

**Q.** Will Waacs be allowed to use make up?

**A.** *Yes, if it is inconspicuous.*

**Q.** What do you consider that to be?

**A.** *I hope their own good taste will decide.*

The subtext of the reporters' questions, however, previewed the challenges that were to come. "Here at this first conference was to begin a never-finished battle," wrote Mattie Treadwell, the official historian of the WAAC, "as to which idea of woman in the Army would prevail—whether the public would get stories mainly of her real work and useful jobs, or of her underwear, cosmetics, dates with soldiers, her rank-pulling, sex life, and misconduct."

From the outset, Hobby enlisted the help of key supporters as she established the program, most notably, her friend Eleanor Roosevelt. The First Lady had been among the earliest advocates for the WAAC and had thrown her support behind it with her typical vigor. It helped that Roosevelt also had known Hobby for over a decade. Years earlier, Hobby had assisted Roosevelt in dispensing with several constituent complaints in Texas, including finding work for a young man after the loss of his baby and investigating an anti-Semitic incident in Houston. With Roosevelt's powerful support, Hobby earned an indispensable ally.

More practically, Hobby also sought out the counsel of the British, who had much to offer from their experience setting up a women's program in the late thirties. Having few other models to turn to, Hobby—with the encouragement of Roosevelt—arranged to meet with British chief controller Jean Knox, the equivalent of a general, and the woman running the Auxiliary Territorial Service in England.

Knox did not suffer fools. She was "charming, intense, typically-clipped-British-speech type of human dynamo," wrote Hobby's aide, "with all the brains in the world and far more feminine appeal than her pictures would lead you to believe." The women were sure to get along.

Hobby's meeting with Knox was both helpful and sobering. She hosted Knox for afternoon tea, but the formality of the occasion soon faded among the like-minded women, as they sat "on the lovely spreads of the White House beds, smoking and talking and generally letting their hair down." Had it not been for the uniforms, the gathering might have looked like any other after-lunch coffee among friends.

Despite the air of informality, however, the conversation was intensely serious. Knox warned that controversy would be the enemy of success for the WAAC. She cautioned, from her own hard-won experience, that difficulties of any type—whether supply shortages, auxiliary status, or run-of-the-mill sexism—would be destructive to morale, recruiting, and, ultimately, effectiveness. More than anything else, however, she emphasized that there could be no questions or insinuations about the morality of the women in uniform. Their character and behavior would have to be above reproach, which meant no drinking, and no men. Hobby and her staff took note.

But the WAAC, by its very existence, was destined for controversy. Hobby could do her best to mitigate the nature and depth of those scandals, but the notion of women serving in Army uniforms proved too enticing for the media and the public to leave alone—and they wasted no time.

Some of the early controversies were hopelessly manufactured. The first, and most superfluous, centered on the issue of the uniforms. The WAAC, for all its good intentions, had been ridiculed—cruelly, in some cases—for their choice of classic, but arguably drab, brown uniforms, topped off with the not-so-affectionately-named "Hobby hats." The outfit soon drew the public's scorn for being especially unflattering.

But most of the public consternation about the WAAC uniform fixated, somewhat inexplicably, on the women's underwear. It became a matter of great public concern, according to many newspapers of the time, that the WAAC was planning to issue women "foundation garments" in the Army khaki. The ridicule was relentless, unfair, and, of course, entirely unwanted. More practically, all the talk of undergarments cast an early shadow on the Army's efforts to paint volunteers as respectable young women. As Bertha Strittmatter, a WAAC based at Stout Field in Indiana, put it, "Our uniform was our worst enemy."

Other early controversies, however, were more substantial. The first serious challenge was the issue of the WAAC's auxiliary status. Though a well-meaning compromise intended to secure the authorizing legislation, it soon became clear that it created a very complicated situation for Hobby and the women in the program. In practice, the WAAC's ambiguous auxiliary status enmeshed it in a web of administrative and legal headaches, many of which were relatively minor but time-consuming to resolve: Were WAACs eligible for postage waivers on their mail? Could they sign up for military life insurance? Could they shop at the post exchange? Was the base chaplain allowed to give them a free copy of the New Testament? Other questions about the WAAC's status, however, had higher stakes: Could WAACs be held liable for service performed on duty? Were they eligible for disability benefits? Could they be buried with a flag and military honors, and would their remains receive a military escort?

Problematically, Hobby had little authority over these questions, and she harbored no illusions about the limits of her oversight on matters big and small. She noted that "more than 1000 different Army agencies were at one time issuing WA[A]C public relations releases—independently, on their own ideas, without centralized control or approval." Until the WAAC's auxiliary status was changed, however, Hobby had to endure this frustrating bureaucratic arrangement.

Finally, adding to the administrative and public relations controversies plaguing the WAAC from the start, Hobby herself presented a serious issue. While Hobby had several traits that made her appeal to the top military brass for the director job, she was also, significantly, a southerner. For most of White America, Hobby's Texan upbringing meant very little, but for Black America, the stakes were different.

Black leaders openly worried that a White southern woman at the helm of the Army women's program would be all too willing to maintain the segregated policies that had already stained the service of Black men in the military, and would depress morale and recruiting. As Martha Putney notes in her comprehensive history of Black women in the WAAC, the downsides of such a policy were well-documented. "There is a definite reluctance on the part of the best qualified colored women to volunteer in the WAAC," wrote one critique, adding that "[t]his is brought about by an impression on their part that they will not be well received or treated on posts where they may be stationed." If segregation in the women's programs were approved by Hobby, argued Black leaders, it would cause the experiment to fail before it began.

Almost immediately, the concerns of Black leaders were realized. At her first press conference, Hobby confirmed that the WAAC would follow the Army's established policy when it came to race, including the segregation of Black soldiers into separate units. While Hobby lacked both the authority and the skill to prevent this from taking place, her southern heritage and unwillingness to challenge the Army's policy of segregation certainly did not discourage the negative publicity quickly mounting among Black leaders about her appointment.

As these controversies—both real and manufactured—began to pile up, so did Hobby's frustration. She quickly discovered that despite being publicly accountable for every WAAC policy and blunder, she had little recourse to correct them, and she was already chafing at her limited oversight. But it would take another year, and much more controversy, for her to gain that rightful authority.

For the first several months of the WAAC's existence, Hobby faced these challenges almost entirely alone, aside from her small staff of loyal supporters. But the Army was not the only service that faced chronic manpower shortages. By 1942, Navy leadership, as well as their counterparts in the Marine Corps and Coast Guard, confronted a similar reality and watched closely as the Army established its women's program. As the sea-based services began to search for new sources of manpower to fill critical support and logistics gaps, they, too, found women ready to answer the call.

# 5

# "BRING HIM HOME SOONER, JOIN THE WAVES"

## WOMEN ACCEPTED FOR VOLUNTARY EMERGENCY SERVICE

"IS THERE ANY LAW THAT SAYS A YEOMAN MUST BE a man?"

It was 1917, and Secretary of the Navy Josephus Daniels, having assembled his advisors to discuss the likely manpower demands of World War I, wanted to know whether there had been a specific prohibition against women serving in the Navy. The answer, responded one of his staffers, was that the Naval Appropriations Act of 1916 "did not contain the restrictive word 'male.'"

Daniels, a lifelong southern Democrat, teetotaler, supporter of women's suffrage, and, notably, White supremacist, replied unequivocally: "Then enroll women in the Naval Reserve and we will have the best clerical assistance the country can provide." By March, women were authorized to serve in the Navy; and by the end of World War I, over ten thousand Yeomanettes had donned the Navy uniform.

But the Navy's progressive attitude toward the integration of women during World War I did not last. By 1925, updated appropriations legislation closed the loophole identified years earlier by Daniels's staff, specifying explicitly that the naval reserve only include "male citizens" of the United States. This provision was carried over into the similar 1938 legislation, and by the start of World War II little appetite existed among naval leaders for a repeat performance of the Yeomanettes.

To be fair, the Navy faced a less dire manpower situation than the Army at the start of World War II, demanding less than half of the personnel than the Army would eventually employ. Still, the Navy had reason for concern. Between 1941 and 1945, the Navy grew at nearly double the rate of the Army, and in 1942 the War Manpower Commission had already indicated they would not be able to meet the Navy's projected demands.

Even in light of these realities, however, naval leaders maintained that they saw little need for uniformed women. In 1941, when Navy leadership solicited its bureaus for ideas on possible job roles for women in the first several months of the war, only the Bureau of Aeronautics and the Chief of Naval Operations responded with suggestions. The remaining branches of the Navy sent back a series of uninspired responses:

> Office of the judge advocate general: "No use for the services of Women's Auxiliary at this time."

> Bureau of Medicine and Surgery: "Do not visualize a need."

> Bureau of Supplies and Accounts: "It does not appear that the establishment of a Women's Auxiliary Corps would be desirable."

> Bureau of Yards and Docks: "Such a corps is unnecessary to assist the bureau in carrying out its functions."

When asked, the answer was clear: women in uniform were not needed in the Navy.

But the Navy did need Dr. Margaret Chung. Chung, the child of Chinese immigrants, had grown up in Santa Barbara with the dream of becoming a medical missionary, and despite the many obstacles thrown in the path of a Chinese American woman living in California at the turn of the twentieth century, she managed to achieve it. By 1916, she had graduated from the University of Southern California's College of Physicians and Surgeons, ready to begin her life of service as a physician, and soon had established an independent practice to treat San Francisco's Chinatown residents, hoping to bring Western medicine to the community. Chung also became well known and respected among the city's White residents as a talented practitioner from her stints as a resident doctor in White hotels.

According to Judy Tzu-Chun Wu, the author of one of the few biographies of this extraordinary woman, Chung found creative ways to survive in the social and cultural landscape of the time despite being an outsider. She began by adopting a masculine style of dress and persona at medical school. "During her early career," writes Wu, "her favorite picture featured her in a dark suit. She sent autographed versions of the photo to her friends and identified herself as 'Mike.'" For good measure, she also adopted the traditionally masculine habits of gambling, drinking, swearing, and driving a flashy blue sports car.

In the known public record, Chung never explicitly identified herself as queer or lesbian—or admitted to romances with women— but considerable evidence suggests that she had several relationships with women throughout her life. Letters and diaries from the time document that she had a series of loving, affectionate, and seemingly romantic relationships with women throughout the period, including with the poet Elsa Gidlow and entertainer Sophie Tucker. Although a well-kept secret, this part of her life sometimes invited unwelcome scrutiny, including a federal investigation into her medical practice, likely born out of the complaints of a competing doctor.

Despite its sometimes challenging consequences, Chung's willingness to buck convention was also one of her greatest assets. Chung's appearance, demeanor, and career choice made her stand out, and soon made her a well-known personality in the area. Word of her presence in California spread to young, eager sailors living in the naval hubs of San Francisco and Los Angeles in the 1930s, who were intrigued by the Chinese American doctor and assumed from her ethnicity that she could help them make connections with the resistance fighters in China battling against the Japanese. While Chung was unable to make such contacts, she did offer the young men a home-cooked Sunday dinner and a much-needed dose of maternal warmth.

Soon, young Navy men were coming to Chung's home in droves. They started calling her "Mom Chung" and referred to themselves as her "fair-haired bastards." Each Sunday, after dinner of ribs and Americanized Chinese food, she would conduct a formal adoption ceremony, including an exchange of engraved rings and a vow that her sons would "dedicate themselves to, and possibly sacrifice their lives for a higher purpose." She restricted membership only to those who were, by her description, "a good guy, who can fly, who's not afraid to die."

By 1937, Chung had adopted five hundred "children," almost all naval aviators and submariners posted in the region, and her dinners were regularly attended by seventy-five to one hundred people. The professional caliber of Chung's adoptive children included extremely influential commanders, policymakers, and celebrities, including: Admirals Nimitz and Halsey; Congressman Melvin Maas; Senators Albert Chandler and Raymond Willis; and even Amelia Earhart. Chung's story also sparked the imagination of the American media, and she soon became the subject of a feature film and a comic book. The additional press made her a local hero, with membership in her adoptive family soon swelling to over fifteen hundred people.

Chung recognized quickly that her maternal bond with the growing, powerful network of American naval personnel—and the attendant media attention that it garnered—could, and would, be put to good use. In early 1942, she would expend much of that capital on behalf of women, like her, who wanted to be part of the US Navy.

As Chung's adoptive family expanded, so did pressure on the Navy to admit women into the service, spurred by Rogers's introduction of the WAAC legislation. "The evidence indicates," reads the offi-

## "Mom" Chung a One-Woman Flyers' Recruiting Force

"MOM" TO AMERICAN FLYERS—Dr. Margaret Chung, San Francisco surgeon and physician, is "Mom" to 465 of Uncle Sam's most brilliant aviators, most of them now somewhere over the Pacific. She's pictured here in her "trophy" room, filled with souvenirs sent her by American flyers.

An article highlighting Dr. Margaret Chung's Navy recruitment efforts. From *The Boston Globe*.

cial Navy history, "that the creation of a Women's Reserve was taken up by the Navy as much because it feared that if it did not move, Mrs. Rogers would, and along lines which the department did not want." Navy leadership understood that they needed to find a solution to the manpower problem before someone else found one for them. With the clock ticking, Secretary of the Navy Frank Knox authorized the initiation of the process to establish a women's program in early 1942.

But the Navy is a bureaucracy, and even senior naval leaders could not force the issue. Weeks after the women's program received the green light, the draft legislation authorizing women for service in the Navy was mired in the worst kind of administrative red tape, a budget dispute. The Navy Bureau of Personnel was stuck in a lengthy back-and-forth on funding issues, specifically over whether the proposed legislation should integrate women as part of the Navy's reserve forces or, as the Army had done, make it part of a separate auxiliary corps. They had gone around and around on the issue for weeks.

But what Knox and his advisors could not—or would not—do, Chung did. Months earlier, on a visit to Irving McQuiston (Beloved Son #465) at the Bureau of Aeronautics, Chung had inquired about where she could sign up to join the Navy. When McQuiston told her that federal legislation would need to be passed for her to serve, Chung was incensed, but not deterred. She started making calls.

First, she rang Representative Melvin Maas (#447), then a colonel in the Marine Corps Reserve and member of the House Naval Affairs Committee, and asked him to introduce the draft of the Navy's legislation that would make women part of the naval reserve. Maas wasted no time. On March 8, 1942, two days after Chung had made her request, he introduced a bill for the women's naval reserve on the House floor with the support of another one of Chung's sons, Senator Raymond Willis (#124).

Chung also enlisted her informal network of influential lobbyists on behalf of the bill. She recruited a distinguished group of advocates, including Senator Albert "Happy" Chandler; Alice Roosevelt Longworth, daughter of Teddy Roosevelt and widow of the former House speaker; and Mary Early Holmes, the sister of Roosevelt's executive secretary. She even put on a dinner for prominent Senate Democrats to generate further support for the bill.

Chung's efforts, combined with the growing public pressure on naval leadership and Rogers's unrelenting demand for legislation in both the Army and the Navy, caused the tide to turn. Finally, the bill was signed into law, and on July 30, 1942, women joined the US Navy for the second time. They were called "Women Accepted for Volunteer Emergency Service," or the WAVES.

Chung was, of course, eager to sign up. Even before the legislation had passed, she had tried twice to secure a commission. In April 1942, when she had submitted her first application for the WAVES, along with the endorsement of Congressman Maas, she was told that until the organization was made public, no commissions would be offered. In June 1942, this time with the endorsement of Senator Willis, she asked to be involved in the planning for the WAVES, one month before the formal announcement of the program. Again, she was asked to wait.

After the legislation passed in July, Chung tried, once more, to gain admission. This time, however, she was denied entry based on her age. At fifty-one, the Navy replied, she was ineligible and they would not make an exception. The message behind Chung's repeated rejection was clear. In 1942, the WAVES had no room for a possibly queer, middle-aged, Chinese American woman—even if it owed its existence to her.

6

# "WISH I COULD
# JOIN TOO!"

## BUILDING THE WAVES

PART OF THE NAVY'S RELUCTANCE TO INCLUDE women like Chung in its ranks stemmed from its concern, above all else, with the public image of its women's program. After watching the Army make a series of unforced errors in the rollout of the WAAC, the Navy understood that the best defense against similar disparagement was a strong offense. With strategy in mind, their first concern was portraying a carefully crafted image of Navy women: White, middle-class, elite, and, above all else, ladylike.

Serving this end, the Navy took the issue of uniforms seriously and, wisely, chose not to issue regulation undergarments, a fact lauded at the time by newspapers, who gleefully announced that the WAVES MAY CHOOSE OWN UNDERWEAR. The Navy leadership eventually settled on elegant blue uniforms designed by the famous American designer Main Bocher, which were an immediate hit. The initial allotment included all the essentials:

Soft, crowned hat, rolled brim, black band.
Short, Navy blue jacket, slightly built-up shoulders, new
    rounded collar and pointed lapel. Blue and white insignia for
    WAVES and gold for the SPARS.

Flattering, six-gored skirt.

Black seaman's tie.

Smart, over-the-shoulder, leather pouch bag (optional).

White gloves in summer, black in winter.

Beige lisle hoes.

Black oxfords, heels not over 1 1/2 inches.

Raincoat and havelock (rainhat); becoming protection for bad
weather.


The summer and working uniforms were equally striking, and most women who joined the WAVES felt they had made out quite well.

Navy leaders, also eager to avoid the issues of auxiliary status that had beset the WAAC, had successfully fought with Congress on the issue, and won, before the authorizing legislation was signed into law. Consequently, Navy women, unlike women in the Army, would have an official rank, with all the protections and benefits that entailed, including the same pay as men.

While the WAVES were still limited in important respects—no woman, for instance, could reach a rank higher than lieutenant commander for the first several years of its existence—the decision to make the WAVES a part of the Navy would prove shrewd in the first year of the organization, since it supplied several practical advantages. In particular, Navy leaders realized that fully integrating the women's units gave them an advantage over the WAAC in recruiting efforts and also made it easier for naval officials to keep a watchful eye on the development of the program. "The theory from the beginning," remembered a Navy commander, "was that if women were going to be in the service, they were going to be in the Navy under the control of the naval officials, rather than being an auxiliary corps that would run its own ship."

Finally, the Navy had taken note of Hobby's selection controversy and aimed to avoid any negative publicity about their director. Recognizing the limits of their own knowledge and understanding, the Navy outsourced their search to the American women best qualified to advise on the matter, deans of women. "The Navy knew enough about the Navy," the logic went, "but they didn't know much about girls."

Under the leadership of Virginia Gildersleeve, dean of Barnard College, the Navy assembled an advisory council for the women's program, which also included Ada Comstock, president of Radcliffe; Meta Glass, president of Sweet Briar College; and the deans of women at the University of North Carolina and the University of Michigan. This distinguished group convened to identify someone with the necessary experience and constitution to lead the WAVES.

After an extensive search, their recommendation coalesced around the recently appointed president of Wellesley College—one of the youngest women in the position nationally—Mildred McAfee. McAfee, an unusually vibrant and effective leader with a sterling reputation, proved to be the ideal choice.

That McAfee found herself under consideration for such an important position came as little surprise to anyone who knew her. She had two degrees, a bachelor's from Vassar College and a master's from the University of Chicago, and everywhere she went she garnered a reputation for being a natural leader. Indeed, in both concept and practice, she took leadership seriously. As a graduate student, she authored a paper titled "Women Leaders and the Family" that profiled the experiences of famous women to draw inferences about whether family upbringing could explain the development of leadership traits. She concluded, "It is impossible to generalize on the type of family in which leaders develop," but, she added, "the essential factor in the preparation of a leader, so far as family is concerned, is the development within her of a sense of independence, of ability."

McAfee had also worked at several colleges with expanding

women's enrollment before finding her way to Wellesley, first serving as the dean of women at Centre College, then working as executive secretary of the alumnae association at Vassar, and later heading to Oberlin College as dean of women. In 1936, having earned a reputation for "intellectual honesty, leadership, tolerance, savoir-faire, sympathetic understanding of youth, vision, and a sense of humor," she was plucked from Oberlin to assume her new post as president of Wellesley College, one of the premier institutions for women's education in the country. McAfee had emerged as the best of the group from a pool of over one hundred candidates.

Wellesley, like most colleges and universities in the country, had undergone its own transformation after Pearl Harbor. "Wellesley College," wrote the campus committee on war activities, "can delay no longer in accepting her full responsibility in this war." Buildings on the grounds were subject to dim-out rules, and air raid precautions were extensive, with a formal emergency response structure, designated wardens, and practice drills. Blackout instructions were distributed around campus, and "Warden's Report" sheets for air raid damage were printed. All the students were invited to meet in the chemistry library every week to assist in sewing Wellesley's monthly quota of 75,000 surgical dressings for the Red Cross, and the campus hosted 124 British children, refugees of the fighting in Europe, for a summer camp.

Given Wellesley's involvement in the war effort, McAfee was not surprised to be invited to attend a conference at Barnard hosted by the Navy and intended to provide college administrators with more information about its women's program. McAfee remembered that the meeting focused on providing a baseline understanding of the program and on imploring the college administrators to assist with recruiting. "We were all eager to do our bit," she would later say, "and everybody was eager to know what would happen to colleges and the students in them." McAfee returned to Wellesley better informed and prepared to encourage her students to consider the WAVES.

It came as a shock, however, when McAfee received a letter from Gildersleeve a few weeks later, not about the recruitment effort but about whether she would be willing to accept an offer to lead the nascent program for Navy women. No one had told McAfee that she had been on the list of candidates, and certainly not that she had climbed to the top of it. Unlike Hobby, who had spent considerable time in the Pentagon and was closely following the developments of women's issues in the Army when she was approached to lead the WAAC, the unexpected request blindsided McAfee.

WAVES Recruitment Poster. Courtesy National Archives, photo no. 513692.

The news of her selection, as surprising as it was to McAfee, galled Wellesley's board of trustees. First, they were skeptical of the intermediary. Gildersleeve was an academic, not a Navy officer. The trustees found it hard to square the urgency and seriousness of her request with her unofficial status and the absence of direct communication from Navy leadership. Second, they were skeptical of the offer. As mandated by the WAVES' authorizing legislation, McAfee would initially receive the rank of lieutenant commander, the highest possible rank granted to a woman. Some of the male trustees, however, questioned the relatively low rank assigned to a position of that authority—as, indeed, it was.

McAfee, with the backing and encouragement of her board, asked for a formal meeting with Admiral Randall Jacobs, the chief of naval personnel, to clarify what exactly she was being asked to do. Jacobs quickly put McAfee and her board at ease. On the issue of rank, he was especially emphatic, clarifying, "Why, think nothing of that," adding, "You'll be in charge, and this will be your baby." With his endorsement, the Wellesley trustees approved a yearlong leave of absence for McAfee, to expire in August 1943. "The theory," she remembered, "was that I would get it set up and then go back to Wellesley." McAfee had her swearing-in ceremony several weeks later and, on August 3, 1942, was commissioned as "an officer and a gentleman of the US Navy."

Even with the Navy's attempts to insulate the WAVES from the early mistakes of the WAAC, McAfee, like Hobby, started at a disadvantage when it came to her knowledge of and authority in the Navy. McAfee and the core group of women charged with running the women's reserve in its earliest days were given no crash course in naval customs and, other than the admirals overseeing their work, had no experienced officers to ask for advice. Having virtually no familiarity with the Navy's regulations, McAfee initially found the institution to be a confusing, unfamiliar, and, at times, hostile place.

But the real and enduring challenge for McAfee was that, despite its professed egalitarianism, the Navy had placed her in a position of limited authority. McAfee's office had been housed in the Bureau of Personnel, where she had direct access to Admiral Jacobs and, at least in theory, full authority over the women's program. But the Navy had failed to mention that most of the policies affecting the women's program overlapped with the responsibilities of other divisions and bureaus. Consequently, when disputes arose between McAfee's staff and competing divisions, it was unclear who would get the final say.

This organizational arrangement immediately caused a host of problems. As McAfee argued in one unsent memo, the structure "assigns responsibility for policy control to the Director of the Women's Reserve and it assigns no corresponding authority" and, frustratingly, "it assigns the Director of the Women's Reserve responsibility without diminishing the duplicate responsibility of the other divisions (e.g. women as enlisted personnel are still the undivided and unshared responsibility of the Division on Enlisted Personnel, etc.)."

The poorly conceived arrangement complicated and compromised how the reserve operated. For example, the assignment of personnel to field positions and grades—a task that McAfee and her staff had assumed they would decide—would actually need to be approved by several other offices. Moreover, when irreconcilable differences of opinion arose, of which there were many, they could only be resolved with a concession from one of the parties or direct appeal to Jacobs.

It also didn't help that, despite Jacobs's assurances that rank would not matter, McAfee's rank nowhere near reflected her level of responsibility and ostensible authority. For instance, early on in the development of the WAVES, she had suggested to Jacobs that she solicit input from the bureau chiefs about where women might best be employed by the Navy. He liked the idea and asked her to consult the chiefs.

When McAfee arrived in the office of Rear Admiral John Towers, chief of the Bureau of Aeronautics, she received an abrupt response. "Where have you been all this time?" he demanded, adding, "We've been clamoring for these WAVES and nobody's ever listened to us." The source of the misunderstanding soon proved obvious. McAfee hadn't known about Towers's request because, as a lieutenant commander, she was too junior to be included in the meetings that he and the other chiefs attended. McAfee didn't just lack a seat at the table, she wasn't even in the room. "As far as general policy was concerned," she said, "that was being done way up in some echelon that I never came in contact with."

Lastly, while Jacobs had given McAfee a direct line to his office, he had failed to tell the rest of the command that she was the point person on issues of the women's units and policies. It took several months, and much explaining, for McAfee to convince the suite of rear admirals that she should be included in decisions about women and that her views should carry some weight. "I really, really, had no authority," she remembered, "except the authority of influence with Admiral Jacobs."

In addition to these bureaucratic handcuffs, McAfee's gender did not help her case for relevance. She soon found that ideas she offered were dismissed, not on their merits, but simply because a woman had proposed them. This pattern seemingly permeated the entire Navy headquarters, and her subordinates reported that nothing was getting done, because the men in charge of their bureaus were simply disinclined to take ideas from the WAVES.

In situations like these, McAfee was forced to find workarounds. "We could go on having just as many ideas as we wanted to," she insisted, "but under no circumstances must they come from my offices to those offices by way of these girls." Instead, she directed, "it would be the fine art of each of these young women, fine intelligent young women, to get the idea to the man in charge" and allow him to think it was his own. McAfee, like the rest of the women, was embarrassed that they would have to employ such a strategy. "How perfectly stupid to resort to this technique when we were there to do a job."

Despite McAfee and her subordinates' clever approach to getting things done, it was neither a sustainable nor an efficient system, and it laid bare the reality that the Navy had not given McAfee the authority or influence she needed to be effective in her role. Instead, McAfee was constantly at odds with her colleagues and lacked the formal rank to override their ill-informed views. She quickly understood that the Navy had not kept its promise to endow her position with the power it required. Instead, it was virtually nonexistent. She would have to find another way to obtain the authority necessary to do her job. "You didn't even earn it," she remembered. "You just had to kind of demand it."

# 7

# "YOUR DUTY ASHORE, HIS AFLOAT"

## MARINE CORPS WOMEN'S RESERVE AND COAST GUARD SPARS

WITH THE ARMY AND NAVY HAVING ESTABLISHED their women's programs, the remaining services—namely the Coast Guard and Marine Corps—soon followed suit. On November 7, 1942, Roosevelt, following the recommendation of Secretary of the Navy Frank Knox, authorized the creation of a women's program for both.

As with the WAVES, the Coast Guard turned to Gildersleeve and her advisory council to identify a woman suitable for heading their women's program. This time, the council already had a handful of vetted candidates. Dorothy Stratton instantly stood out from the rest.

Stratton was a midwesterner through and through. The daughter of a Baptist preacher, Stratton was born in Missouri but spent most of her childhood moving between small towns in the region. Her itinerant upbringing meant that she quickly developed an ease with people, and she was known among close friends for her "inherent kindness, sensitivity to people, and an open, frank attitude of friendliness." She was, in other words, a delightful person to be around. Stratton, however, also had an ambitious and mischievous streak. When asked by a reporter whether, as a minister's daughter, she was "ever a bad little girl," she replied with a laugh, "Was I ever a good little girl?"

Stratton's father had encouraged her interest in education, and after graduating high school, she went on to pursue a bachelor's from Ottawa College, a master's in psychology at the University of Chicago, and, finally, a doctorate in student personnel administration at Columbia University. Her decision to continue her education was a practical one: "I found that employers wanted firstly, a man with a PhD degree; secondly, a man with a master's degree; thirdly, a woman with a doctoral degree, and very fourthly, a woman with a master's degree." It was a welcome development when Stratton, third in line for any academic positions according to the ranking she had observed, got a call from the president of Purdue University in the summer of 1933. Stratton, with her three advanced degrees, was invited to an interview in West Lafayette, Indiana.

Under the visionary leadership of President Edward Elliott, Purdue University had established itself in the early twentieth century as one of the top institutions for science and technology in the Midwest. Enrollment had skyrocketed, and with hundreds of women now on campus, the staff struggled to keep up. In 1933, Elliott called Stratton, brought her to campus for a tour, and asked her to be the first full-time dean of women for the university. She accepted on the spot, and, days later, she purchased her first car—a beat-up secondhand Dodge—packed it to the roof, and made her way through the seemingly endless cornfields of Indiana to her new home.

Stratton and Elliott proved to be an effective team: he gave her the leeway she needed, and she delivered time and time again. Once she settled in, Stratton hired a small staff to support her expanding initiatives. First among them was Helen Schleman, who would later be appointed dean of women at Purdue and became a longtime friend, confidante, and partner to Stratton. But just as Stratton was making her home in West Lafayette, the war preparations on campus began in earnest. "If there was an opportunity for me to do my little bit," Stratton remembered, "I wanted to do it." And so, at forty-three years old, Stratton resigned her post at Purdue and headed to boot camp.

Despite Stratton's attempts to blend in among the young Navy recruits, she soon got noticed by the women serving on Gildersleeve's advisory council, who were now looking for a director of the Coast Guard women's program. As a former dean of women, Stratton was a known and trusted quantity, and, as a freshly minted WAVE, she had valuable exposure to the Navy and its customs. Stratton's combined experiences made her the ideal candidate, and the advisory council enthusiastically pursued her to head the Coast Guard women's service.

After Stratton was selected by the advisory council, McAfee set out to pitch the job to her in person. Reluctant but intrigued by the opportunity, Stratton returned to Washington for an intimidating, but successful, meeting with Admiral Russell Waesche, commandant of the Coast Guard. Within weeks, Stratton found a room in Washington—"a sort of enlarged closet"—and settled in.

As her first order of official Coast Guard business, Stratton started thinking up a name for the women's program. She sat down in her new office, situated in "one of those hard-to-get-around-in older buildings of the capital" with "that old linoleum everybody hates," and began playing with acronyms. Eventually, she settled on the SPARS, inspired by the Coast Guard motto, "Semper Paratus—Always Ready."

Stratton knew that she faced a steep learning curve when it came to understanding and enforcing rigid Coast Guard customs. McAfee and Hobby had warned her of the difficulties she would face, and Stratton had listened closely. Her second move, then, was to request a Coast Guard officer to be assigned for any protocol questions that might arise. Following that, she called up her old friend, Schleman, and insisted that she come to Washington to serve as her executive officer. Together, with the help of McAfee, they recruited twelve officers from the graduating class of WAVES to become the first ever Coast Guard SPARS.

While the Marine Corps took a different approach to establishing its women's program than did the rest of the services, it began the process with the same reluctance. Like the Navy, the Marines, up and down the chain of command, initially had little interest in trying to find a way to integrate women. Lieutenant General Thomas Holcomb, commandant of the Marine Corps, was especially suspicious of the idea. He dismissed it out of hand as exactly the type of social experiment he loathed.

Holcomb had been commissioned into the Marine Corps in 1900 and was a highly decorated commander of Marines in France in World War I. He was appointed commandant in 1936, and Roosevelt had reappointed him in 1940 and promoted him to lieutenant general, the highest-ranking officer to command the Marine Corps in its long history. Holcomb was incredibly well respected by his fellow Marines, especially for his single-minded focus on preparing the Corps for the unprecedented combat on the horizon.

For all his accolades and experience, however, Holcomb entirely lacked the foresight to recognize the value in expanding the Corps to include non-White men and women. When it came to Black men, he famously quipped that he would prefer 5,000 White Marines to 250,000 Black Marines. The suggestion that women be integrated into the Corps was equally, if not more, insulting. "I didn't believe," he admitted at the time, "women could serve any useful purpose in the Marine Corps." He reasoned that the women's programs were born of political, not practical, motives and loudly resisted the change. "From Holcomb down to the ranks," wrote one Marine historian, "there was considerable unhappiness about making the Corps anything but a club for white men."

By the end of 1942, however, two realities were pressing down on Holcomb. The first was, as he had feared, a political one: the rest of the military services had already integrated women into their ranks. Even the recalcitrant naval leadership had relented to the pressure coming from the president and Congress, and it was becoming difficult to resist what increasingly appeared to be a fait accompli.

The second reality was decidedly a military one: the Marine Corps was losing battles and personnel at an astonishing rate. In late summer 1942, the Corps had its first trial by fire during the Battle of Guadalcanal in the Solomon Islands, and it had rapidly devolved into a six-month slog. Although the Marines eventually prevailed in their first outing against the Japanese, they lost over one thousand men. Guadalcanal proved to be a rude awakening.

Adding to the alarm of the Marine Corps' early battlefield performance, Holcomb faced the same daunting manpower projections that had nudged the Navy into action on its women's program. In 1942, this reality became more dire when the Joint Chiefs of Staff authorized another increase in Marine manpower, directing it to double in size within a year. This directive, which amounted to a tenfold increase from the Corps' strength in 1939, backed Holcomb into the same corner with Army and Navy leadership, all facing the need to undertake a massive personnel expansion in incredibly short order.

Committed to preserving the elite reputation of the Marine Corps, however, Holcomb refused to lower admissions standards. This left him in a seemingly impossible predicament at the end of 1942, since there were simply not enough White men left who met the qualifications. This dilemma forced Holcomb—arguably the most reluctant holdout of the US military leadership—to concede that the Marines would need women.

In late 1942, the Marines got to work creating a women's program. Hewing closely to the precedent set by the Navy, Holcomb ordered that the process of integrating women be studied closely by his Division of Plans and Policies. They submitted their report in October 1942, concluding that women could effectively take over shore jobs, if they were carefully and strategically integrated into the force. Within a month, Holcomb approved the initial plan for the program and authorized a search to fill its most critical post, director. Seeing the Navy's success in using Gildersleeve's network to identify both McAfee and Stratton, Holcomb turned to the same list. Discreet interviews and background checks quickly coalesced around one name: Ruth Cheney Streeter.

Streeter, while not as prominent in academic and political circles as the other women's directors, had exactly the polished disposition that the Marine Corps sought for its women's program. Born in Brookline, Massachusetts, Streeter had attended Bryn Mawr College in Pennsylvania, where she was class president. After graduating, she moved to New Jersey and focused on being a housewife and mother to her four children.

As for so many women who signed up to serve, however, Streeter's traditional home life belied her more atypical character traits. For instance, although Streeter was a mother and a housewife, she was also an accomplished pilot. She received her license in 1940, served on New Jersey's Committee on Aviation, and, once the war began, offered her services to the US Army Air Forces five times. Rejected each time, Streeter briefly considered joining the WAVES but, learning that she would not be able to fly for the Navy, decided not to sign up. By the end of 1942, with her flying hopes dashed, she found herself with another, better opportunity in hand—leading the integration of women into the Marine Corps. In January 1943, she was commissioned as a Marine officer and became the head of the Marine Corps' women's outfit.

For all his protestations about integrating women into the Marine Corps, Holcomb was adamant from the start that if women were going to be a part of the organization, they would be Marines, full stop. Given his stance, Holcomb had been dismayed by the proposed nicknames for the women's Marine Corps: "Femarines,

WAMS, Dainty Devil-Dogs, Glamarines, Women's Leatherneck-Aides, MARS, and Sub-Marines," among others, had been proposed, and he found them all absurd. In a prototypically Marine fashion, Holcomb immediately put the matter to rest. "They are Marines," he retorted to a *Life* reporter when questioned about the name. "They don't have a nickname and they don't need one. They get their basic training in a Marine atmosphere at a Marine post. They inherit the traditions of Marines. They are Marines."

Bypassing catchy slogans and nicknames altogether, the Marines called the women what they were: women reservists (WRs), or, more simply, Women Marines. The organization itself would be called, matter-of-factly, the Marine Corps Women's Reserve (MCWR). There was nothing cutesy about the name because there was nothing cutesy about the Corps.

With the establishment of the MCWR in early 1943, all of the American military services possessed a women's program and were now sending them to the field to replace men in support roles. There was, however, one domain where women in uniform were still missing: the air.

# "THE ARMY AIR FORCES WANT YOU!"

## WOMEN'S AIRFORCE SERVICE PILOTS

ON NOVEMBER 2, 1929, A GROUP OF TWENTY-SIX women sat assembled in a dark, musty aircraft hangar at Curtiss Field in Valley Stream, New York. It was loud and cold, with a persistent hum in the background, as Curtiss mechanics got to work repairing six-cylinder Challenger engines. The day had seen bad weather, so most of the women had arrived by train or car, bundled in winter furs and leather gloves, and were now passing around a tea cart that was actually just a kettle balanced precariously in a toolbox.

In a photo taken on the day of the meeting, most of the women were adorned with cloche hats, furs, and oxford pumps—all typical of the time. Some are looking in the direction of the camera, but others are turned away, clearly enjoying each other's company. Aside from the setting, the gathering could have easily been mistaken for a luncheon, except for the presence of one woman, off to the side and staring directly at the camera. Fresh off the flying line, outfitted in grease-stained coveralls, a flying cap, and goggles, clipboard in hand, she was clearly a pilot. And so were the women dressed in furs.

The photo depicted the inaugural meeting of what would become known as the Ninety-Nines—named for the number of its charter members—the small but growing organization of women pilots in the United States, whose goal was "good fellowship, jobs, and a central office and files on women in aviation." The Ninety-Nines had been founded in August 1929 after the first annual Powder Puff Derby, when nineteen women pilots took off from Santa Monica, California, and raced to the finish line in Cleveland, Ohio, just over a week later.

The Ninety-Nines sprouted from the growing sense of community among women pilots, who numbered just over one hundred at the group's founding. Although they were as fiercely competitive with each other as they were with the men, the women had an undeniably strong bond as the forerunners of women in aviation. Each of them was daring, fearless, and talented, and each recognized the same traits in their counterparts.

The inaugural class of the Ninety-Nines included several women who had become minor celebrities for their flying prowess,

Inaugural meeting of the Ninety-Nines. **Courtesy of the 99s Museum of Women Pilots, Oklahoma City, Oklahoma.**

both in stunt flying and racing. The most famous at the time, and now, was Amelia Earhart, still years away from her final flight and the peak of her fame. Also in the group and only slightly less well known at the time, however, was Jacqueline Cochran, the brash, beautiful, and exceedingly talented wife of a self-made millionaire, who would soon be in charge of American women pilots during World War II.

Born Bessie Lee Pittman in Pensacola, Florida, in 1906, Cochran described herself as a refugee from Sawdust Road. "Until I was eight years old, I had no shoes," she would state years later, and "my bed was usually a pallet on the floor and sometimes just the floor. Food at best consisted of the barest essentials—sometimes nothing except what I foraged for myself in the woods or in the water of the nearby bayou."

The details of Cochran's early life are sketchy, in part because she was known to fabricate or omit certain parts of her biography, but no one would contest the difficulty of her upbringing, which she remembered as "bleak and bitter and hard." At fourteen, Cochran had been married to a twenty-year-old salesman, and three months later she gave birth to a baby boy. Seven months after that, she left the boy and his father and moved to Montgomery, Alabama, where she worked alternately as a beautician and a nurse for several years, until returning home four years later when her son was killed in a fire. Two years after the tragedy, she and her husband divorced, and, with nothing left for her in the South, she bought a train ticket to New York.

By the start of World War II, Bessie Lee Pittman had changed her name to Jackie Cochran, met and married Floyd Odlum—a millionaire who had acquired his fortune buying up companies during the Great Depression—and started her own cosmetics brand. Observing her business's breakneck pace of growth, her husband had encouraged Cochran to get her flying license, joking it was a more efficient means of travel for a woman with her ambitions, and so she got it.

Flying soon became more than a savvy business move: it was an obsession for Cochran. After devoting months to training and licensing, Cochran began competing in air competitions in the 1930s and quickly became one of the best-known women pilots in the country. An exceptional flier and a media darling, she always insisted on changing out of her flight gear and adorning the signature products of her cosmetics line before granting any interviews.

In 1938, Cochran achieved a triumphant success for both her and the Seversky P-35 she flew, winning the Bendix race, one of the most popular air competitions of the time. Cochran landed her plane among a crush of reporters and in her typical fashion, "kept them waving their notebooks and press cameras while she put on fresh face powder and lipstick." Cochran's first question after opening the canopy, writes historian Sally van Wagenen Keil, was, "Where's my husband?" Her second: "Does anyone have a cigarette?"

Behind the scenes, however, Cochran's reputation was mixed. She harbored a deep feeling of inferiority within the often-elitist world of professional flying, which could make her seem sharp-elbowed, particularly in the face of perceived disparagement of her intellect or skill. Though Cochran had come into money through her marriage to Odlum, she never forgot where she came from, and despised the upper-crust elitism found in women's flying circles before World War II. Cochran's distaste for the wealth and privilege of this community proved especially challenging during the war, since her primary counterpart, Nancy Harkness Love, came from precisely that rarified set.

Love was, in almost all respects, Cochran's opposite. The daughter of a doctor, she had attended Milton Academy and Vassar College, and had started flying at a young age with the full support of her family. Her father had responded to her request to take flying lessons with a simple statement, "Do it well, or not at all."

But even with her starkly different upbringing, Love did share one attribute with Cochran, ambition. Love received her pilot license at sixteen and soon after became qualified as an instructor and test pilot. With her husband, Robert Love, she built an impressive aviation-sales company in Boston and began competing in air races. She was a businesswoman, flier, and visionary—and perhaps not so different from Cochran after all.

The B-17 Flying Fortress, the United States' first operational four-engine bomber, had started development in the mid-1930s and reflected the expanding mandate of American airpower at the time. Whereas aviation in World War I was intended primarily to enhance the effects of ground forces, American air commanders during the interwar period saw airpower as having its own independent effects. This vision formed the basis of strategic bombing doctrine, which employed airpower to cripple the productive capacity of Japanese and German industry and required a fleet of long-range bombers packed with munitions to enact it.

Under the leadership of General Henry "Hap" Arnold, the Army Air Forces devoted considerable resources to building such a fleet over the course of the conflict, and the B-17 was among the first of the American bombers to be given this mission. It looked the part. "With all those guns," Arnold remembered someone saying, "it looks like a fort that can fly."

By 1942, as the first murmurs about a women's flying program started circulating, the war had crept to the far corners of the globe. Pearl Harbor ushered in a wave of Japanese victories, culminating in May with the fall of Corregidor. In Europe, the Germans and Italians took advantage of the momentum at their backs and continued to open new fronts.

But the news was not all good for the Axis. While the Nazis had occupied France with relative ease, they had been rebuffed in their cross-Channel attempt to invade England during the Battle of Britain, due largely to one of the best performances in the Royal Air Force's storied history. The Allies, seeing this success, took note of the important role airpower could play in future battles.

The loss, however, had done little to temper Hitler's seemingly endless ambitions. He quickly moved to advance on Yugoslavia, Greece, and Crete, only to then turn his attention to the Soviet Union, where he began a grueling assault on his former ally. The Italians, similarly undeterred by some early missteps in North Africa, were reinforced in that theater by the formidable German Afrika Korps, under the infamous "Desert Fox," Erwin Rommel. The British, spread too thin and struggling to prioritize, found themselves unable to keep up with the growing scope of the conflict. They waited, impatiently, for the United States to meaningfully commit trained men to fighting on the ground.

As the war spread to farther-flung corners of the globe, both Jackie Cochran and Nancy Love were aware that airpower was only growing in importance. Over the course of several months, the war had become truly global, crossing through dozens of borders, climates, and terrains. Many people, including most of the leaders in the US Army, understood that airpower had the unique capability of seamlessly crossing these varied thresholds.

As 1942 unfolded, Love and Cochran watched closely when the Army, recognizing the important role that airpower was playing on the battlefields in Europe and the Pacific, elevated its Air Corps to a semiautonomous organization within its ranks. The new organization was called the Army Air Forces—the predecessor to today's independent Air Force—and it consolidated all American air pilots and air assets under a single chain of command. Cochran and Love had also heard the pleas from politicians and military commanders for increased aviation resources, including Roosevelt's public demands for more planes. They had watched male pilots sign up to serve, noting that they often received a direct assignment to the Army Air Forces, their flying skills at a premium. They had seen many of the remaining men enroll as instructors and civilian ferrying pilots, contracted with the Army to move the surge of planes from manufacturing facilities to bases and, eventually, to the field. They had heard rumors about the WAAC and had seen the legislation moving through Congress. And they both wondered, to themselves and to their high-placed friends, could they find a way for women to fly too?

Though motivated by the same vision of establishing a women's flying corps within the Army, Love and Cochran took very different approaches to the task. Cochran quickly found her way to the ear of General Arnold, the senior air commander in the Army and freshly appointed head of the Army Air Forces. For several months, Arnold rebuffed her requests to begin setting up a women's flying corps, insisting that existing manpower and training rates would be sufficient to meet the Army Air Forces' needs. He did assure Cochran, however, that if the time came for a women's pilot organization, she would be asked to develop and command it.

As Cochran worked the upper echelons of the American flying establishment, Love had insinuated her way into a lower-ranking but still powerful element of that same community, Air Transport Command (ATC), the hub of the Army Air Forces' flying in the United States. ATC was responsible for two primary missions: air-lifting equipment and personnel into the field and ferrying military aircraft from manufacturing plants to bases around the country. By 1941, ATC was dealing with an exponential increase in demand for its services, and, within a year, they needed more pilots than even existed in the Army Air Forces. In the immediate aftermath of Pearl Harbor, they had hired over 3,500 civilian pilots to fill the gap, but they still struggled to keep up. Within weeks of her introduction to the command's senior leaders, Love had convinced ATC commander Brigadier General Harold George that women pilots could help ease the burden of transporting aircraft around the country, freeing up men for other duties. Overwhelmed by the sudden swell of aircraft and the limited number of pilots qualified to move them around the country, he jumped at the idea.

Under Love's guidance, ATC recommended the establishment of an organization of highly experienced women ferrying pilots—

ideally with over one thousand hours in the air—with Love as their commander. "I have been able to find forty-nine qualified women pilots I can rate as excellent material," she reported to Lieutenant Colonel Robert Olds of the Army Air Forces' Plans Division, adding, "I really think this list is up to handling some pretty complicated stuff."

By the end of 1942, informal negotiations about establishing a group of women pilots to be used for domestic Army Air Force tasks were progressing steadily on parallel tracks—the first under discussion between Cochran and Arnold, the second being hashed out between Love and ATC. But this introduced two problems. First, conflicting promises had been made. Both Cochran and Love expected that they would oversee efforts to build a women's flying organization, and both had been promised the coveted appointment to lead the new organization.

Second, and more problematic, Cochran and Love had competing visions of the scope for militarized women fliers. Love advanced a narrower proposal. She believed women pilots' primary contribution to the war effort should be to support the domestic aviation tasks of ATC. Therefore, she wanted to recruit women who met the high standards necessary for cross-country flying.

Cochran, on the other hand, had a far more expansive vision. She advocated for women with limited flying experience but exceptional competence and verve to be trained by the Army, not just to ferry planes, but to undertake any and all stateside duties that could release male pilots into combat. "We have about 650 licensed women pilots in this country," Cochran noted, adding that "most of them would be of little use today, but most of great use a few months hence if properly organized. And if they had some official standing or patriotic initiative (rather than just flying around an airplane occasionally for fun), there would be thousands more women pilots than there are now."

Although these two visions were equally valid approaches to the challenge at hand, it would have been difficult if not impossible to sustain both. And, clearly, two women could not be tasked to head a single women's flying unit. The conflict came to a head in mid-September 1942, when Love, attending a ceremony with George and Secretary of War Henry Stimson, was publicly announced as the new leader of the women's ferrying organization. The *New York Times* summed it up: WOMEN WILL FORM A FERRY COMMAND; ARMY AIR FORCES SET UP A SQUADRON WITH MRS. LOVE AS COMMANDER; FIFTY IN THE FIRST GROUP; MEMBERS WILL RECEIVE $3,000 A YEAR AND HAVE A CIVIL SERVICE STATUS.

Noting that the women's flying organization would have exacting standards, the article went on to detail Love's qualifications: "Mrs. Love has been flying for twelve years and has logged more than 1,200 hours of flying time. She has passed tests qualifying her to handle planes with engines of 600 horsepower, is an expert in flying with instruments and is also rated to fly seaplanes." By the look of it, the issue was settled. Love was certainly qualified, and the presence of War Department and ATC leadership at her swearing-in indicated their support of the venture. ATC had beaten Cochran to the punch, it seemed, and Love would oversee the newly created Women's Auxiliary Ferrying Squadron (WAFS).

Unfortunately for ATC, however, the head of the Army Air Forces, Arnold, did not agree. Cochran had immediately confronted him after the announcement and demanded an explanation of whether and how she was going to figure into this arrangement. Arnold claimed that the WAFS had been announced without his knowledge or approval and, surely recognizing that he had offended and humiliated a woman with influential friends, did what any commander in his position would do: he ordered that the mess be cleaned up. "He called General George . . . to his office," recounts one history of the women's flying program, and told him the WAFS would need to be revised. Then, pointing to Cochran, he instructed George to work it out with her.

Four days later, and much to the dismay of Love and the ATC,

SHE WILL DIRECT THE WOMEN FERRY PILOTS

# WOMEN WILL FORM A FERRY COMMAND

**Army Air Forces Set Up a Squadron With Mrs. Love as Commander**

**FIFTY IN THE FIRST GROUP**

**Members Will Receive $3,000 a Year and Have a Civil Service Status**

Special to THE NEW YORK TIMES.

WASHINGTON, Sept. 10—The Army Air Forces today formed a Women's Auxiliary Ferrying Command, although withholding military recognition from the service.

A War Department announcement said that the command would begin with about fifty women, of whom ten would do administrative work and forty would fly airplanes.

The commander of the squadron will be Mrs. Nancy Harkness Love, 28-year-old pilot and the wife of Lieut. Col. Robert M. Love, Deputy Chief of Staff of the Air Transport Command. While Mrs. Love was referred to as "commander" and

Mrs. Nancy Harkness Love being congratulated by Major Gen. Harold L. George, Chief of the Army Transport Command.

The New York Times (U. S. Army Air Forces)

*New York Times* headline announcing WAFS. **From the *New York Times*.**

Arnold announced that Cochran would head up the newly established Women's Flying Training Detachment (WFTD), a civilian organization that would find and train women to conduct a wide range of domestic tasks for the Army Air Forces, including but certainly not limited to ferrying planes.

Behind the scenes, Cochran had acknowledged that eliminating the WAFS so soon after its establishment would only serve to further confuse matters. Instead, she agreed to allow Love to remain in charge of the unit, ostensibly under the umbrella of Cochran's WFTD. In the meantime, the press release cleared up any confusion that the announcement of Love's appointment days earlier may have caused. "The formation of the Women's Auxiliary Ferrying Squadron, which was announced September 10," it was clarified, "is part of the program for the utilization of this additional reservoir of trained pilots."

It served as a useful, if tenuous, compromise for both women.

Cochran's vision of a broader women's flying command had been embraced, while Love retained her command over an elite corps of highly capable women ferrying pilots.

It was certainly not the last compromise that either woman would have to make.

Suddenly, it seemed, women were everywhere—and just in time.

By the end of 1942, the United States was fully engaged in the rapidly growing war effort and was beginning to see the exact contours of what it was going to demand. First, and most urgent, there was the fighting in Europe. Before the attack on Pearl Harbor, the British and American leadership had agreed, with some reluctant holdouts in the US Navy, that Allied effort should focus primarily on defeating Germany. The "Germany first" strategy, the argument went, would strike at the Axis power center: Hitler and the Nazi regime. Drawing on the assumptions of this strategy, American war planners began to develop estimates for creating, outfitting, and sustaining a force that would be able to defeat Germany as early as 1941. The planning, undertaken at the president's direction and eventually leading to a report called the Victory Program, was intended to be a top-secret document outlining the broad contours of what the American military would need to beat Germany.

Defeating Germany, the planners admitted, would require a hulking force of over eight million men and two hundred divisions that relied heavily on airpower, armor, and motorized forces. With a force of this size and composition, it was clear to many military planners that the supply and support elements of these units would be critical. Training, security, maintenance, and administration would ensure the effectiveness of frontline units.

By force, if not by choice, however, the Japanese attack in the Pacific ensured that the estimates for what the United States would need to produce—and the accompanying demands on combat support forces—would be even greater than those that the planners had assumed were necessary to defeat the Germans. A war with two fronts, and double the demands, was all but assured.

Roosevelt, perhaps more than anyone else, was willing to turn the screws on American productive capacity to meet these dual requirements. In his 1942 State of the Union address, he called for the production of 60,000 planes, 45,000 of which would be combat aircraft, that year alone. The next year, he stated, the United States would produce double that number. He went on to insist the United States would produce 45,000 tanks in 1942, and 75,000 in 1943; 20,000 antiaircraft guns in 1942, and 35,000 in 1943; and 6 million deadweight tons of merchant ships in 1942, and 10 million deadweight tons in 1943.

Most military and industrial leaders considered the request ludicrous. They believed there was simply not enough infrastructure and raw material to produce on this scale. Roosevelt knew, however, that with enough money and effort, enabled by the immediate and extreme expansion of US federal investment, the military could, and would, do a great deal more than they claimed possible.

The process was bumpy, but it worked. By one estimate, the expansion of American floorspace devoted to aircraft, engine, and propeller production had quadrupled in the two years from 1940 to 1942. In the same period, American air-combat strength had grown tenfold: from just over 3,000 combat aircraft at the end of 1940 to over 33,000 at the end of 1942, and by 1943 the United States would well exceed Roosevelt's initial request for 45,000 combat aircraft. By the end of the year, American production of TNT alone had gone from a prewar peak of 100,000 pounds a day to over 4 million pounds a day. Rubber production—which had suffered real and persistent shortages at the start of 1942—would quadruple within a year. Artillery production in the US would soon reach its wartime high of 120,000 pieces, alongside 14 million shoulder weapons. As Marshall put it years earlier, the "convulsive, expensive expansion in an emergency" had arrived.

Recruitment and training of military personnel was also surging in the United States. By the end of 1942, the US military had grown from 1.8 million personnel to 3.9 million personnel, and it reached over 9 million in 1943. The Army alone had grown from 1.4 million personnel to almost 7 million; the Navy had grown from a force of just over 280,000 to nearly 2 million in the same period; and the Marines had gone from just over 50,000 men to over 300,000. The first American peacetime draft had been authorized in 1940, and in 1942 it had enrolled almost 10 million men. The training apparatus was also starting to find its footing and had begun to churn out trained personnel in fully equipped units.

With all this progress, military planners knew it was time to start filling the gap between the home front and the front line. All this equipment and trained combat personnel would be compromised without the required support forces ready to enable its use in the field. "One hundred thousand airplanes would be of little value to us," noted chief of the Army War Plans Division, Major General Leonard Gerow, "if these airplanes could not be used because of lack of trained personnel, lack of operating airdromes in the theater, and lack of shipping to maintain the air squadrons in the theater." With women's programs established—and under the command of exceedingly capable leaders—it was time to redouble the effort to get women into the essential noncombat roles that would support this mammoth force. At freshly painted recruiting stations across the country, the women of America joined the line.

# 9

# "ARE YOU A GIRL WITH A STAR-SPANGLED HEART?"

## RECRUITING AND TRAINING WAACS

THE US ARMY HAS A REPUTATION FOR FINDING EF-
fective, if not elegant, solutions to unanticipated problems. When
it came to WAAC recruiting in late 1942, that solution was, literally, bananas.

The problem was, at least in part, of the Army's own making.
Despite months of careful preparation for the incorporation of
women into the Army and the meticulous development of requirements for admission, the Army had failed to consider that
some women are, by nature, petite. This reality proved to be an
issue, since the Army had set the weight cutoff for prospective
WAACs firmly at one hundred pounds. While many WAACs
met this standard, many others found themselves standing on a
scale in an Army recruiting office only to receive the devastating
news that their interest in joining the WAAC ended before it even
began.

Army recruiters were equally disappointed. Not only did this
requirement stymie their monthly enlistment targets, but they, like
most of those turned away, questioned why on earth weight even

# VALIANT WOMEN

mattered when the Army had been clear that most WAACs would be assigned to combat support duties.

So, they found a deceptively simple workaround. If a slightly underweight woman came into the recruiting office, she was instructed to go home, eat as many bananas as possible, and come back at the end of the day to be weighed again. Usually this would increase her weight within a pound or two of the requirements. As a final recourse, they told the most petite women to try milkshakes, harder to come by but even more effective.

Other tricks quickly emerged for women eager to volunteer but found lacking in some respect. Teased hair would beat the height requirement, a letter from a well-placed family friend or colleague could bypass the upper age limit, and a recruiter's visit to church, or better yet Sunday dinner, could overcome the parental-consent requirement for women not yet old enough. "The men lie like anything to stay out of the Army," reported one Army recruiter as he took a WAAC's measurements, "and you girls lie like anything to get in."

This enthusiasm was a welcome development, since senior leaders across all the women's programs felt a great sense of urgency around growth. They reasoned, correctly, that near-constant recruitment would be paramount for women's units to make a dent in the manpower balance. Part of the recruitment challenge, however, was that the programs were looking for a very specific type of woman—generally no younger than twenty or older than forty-five, in good physical health, with no dependents under eighteen and, ideally, White and middle-class. Finding women who fit this description and who were willing to uproot their lives, for the duration of the war plus six months, proved extremely difficult. What's more, the women's services were also contending with the rapidly growing and well-paying manufacturing industry, which faced its own shortages and recruited from the same pool. Women, suddenly a hot labor commodity, could take their pick: Army? Navy? Nursing? Red Cross? Civil Air Defense? Industry? All were hiring.

98

Understanding these demands and having a head start over the other women's services, Hobby soon began what would become a signature of her leadership for the next three years: road tours. Over one particularly busy two-month recruiting trip for the WAAC, Hobby traveled to Baltimore, San Antonio, Fort Worth, New York, and Des Moines; made three stops in Missouri; and then stopped in Commerce, Texas, before returning to Washington. The relentless travel, though exhausting, provided Hobby the opportunity to keep an eye on national recruiting efforts.

As the first and largest service, the WAAC was in a difficult recruiting position—and so, therefore, was Hobby. Not only did the WAAC have the highest manpower targets, but there was no existing model for how to compete. Hobby, following her intuition, reasoned that the best strategy was to get the program on the front page of local papers, and stay there. In service of this goal, Hobby insisted on conducting endless interviews with local media as she traveled the country, highlighting the important work that women were already doing in the Army and using her own newfound stardom to attract enlistments at community organizations.

Her pitch consistently followed the same arc. She would first outline the progress that had been made in setting up the WAAC, reporting on the jobs that women were fulfilling across the country. She would recount the harrowing figures about the strength of the Axis forces. Then, and often quite forcefully, Hobby would note that the stakes were too high for anyone to sit this war out, man or woman.

She did not mince words:

The freedom of man is once again at stake. Every man, and every woman throughout our land has a personal share in that stake. They all are needed, in some way, to protect it. We of the Women's Army Auxiliary Corps know the part that we must take. We do the things which otherwise would be done by men—thousands of men from the fighting ranks—men whose presence in the battle line may mean Victory—men whose absence might mean defeat. I say to every American woman who is available and eligible to serve with us, if she will come forward and cross the line, together we shall take our stand, for Freedom.

Hobby's urgency was well placed since, in early preplanning discussions for the WAAC, the Army had set a high bar for recruitment. While Army planners wanted to create an elite corps of women who would meet exactingly high-qualifications standards, they also recognized that the pressure of rapidly increasing manpower demands would soon expand the need for women. Given these considerations, the overwhelmingly male planners hoped to persuade around eleven thousand highly qualified women to sign up to serve in uniform. Although the number was high, they pinned their hopes on a vigorous recruiting effort.

In the end, their estimate for the WAAC's first year missed the mark, underestimating it by almost six hundred percent. In the Corps' first year alone, over 60,000 women signed up. On the first day of recruiting in New York City, for instance, 1,400 women arrived at the recruiting office. Across New York State, over 5,000 women submitted applications, even though the WAAC was only authorized to take 30 women from the entire mid-Atlantic region. Clearly, American women were ready to serve.

The overwhelming response to the early recruitment drives created an impressive pool of candidates, from which the Army selected a truly exceptional group of women. According to the official military record, of the three hundred and sixty WAACs in the inaugural training class, ninety-nine percent were employed before joining the WAAC, ninety percent had college training, and several of the group had advanced degrees. They were among the most accomplished women in the country: "a dean of women, a school owner and director, a personnel director, a Red Cross official, a former sales manager, and several editors . . . reporters, office executives, lawyers, social workers, Army employees, and teachers."

The combined quality and number of women signing up proved to be a welcome surprise to Army planners, since demand for women in uniform continued to increase. The early enthusiasm was so encouraging that, only three months after the WAAC was established, the Army started making plans to recruit over one and a half million women.

With overflowing rosters of recruits in hand, Army officers now needed to train them.

When Doris Samford arrived at Fort Des Moines, the former cavalry base that had been retrofitted as a training facility for WAAC, she worried about her iron. The Army had required her to bring several essential items to basic training, among them "hairpins, comb, toothbrush, shower cap, shower clogs, bathrobe, pajamas, safety pins" and an electric iron. The state of hers had kept her up all night on the train ride from Colorado to Iowa.

Wartime rationing had made some electrical items, like irons, exceedingly difficult to acquire. Factories no longer produced them, as they were now making navigational aids and radios, and used irons were hard to come by. Samford had finally found a temperamental one at a secondhand store, ugly as sin with its yellow handle and checkered black-and-white cord, but she worried that her dilapidated equipment would immediately disqualify her in the eyes of her superiors. As she pulled up at the train station, however, Samford forgot about the iron entirely.

Arrival at Fort Des Moines, the first WAAC training center, could be an ordeal. Nearly the entire town turned out for the monthly shipment of WAACs arriving by train. "I don't know what they expected to see, but I am sure they were heartily disappointed," remembered one WAAC. "We were not exotic, not startling, not queer, just average women who looked awfully tired and train weary."

Samford was in for quite a scene. Having disembarked from the train, she was abruptly brought to her senses by an officer with a WAAC armband ordering her—and her fellow confused companions—to collect their suitcases, form a line, and march in unison to the olive Army truck that would take them to the base. A short ride later, they were deposited at the new WAAC barracks, the infamous Stable Row, a building that had been speedily upgraded from a horse stable into suitable housing for human occupants.

From there, each woman moved through the various phases of basic training in essentially the same sequence. On arrival at Des Moines, or one of the other four bases set up to manage the influx of recruits, the women were assigned to their bunks and then sent off for processing. There, they received their uniform, or whatever parts of the uniform were still available in their size, and lined up for the first of many rounds of shots, which left most women staggering out of the processing center. Soon after, each woman was scheduled for an aptitude test, intended to give the Army a sense of their particular strengths and weaknesses: "There is no sloppy guesswork in the Army," wrote one WAAC. "They know exactly what you can do, and how well you can do it."

Once processed, their new lives began. Made clear on day 1, the Army routine did not deviate for two months. The women woke up at 0530 and were expected to be at the morning flag raising by 0630. They had about an hour to clean and organize the barracks, with the reserve of that time left for a hurried breakfast, surprisingly filling and, often, quite tasty. The rest of the day was split between classroom instruction and outdoor activities— notably, calisthenics and marching. The calisthenics generally followed a similar structure as the men's training, and, for the most part, the women were able to keep it up, despite some unexpected challenges. "It wasn't so bad," remembered one Army nurse, "but the jumping exercises wrecked the dignity of some of the heavy chested girls." By 1630 it was time for a quick dinner and then back to the barracks for studying and, if time allowed, letter writing or a quick shower, followed by lights out at 2200.

"I feel as if I were riding a rocket," wrote one bewildered woman.

Prior to establishing the WAAC, male members of Congress and the public had worried about how the women would respond to the rigid uniformity of military service. Many of the men, skeptical of the women's program, feared that recruits would be driven to hysterics by the constant threat of inspection, the yelling of senior officers, and the loss of independence and individuality.

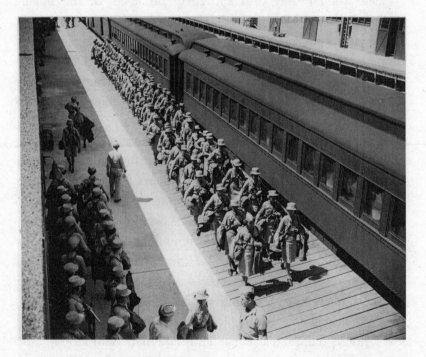

WAACs arrive for duty at Camp Patrick Henry, Virginia. **Courtesy National Archives, photo no. 138926094.**

They were, again, wrong. Surprising many of their male superiors, but probably few of their fellow volunteers, the first WAAC classes often had standards for cleanliness, uniformity, and discipline that far exceeded Army regulations. In one case, a young woman had to be reprimanded for making up the beds of her bunkmates, simply because she "liked to make beds" and wanted the unit to pass inspection. Entire barracks of women slept on top of their covers the night before inspection so that they would have more time the following morning to prepare the rest of their equipment and uniforms. And, as it turned out, Samford's concern about her iron was shared by many other WAACs. Women often requested additional irons, laundry tubs, and drying racks, since they deemed the normal allotment inadequate to meet their high standards.

The women were also extremely proficient at the much-maligned drill. "We have found that women respond more quickly and rhythmically to drill and marching than men do," said one training officer, a fact confirmed time and time again by the public displays of military women marching in sharp formation. As another male officer at Fort Des Moines put it, "You couldn't make them complain."

The first class of recruits at Fort Des Moines in the summer of 1942 set a high standard, and provided the earliest and best evidence against any doubts about women's adaptability. In the inaugural class, the commanding officer at Fort Des Moines, Colonel Donald Faith—tough but beloved—implored the officer candidates to take things less seriously, remarking that he "had never seen such a spirit in a group." The women, he continued, should be ashamed for "not having more sense than to go to bed when they have to get up at 5:45" and were "too tense and too competitive." By all accounts, Faith's pleas for the women to take their jobs less seriously fell on deaf ears. "From the first," said Hobby, "the WAACs have been eager to prove that they required no quarter in discipline, no special comforts, no concessions to chivalry. This selflessness had its root in their united determination to be good soldiers—its fruition is the WAAC esprit de corps."

Overwhelmingly, the recruits—including the more distinguished among them—adjusted well to basic training. After all, the deans, professors, and businesswomen who signed up for the WAAC had been humbled, and sometimes humiliated, on the way up the ladder in their respective fields. At least in this case, they could draw a straight line between the inconveniences and hardships they endured at training and the contribution they were making. "When a woman in her middle thirties who has formerly had an important post in a large university," remembered one WAAC, "tells you that during indoctrination she had thirteen different roommates and six different rooms in a month, you may be sure she did not take this lightly." The women willingly endured a little indignity and discomfort as the price of admission to serve their country.

However, in a small number of cases, some women never quite made the adjustment. Military training, even when executed by well-intentioned and effective officers, could be difficult to tolerate. Marcelle Fisher alleged her commanding officer played favorites, writing her mother, "I have been very unhappy here," and adding, "I contemplated quitting entirely. I have worked until I could drop and it seems that the ones that are apple polishers get farther." Adeline LaPlante shared Fisher's frustration with the perceived playing of favorites, telling her parents, "If at the end of November I don't have a decent job, I am going to raise a big row to find out how I can get out of the corps," adding that "the whole thing is politics, if you're not well connected it's too bad."

For other women, the stress and pressure to perform well proved difficult to bear. Roberta House wrote in a note to her family, "I've never felt so inadequate in meeting requirements," adding that "we must make good. The WAACs have to be tops." Jean Holdridge Reeves had almost received a medical discharge "on account of nerves" during her time at basic training. Still others, facing the difficulties and disappointments of military life first-hand, quit the Corps, either because they were lured away by the defense industry or faced complications of dependents.

Whatever the reason, the WAAC did their best to find an arrangement for the small group of women that struggled. But, overwhelmingly, most women withstood the rigors of basic training, especially given the payoff. As Jenny Lea put it after graduating from officer candidate school in September 1942, "Getting those gold bars meant more to me than anything I've ever done. It cost me more hell than I ever thought I could bear but now I've made it. I'm so d[amn] proud of it I could die."

# 10

# "LEARN A SKILL YOU'LL VALUE ALL YOUR LIFE"

## BLACK WOMEN JOIN THE WAAC

FOR MANY BLACK WOMEN IN THE FORTIES, SEGRE-gation animated every moment of their existence in the public sphere—and Black WAACs were no exception. This reality confronted them almost immediately upon joining the Army, as they stepped off the bus at Fort Des Moines and were greeted with a stark reminder: "Negroes on one side! White girls on the other!" Among the thousands of Black women who arrived at Fort Des Moines only to be greeted by an officer directing her to get into a different line stood Vivian "Millie" Corbett.

Corbett knew segregation well. Born in Washington, D.C., but raised in Tulsa, Oklahoma, she remembered Tulsa as having an invisible line that ran through it—on one side, the Black part of the town; on the other side, the White. "Segregation was nothing new to me," she stated firmly in our interview years later. "All my life I had been segregated."

Corbett's father and mother divorced when she was too young to remember much about her father. His absence, however, paled in comparison to the presence of her mother, Leona Bell Corbett. She was a force. In the aftermath of World War I, she became a businesswoman, doing whatever it took to support Corbett and her sister, whether that meant running a rooming house or working as one of the most talented seamstresses in town. "She didn't take any guff from anybody," said Corbett, adding, "I got that from her." But Corbett's mother was also kind and warm: "She didn't have a lot to give," Corbett remembered, "but she was a giving person." It was that combination that Corbett envied and emulated her entire life.

The Corbett girls, Millie and her sister, Ione Thelma, were smart. Ione had been valedictorian in 1933; Millie, in 1934. But Millie faced limited options, despite excelling as a student. Working in the White part of town as anything but a service worker—domestics, chauffeurs, and so on—was unusual, and although businesses and professionals did exist in the Black neighborhoods, Corbett was capable of a great deal more than the opportunities in Tulsa could offer her.

Corbett had heard about the WAAC from her cousin, who joined several months before Corbett graduated from high school, along with another woman in town. Corbett didn't have much information about the military but, at a minimum, she figured it would give her experience that would be useful after the war. She knew the Army would be segregated, but so was Oklahoma and, for that matter, most of the United States.

From the moment Black women like Corbett set foot on base, they were required to serve in different units and housed in different barracks. The segregated housing was a particularly wasteful and absurd arrangement. Since Black WAAC officers needed to be housed separately from Black enlisted women, and both were required to be housed separately from White WAACs, this meant that the Army sometimes built double the housing units for the handful of Black WAACs on base. It was an expensive and illogical solution to a problem purely of the Army's own creation.

Even in the face of this brazen discrimination, however, Black leaders, and especially Mary McLeod Bethune, one of the most powerful and well-known Black women in the country, encouraged Black women to sign up for service in the WAAC. Bethune, a formal advisor to Hobby on issues facing Black WAACs and informal champion of the women who served, understood that while communities of color often bore a disproportionate share of the costs of war, the circumstances of conflict could also present unique opportunities for Black Americans.

First, as a symbolic rejoinder to American racism, Black Americans understood that their military service, in part, could be used as a tool to force White America to acknowledge the contradiction of Black soldiers fighting for democratic ideals abroad while being denied them at home. By sacrificing their lives and livelihoods for the cause of freedom, Black Americans in uniform were a powerful reminder of America's shameful failure to realize that cause within its own borders.

More practically, Black Americans also knew that war could be a catalyst for expanding professional opportunities. In the 1940s, few opportunities for economic and professional advancement existed for Black Americans. Black women, especially, were stuck at the bottom of the economic ladder. But military training, the thinking went, could provide them with valuable skills for the postwar job market and, potentially, lift them into a new economic tier. Sandra Bolzenius, a historian of Black women's service during this period, remarked that "the corps offered servicewomen opportunities to acquire meaningful job skills, demonstrate their abilities, and directly contribute to the war effort," adding that "any one of these possibilities was a rare occurrence for most African American women, so when they came as a packaged deal, many sought to take advantage."

\* \* \*

Several months before Corbett had departed for Des Moines, another group of young Black women descended onto the same train platform to see what opportunities the Army might offer them. Charity Adams, a tall, striking woman from Columbia, South Carolina, was among them.

Like Corbett, Adams had lived in the shadow of racism her entire life. As a toddler, she sat on her father's lap and watched one of the nation's largest Ku Klux Klan parades march through her hometown. She was accustomed to taking a seat in the rear of public transportation and to seeing the COLORED signs affixed to most public places. As a child, she was devastated when her best friend, Mitchell, a Greek neighbor with whom she played, started attending a different school.

Despite the segregated environment, Adams fondly remembered her upbringing in the South. The daughter of a preacher, Adams was an excellent student and enjoyed a warm childhood surrounded by family and community. When she got a coveted scholarship to attend Wilberforce University, she jumped at the opportunity and went on to get a degree in education. By 1942, she had settled into a comfortable life teaching math and science at a junior high school in Columbia.

For a woman—Black or White—she had built a respectable, stable career. But Adams, like many of her contemporaries, chafed at the small-town life that threatened to suffocate her growing aspirations. So, when a personal letter arrived from the dean of Wilberforce inviting her to apply for a position in the WAAC, it felt like a lifeline. "The uncertainty of the Army," she would remember in her memoir, "was far more appealing at this point than the certainty of dullness and rigidity that the teaching profession had offered."

Adams was also confident, and rightly so. With all the world had thrown at her, she entered the WAAC as an assured young woman, fitting exactly the description the Army had claimed it was looking for: highly educated, accomplished, intelligent. Since Adams was a Black woman, however, her confidence was often perceived as a threat as much as an asset. In her initial interview with the WAAC admissions panel, she overheard one of the interviewers remark, "Let's take her and see if she is as good as she thinks she is."

It turned out that Adams was exactly that good. Before the war's end, she led the only unit of Black WAACs to serve overseas in World War II, the 6888th Central Postal Battalion—known as the Six Triple Eight—and became one of the few women in the Army, Black or White, to achieve the rank of lieutenant colonel during the war.

Her future achievements, however, did not compensate for the demoralizing segregation that she and other Black women endured at Fort Des Moines. Even Adams, who had seen the worst segregation had to offer, was surprised at her treatment. Having spent days traveling with a cadre of White women on her way to Fort Des Moines, she remembered, warmly, that they "had some feeling of closeness because we had started out together on our adventure," adding that "the Army soon shattered whatever closeness we had felt."

Like Corbett, Adams had known to expect segregation and racism in the Army when she signed up. But she calculated that the prejudice and hardship would ultimately be outweighed by the opportunities that military service presented. As Bethune said when she visited one of the first classes of Black recruits, "Here at Ft. Des Moines we have democracy in action. We are seeking equal participation. We are not going to be agitators." The Black women who had joined the Army were making a point, to be sure, but they mainly wanted to do their duty and do it well. The times, and their consciences, demanded it.

As the Army received its first Black women into segregated units, the Navy, again, watched closely. In June 1942, the Navy had reluctantly allowed a small group of Black men to join their ranks but remained staunchly opposed to recruiting Black women into their women's program. Instead, they focused on building a recruiting and training apparatus that would appeal to middle-class White women, and they hoped that recruiting these women in sufficient numbers to address their manpower shortfalls would prevent them from having to open their doors any further.

Women's Army Auxiliary Corps (WAAC) officer Charity Adams (*center*) at the first WAAC training center in Fort Des Moines, Iowa. **Courtesy National Archives, photo no. 531334.**

# 11

# "THAT WAS THE DAY I JOINED THE WAVES"

## RECRUITING AND TRAINING SAILORS

"CAN I HELP YOU, LITTLE LADY?"

The redcap porter had seen the young woman lugging her suitcase across the platform, and years working in the bowels of Penn Station had made him an expert at rescuing a fish out of water.

Joy Lemmon had just arrived in New York City for the first time, and was certainly out of her depth. She had journeyed to New York from her small hometown in the shadow of Tennessee's Great Smoky Mountains, taking the Clinchfield Railroad to Johnson City, then transferring to the Southern Railroad en route to Pennsylvania Station. It was a long trip, but, being unfamiliar with cross-country train travel, she never used the sleeping berth that had been assigned to her. Groggy and bewildered, she stepped off the train into the commotion of the busiest train station in the busiest city in the country.

Lemmon did indeed fit the description of "little lady." She weighed just under a hundred pounds, stood barely five feet tall, and wore a size 2 shoe. Like many WAVES, Lemmon had initially been judged too small by the Navy recruiter reviewing her qualifications in an unassuming Knoxville post office. But he had seen her potential, and gave her the well-worn counsel that had worked for so many other women: "Drink a milkshake," he advised—and then, looking back, he added, "and have a banana split." Lemmon did as instructed and weighed in again. She barely made the cut.

Lemmon remembered in our interview that she had known for some time that she wanted to join the military. Most of her family had joined the service, including her twin brother, who had recently joined the Navy, and she wanted to do her part. For most of the war, she had been painting dishes in Tennessee for forty cents an hour. "I can't just keep painting these teacups," she thought, feeling at her wit's end. Now, as she stood in the center of Penn Station, she wondered whether she would make it to boot camp, let alone through it.

Lemmon told the redcap in her infectious Appalachian drawl that she was looking for the WAVES meeting point. A spark of recognition lit his face. He knew the spot well, as by then seemingly countless women had arrived at the station en route to training. He grabbed her things and started on his way, headed just one floor up on the escalator.

When he reached the top, however, Lemmon had vanished. Looking over the edge, he noticed her frozen below, dumbfounded by the moving staircase. She had never before seen an escalator.

He went back down, helped her onto the first step, and said gently, "We'll make it."

Lemmon was heading to Hunter College, then nicknamed the USS *Hunter*, where the Navy had just transferred training for enlisted WAVES. Located on Manhattan's east side, the college undertook many changes to function as a training center, including retrofitting the dorms and the recreational spaces to accommodate the recruits. The Navy jargon also crept into the daily vocabulary:

on campus: quarterdeck (lobby), billet (room), mess (dining hall), and even a term for the new recruits, "ripples" (little WAVES).

The WAVES training facility at Hunter provided a welcome upgrade to the initial Navy boot camp experience. Against the strenuous objections of McAfee and her team, the director of training in the Bureau of Personnel had initially decided that the WAVES recruits did not need to go through the rigors of boot camp. Rather, for the first several months of the program, the WAVES boot camp was truncated, simply tacked on to more specialized training at facilities around the country. This resulted in new enlisted WAVES being sent directly to, say, yeoman's school, and only receiving two weeks of general Navy instruction before starting a specialized course.

This approach proved to be seriously misguided. Boot camp, and its equivalents across all the services, is one of the most foundational and critical elements of military training. It instills a sense of shared purpose, community, and esprit de corps. It also provides a standardized lexicon and baseline understanding of complex military customs and regulations, both formal and informal. Without this training, enlisted WAVES found themselves confused and ill equipped for the jobs to which they were assigned. It only took six months—and near-constant pleas from WAVES leaders—for the Bureau of Personnel to realize its mistake.

Uniform and consolidated training was especially important given the numbers of women who were now flooding into the WAVES recruiting stations. As for the WAAC, the announcement of the WAVES and McAfee's vigorous recruiting campaign had resulted in a surge of enlistments at the close of 1942. Although the Navy had decided on a slightly more discerning strategy for recruiting, asking women to apply in writing before coming in for an interview, the numbers of volunteers who met the Navy's standards still managed to astonish many naval leaders. "The Navy, at no point, thought in big terms," said McAfee, and instead believed the program would start out small and grow gradually. And grow it did. In its first year alone, the WAVES swelled to almost thirty thousand women.

When the Navy's training division finally realized the wisdom of a unified, streamlined means of indoctrination, however, they took a slightly different tack than the Army. Rather than build their own facilities, as the Army had done, the Navy chose to commandeer existing college campuses around the country and retrofit them to meet their needs. The choice was both practical and symbolic. The Navy wanted to create the impression that joining the WAVES was just as respectable and prestigious as going to college, and what better way to do so than to, literally, take over a college campus.

Hunter College, now under the leadership of Captain William Amsden and Lieutenant Elizabeth Reynard, a former professor of English literature at Barnard with a flair for the dramatic, grew into a formidable naval training base. Like the WAAC at Fort Des Moines, the WAVES followed a relentless schedule. Reveille came at 0530, followed by breakfast at 0620, with the remaining balance of the morning reserved for cleaning, before the recruits reported to their duty stations at 0830. They were expected to march to meals and classes, conduct two to three hours of drill, and attend at least five hours of classes daily. Instruction started out with the basics: military courtesy, salutes, pay and accounting, officer insignia, ranks and protocol, identification of rated and nonrated men, military discipline, identification of aircraft, and identification of naval vessels—and only deepened from there.

The Navy kept a watchful eye on the women, and nothing seemed to escape the attention of senior officers. "It has been brought to the attention of the Bureau," wrote one scolding memo, "that WAVE personnel are wearing play shoes and other casual-type shoes. In particular, the wearing of moccasins has been noted." The memo reminded women that Uniform Regulation, paragraphs 14 and 15, dictated only black service or dress shoes were allowed. "Telephones are to be used sparingly," directed another official pronouncement. "Make conversations brief, and dispense with amenities," it recommended, adding: "Conversations should be completed within three minutes."

Just north of Hunter, the first officer class of the WAVES were also settling into their newly retrofitted military barracks at Smith College in Northampton, Massachusetts. One of the top women's colleges in the country, Smith had been selected by the Navy as the location for training officers primarily because it was one of the few colleges that could quickly adapt its existing infrastructure to handle the expected influx of hundreds of Navy recruits arriving for training each month. Just as important, the college's administration was highly supportive of hosting the WAVES. Although Smith was stretched to the limit of its capacity, its president, Herbert Davis, had not been shy about his enthusiasm for supporting the WAVES. "President Davis," remembered McAfee, "said to the Navy 'Anything that you want, we'll be just delighted to do.'" McAfee—as a college president herself—immediately asked whether he had discussed the matter with his administrative officers. "Oh no," he replied, "[b]ut they will be glad to do anything they can for the service."

He was right. On being notified that Smith was in the running to house the officer-training facilities for the WAVES, both the administrative staff and the board of directors were elated. The board members enthusiastically provided their consent to have several campus buildings renovated and handed over to the Navy for the duration of the war. "It sounds to be perfectly splendid," wrote famed attorney and Smith board member Dorothy Kenyon. Eleanor Edson, metropolitan director of the Girl Scouts of New York, also lent her endorsement: "With all possible haste, I send my most enthusiastic approval." She added, "I cannot see any drawback to accepting such an idea."

But even as the WAVES settled in at Smith, more space was

needed to handle the rapidly expanding service. Mount Holyoke College, ten miles down the road from Smith, soon offered its facilities, used primarily to train WAVES selected for the elite communications units that would head to Washington to break Axis codes.

In addition, the extra space allowed the WAVES to accommodate an unexpected, but welcome, influx of their sisters in the Coast Guard and Marine Corps, who faced the same challenges of finding space for the sudden flood of recruits. The two services, established months later than the WAVES, had worked diligently to increase their numbers from the outset, and had also succeeded beyond expectations. Within months of their establishment, the MCWR and SPARS outgrew their shared space with the Navy and started to search for another arrangement.

Given the broadening scope of the war, the growth of the women's services became increasingly important. The steady advance of the Axis had hit its peak at the end of 1942, but, by then, the United States was finally prepared to respond. At the end of the year, the United States had moved to reinforce the British in North Africa and, after a faltering start, managed to regain the momentum there, stopping the combined German and Italian forces and reversing months of Axis gains in Egypt, Libya, and Tunisia. But the Allies did not stop at this important victory. They knew they needed to exploit their gains in North Africa and keep the Axis off balance, or the Axis forces would surely regroup and inflict a punishing counterattack. To avoid this outcome, the Allies pressed forward and attempted to pin the Axis forces at the edge of the Mediterranean.

With 1942 coming to a close and the Axis beginning to show its cracks in North Africa, the Allies had also started to make progress in the Pacific theater. Over the summer, they had slowed the Japanese advance in the Pacific with a critical victory at the Battle of

Midway, executing a stunningly effective defense of the island and striking a major blow against the Japanese fleet. Aiming to exploit this momentum, American commanders began planning for a series of sequential assaults on strategic Japanese-held islands in the Pacific.

With near-constant advances on so many fronts in the offing for 1943, the United States needed to send unprecedented amounts of resources—including, above all else, personnel—to meet its growing global commitments. At the end of 1942, the manpower reckoning that American service leaders feared had finally arrived.

WAVES walk to the target range while attending the Naval Air Gunners School. **Courtesy National Archives, photo no. 520612.**

# 12

# "THE GIRL OF
# THE YEAR IS A SPAR"

## SPARS AND MCWR RECRUITMENT
## AND TRAINING

AMONG THE MANY WOMEN CAUGHT UP IN THE RE-
cruiting and training surge of 1942 and 1943 was Merle Jean
Selma. Selma grew up five miles from the Mississippi River in Arlington, Kentucky, then a town of about three hundred people.
Although there wasn't much to be said for it, Selma remembered
that the town had everything she needed: a grade school, a high
school, two churches, a main store, and a barbershop. Selma's
mother had moved there from Kansas City to be closer to home
after having five children in as many years. But even with family
nearby, her mother struggled, especially after Selma's father left.

In the wake of the Depression, with no way to care for her
children, Selma's mother faced an impossible choice: give some
of her children up for adoption or risk being unable to feed them
all. She chose the lesser of two bad options and placed three of
her kids with other families, including Selma. But it didn't take. All
three times that her mother tried to give her away, Selma found
her way back.

Selma soon understood why her mother had worried about

raising so many children on her own. They experienced stark and constant poverty. Her mother sewed and took whatever work she could find, but she found supporting three children on odd jobs to be a nearly impossible task. "The Depression was tough," remembered Selma in our interview, and it was as simple as that.

But Roosevelt's inauguration proved to be a boon for the family. Selma's mother enrolled in the Works Progress Administration (WPA) as a seamstress, and their situation started to improve, helped by Selma and her siblings finding work babysitting and mowing lawns. Still, by the time she finished high school, Selma knew she had to leave Arlington. She graduated just as the war got underway, and most of her girlfriends went to work for the defense plants across the border with Tennessee. With war jobs available nationwide, however, Selma saw an opportunity. She found work at a munitions plant a bit farther away in Saint Louis, quality checking .50 caliber bullet cores.

Selma received more money in her first paycheck than she had ever seen in her life. She sent most of it home to her mother but, occasionally, spent some of it on clothing or a new pair of shoes, with the help of her ration cards. Since silk and nylon stockings were impossible to find, Selma settled for the paint-on variety—"liquid stockings," as they were known—falling somewhere between tint and foundation, topped off with a ruler-straight line of brown pencil to mimic a seam.

With her "stockings" applied, Selma walked a short block and a half from the nearest streetcar stop to the defense plant where she worked each morning. On her way, she remembered being intrigued by the Army, Navy, Coast Guard, and Marine Corps recruiting stations lined up in a row on the strategic block between the station and the plant.

Within weeks, Selma had stopped at each stall. She was fixated on the different styles of the hats, and had soon tried on all of them. She liked the Marine Corps version best, with its brass globe resting against an olive-green base and "Montezuma red" rope.

But each time she admired herself in the mirror of the recruiting booth, her hand would drift up to her shoulder, finding its way to her prized possession, her hair. The recruiters told her that she would have to cut it into a sensible shoulder-length style to join any service, and she couldn't bring herself to do it.

But sacrifice takes many forms. Selma knew she wanted a change, and she wanted to contribute to the war that had become all-consuming. She took one last look at her long hair under the Marine Corps cap and signed up.

Both the Coast Guard and Marine Corps had started at a disadvantage when it came to recruiting and training. They were dwarfed in size compared to the other services, and they had gotten off to a later start. Both Stratton and Streeter, just starting as directors of the SPARS and MCWR, were well aware of their handicap. "It is probable," reported a Coast Guard study on joint publicity with the Navy, "that both the WAVES and SPARS have suffered somewhat because they could not play up the distinctive features of their own individual service." The Marine Corps leadership agreed, noting that the other services had "considerably more that was spectacular and newsworthy to offer."

The SPARS and MCWR recruiters faced a difficult challenge: "In stiff competition with the other services and their snazzy station wagons," wrote historians Mary C. Lyne and Kay Arthur, the recruiters "careened about the country in mobile units, leaving laundry and dry cleaning in their wake, ironing shirts on top of suitcases, battling with primitive plumbing and cockroaches, and being of necessity constantly cheerful and perpetually enthusiastic."

Although the Coast Guard and Marine Corps faced several recruiting challenges, they did have one advantage working in their favor. Both of the services had capped the size of their programs well below the Army and Navy, with the Coast Guard initially limited to just over eight thousand women, and the Marine Corps restricted to nineteen thousand personnel. These limits provided some relief from the otherwise unrelenting competition for talented recruits.

With the benefit of these lower caps, both services had gotten off to a strong start. In their first six months, the SPARS reported an almost tenfold increase in enlistment. The MCWR also did well, with close to 2,500 women enlisting in the first eight weeks, and 15,000 women by the end of the first year, only a few thousand women short of its authorized maximum for the entire war.

Even as the SPARS and MCWR gained momentum, however, they still relied on the training facilities provided by the Navy. For the first several months of their existence, the enlisted Women Marines and guardsmen trained at Hunter College, and their officers at Smith College. As their units grew, however, the directors of both services began to feel cramped.

The issue of dedicated training facilities was both practical and cultural. Although the SPARS and Women Marines were typically assigned to units composed of other women in their services, they were surrounded by Navy WAVES. In the early days, this served as a helpful socializing mechanism, particularly given the many shared regulations and traditions across the Navy, Coast Guard, and Marines Corps. But while the SPARS and MCWR leaders were certainly grateful to the Navy for sharing their facilities and best practices during the first several months of their creation, as their ranks swelled both services felt they needed their own dedicated facilities. So, in their first real declaration of independence from the Navy, the leaders of SPARS and MCWR decided to establish their own training organizations.

The first to cast off from the Navy, the SPARS identified and relocated their enlisted women's training course to Palm Beach, Florida, at the Biltmore Hotel, affectionately referred to as the "Pink Palace." Although the Biltmore was known locally as a luxury vacation destination, the SPARS leadership had warned their charges not to emphasize the glamour of the relocation.

The warning was well deserved. By the time the Coast Guard

revamped the Biltmore, it was barely recognizable. The white linen service and ornate wallpaper adorning oversize rooms with balconies had been unceremoniously torn out, and "with walls knocked out, partitions built in, rich appointments removed, and over 900 girls installed, the Biltmore's decks were cleared for action." The basement housed classrooms; the first floor had a mess hall, library, clothing store, sick bay, and dentist; and atop it all sat rooms filled with cots for the women arriving from around the country. The Pink Palace may have lost some of its luster, but it buzzed with the energy of the women who occupied it.

While the enlisted women of the Coast Guard settled into their

SPARS give their first salute after graduating from the US Coast Guard Academy. **Courtesy National Archives, photo no. 205572892.**

training at the Biltmore, their counterparts in the officer corps found their new home to be both entirely routine and unprecedented. The SPARS officer corps, which at its peak totaled fewer than one thousand officers, presented a logistical challenge for Coast Guard leaders; it was just small enough not to warrant a devoted facility, but just large enough to make training the women with WAVES unsustainable. Two training options existed for the small group: continue the confusing practice of training the SPARS alongside the WAVES at Smith College or allow women to attend the all-male US Coast Guard Academy. The Coast Guard, ever practical, chose the latter. When, in 1943, the first class of SPARS arrived in New London, Connecticut, they took their seats next to several hundred men and started training to become officers. Surprisingly, the choice raised few eyebrows, given that it marked one of the first times women received training at a military academy.

Within a month, the MCWR followed suit. Rather than establish an entirely new training facility for the women, MCWR leadership decided that the women—enlisted and officer alike—would be trained with male Marines at Camp Lejeune.

The Women Marines immediately saw the benefits of being colocated with their male counterparts. In addition to being fully immersed in the Marine experience, the women regularly attended demonstrations of prized weapons and equipment that the men were training on, including "mortars, bazookas, flamethrowers, amphibian tractors, landing craft, hand-to-hand combat, camouflage, even war dogs." The demonstrations provided the women with a more comprehensive and immediate sense of the Corps' mission, allowing them to observe the realities of combat that they would support in their jobs. As an added benefit, the men tended to perform better when a group of women were watching them.

Even with these advantages, however, the reality at Camp Lejeune often fell short. With little support for the women recruits coming from senior Marine Corps leaders, who were themselves reluctant to accept women into their ranks, the young men arriving at training openly displayed their disdain for the women. The insults came fast and furious. In the absence of an official nickname for the women, the men delighted in calling them "BAMs"—short for broad-assed Marines—and went so far as to spray-paint the epithet on stray dogs and send them scurrying into an MCWR graduation ceremony. More than one woman remembered some iteration of an insult equating the women with "dogs and n[****]rs."

The women, who had been told they would be treated as Marines, handled their unwelcome reception as best they could. Some met the remarks with indifference, while others addressed the insults head-on. Still others, particularly the victims of the worst types of harassment, found it more difficult to bear. One woman, working at the post exchange, was ceaselessly maligned by a group of Marines who had recently returned from Hawaii and insisted that they knew her from their deployment—referring to her as a famous prostitute from Oahu. "They would not leave her alone," remembered her friend, Mary Rieger. "It was unbelievable. Her life was made miserable. She was finally moved out of the PX and put on barracks duty. She rarely left the barracks to go anywhere. It ruined her life."

To his credit, when, in 1943, the commandant of the Marine Corps, Lieutenant General Holcomb—once a vocal skeptic of the women's program—heard reports of the mistreatment, his response was forceful. "Information reaching this Headquarters," he wrote, "indicates that in some posts and stations officers and men of the Marine Corps treat members of the Women's Reserve with disrespect." The behavior, he added, "indicates laxity of discipline which will not be tolerated." He informed his charges that any further reports of such conduct would be dealt with directly by his headquarters. After all, while Holcomb may not have been particularly enthusiastic about the Women Marines, he would not tolerate indiscipline. With his public endorsement of the women's program, some of the men softened their views. Others simply expressed them in quieter, more pernicious ways. But, slowly, the derision of the women began to ebb at Camp Lejeune.

Selma, for her part, took the good with the bad. Even with the occasional disparagement from her fellow Marines, Camp Lejeune was practically luxury compared to the life she had left behind. Three square meals, all the milk she could drink, and a shower every day; those were extravagances "practically unheard of in Arlington, Kentucky." But, above all else, there was little time to dwell on the men's hostility. Selma had work to do, and she figured they'd come around, eventually: "We were here to stay, and to do our jobs."

# 13

# "IF YOU WANT TO FLY"

## RECRUITING AND TRAINING

## THE WASPS

LIKE SELMA, FLORENE MILLER, A NEWLY MINTED member of the Women's Auxiliary Ferrying Squadron, had little time to dwell on the naysayers. She was too fixated on the P-47 Thunderbolt fighter plane that was parked on the runway in front of her.

The P-47's resilience was legendary. The Thunderbolt had returned from enough combat engagements still flying despite its pockmarked wings, missing propellers, and gaping holes through the fuselage that there was an aura of invincibility around the fighter. Rumor had it that the plane could fly into a brick wall and still make it through to the other side.

Simply on its technical merits, it was an impressive plane. One of the largest and heaviest fighters used in World War II, it was powered by the eighteen-cylinder Pratt and Whitney R-2800 engine with an equally powerful propeller, armed with eight .50 caliber machine guns. The plane was so advanced that the government worried about its description falling into enemy hands and prohibited *Life* magazine from including it in their February 1942 aircraft spotting guide.

Every pilot wanted to give it a try, and when Miller, posted to

Love Field in Dallas, Texas, was offered the chance to take the Thunderbolt for a test run on a sunny afternoon in December 1943, she quickly and unequivocally replied yes.

But the P-47 was a tricky plane to fly. The huge engine and propeller obscured the view from the cockpit, requiring a set of complex maneuvers during takeoff and landing to get it up and down safely. Moreover, Miller had to fly the plane solo, since it was a single-seat aircraft.

Love Field was also an Army Air Forces testing and training hub, and it was a hectic afternoon there. Several dozen new planes had

Florene Miller at Love Field, Dallas, Texas. **Courtesy of WASP Archive, Texas Woman's University, Denton, Texas.**

just been delivered to the base and were parked at the edge of active runways, adding to the usual crowd of power lines, telephone poles, buildings, homes, and traffic lanes surrounding the airfield. The huge P-47 required the entire crowded airstrip to get up and down and left virtually no room for error on takeoff and landing.

The weather had been clear enough when Miller took off in the Thunderbolt, but just as the sun began to set, a thick haze descended over the airfield. The air-traffic controllers grew worried and instructed all pilots to return for landing. By the time Miller had lined up, however, the descent had become especially difficult. Not only had the haze thickened, but the angle of approach forced the pilots to land straight into the sunset. That might not have been a problem in a smaller plane, but the obstructed cockpit view from the P-47 reduced the visibility to near zero.

The sound of impact was deafening. Miller had not seen the pole until it had already sliced through the fuselage of the plane midair. In seconds, the nose of the Thunderbolt shot up and the entire aircraft lurched backward.

Miller remained focused. After a tense minute, with the plane still miraculously in the air, she looked around to survey the damage. The instrument panel was unintelligible, the wing and tail were torn apart, and the radio returned only static.

She weighed two options: bail out or try to get the plane on the ground. With no instruments, Miller had no way of knowing how long the plane could stay in the air, but given the extent of the damage to the aircraft, she thought it was coming down sooner than later. Although it made the most sense to bail, doing so meant the plane would be destroyed and would surely invite the Army's wrath. In the high-stakes airpower competition of World War II, Miller knew that no planes were disposable. She had to try to land it.

Miller first had to figure out how to get the control tower on the radio to guide her in for landing. It was now after dark, and the accident had apparently knocked out most of the lights on

Love Field. After several minutes of frantic frequency hopping, Miller made contact with a nearby Lockheed mechanic, who relayed messages to Love Field's control tower. They immediately scrambled to get light on the runway. The base-operations officer radioed for his transport section to position several jeeps along the edge of the runway—high beams on—and the faint strip of concrete emerged from the shadows.

Before bringing the plane down, the control tower asked Miller to do one pass of the tower to visually confirm the landing gear was in place and then circle back around for a landing. But she knew better. The plane needed to get onto the ground. Instead of making a high pass over the tower, Miller decided to land the aircraft on the first try. She manually pumped the emergency hydraulic system to maintain pressure in the landing gear with one hand and, with the other, pulled down the throttle at the start of the dimly lit runway to guide the Thunderbolt down. The fighter landed with a thud, swept through the dangerously narrow gap between jeeps and planes on either side of the runway, and lurched to an abrupt stop.

At this point, the emergency lighting in the nearby hangar had come on, and dozens of airmen waited for Miller to taxi in. She slowly got down from the cockpit, turned around, and surveyed the fighter: it looked like she had flown it through a brick wall.

After their rough start, both the WFTD under Cochran and the WAFS under Love had settled into their own lanes by 1943. The WAFS, composed of pilots like Miller, had especially hit its stride.

Love managed to recruit an initial group of the most qualified women pilots in the nation to fill out the WAFS' first class of trainees, and they were already arriving at airfields in several states. The recruited pilots had to meet Love's exacting standards to even be considered for the WAFS. They needed to have five hundred hours of flying time, along with "cross-country experience, commercial licenses, high school educations, American citizenship, and be between the ages of twenty-one and thirty-five." From an initial group of eighty women that met her criteria, Love convinced twenty-eight women to join the first class. They were instructed to report to New Castle Army Air Base in Wilmington, Delaware, to form the nucleus of the new corps: the Second Ferrying Group.

Since the recruited women already had extensive flying experience, they were rushed through an abbreviated monthlong course in military aircraft. They flew training aircraft and attended classes in all the basics—instrument flying, navigation, meteorology, military courtesy and law, and Morse code. Even though they were civilians, they lived the military life. They were billeted in Bachelor Officer Quarters (BOQ) 14 and were issued the standard military allotment of furniture—"an iron cot, maple bureaus, a large pine wardrobe, and blue scatter rugs." They were expected to be in formation for roll call each morning at 8 a.m. and got the same perks as the male officers—namely use of the mess and the officers' club.

With their speedy indoctrination complete, the first groups of WAFS started ferrying thousands of military planes around the country. Miller was sent to Dallas to be the commanding officer of the women assigned to ferry planes out of Love Field, including the P-47 Thunderbolt. The schedule was unrelenting from the start. Either the women started their trips from a manufacturing plant, or the manufacturer delivered the planes to them at various airfields. Either way, once the plane was received, the women piloted it to the base where the aircraft was required, checked it in, and reported to the commanding officer. If another plane stationed at the base needed to be flown elsewhere, the WAFS pilot would, if qualified, depart to deliver it as soon as feasible, usually leaving on the same day she arrived. The women continued crisscrossing the country from base to base, returning home only after they found one with no deliveries required or one with no planes they could fly.

When they did run out of steam, the women were instructed

to return home by whatever means available. Often, that meant taking a commercial flight, but occasionally they took a military transport headed in the right direction. Miller, for her part, did not like taking military aircraft. She didn't always trust the male pilots, since some were known to be cowboys in the air, and as she frankly put it: "I didn't want those pilots to kill me." If she was going to die in the air, she added, it would be her own doing.

The risks of flying the planes were numerous, and Miller knew them well. Not only had she experienced several of her own close calls—including her miraculous landing of the P-47—but her father and brother had been killed in their family airplane before the war began. Most aviators understood that fickle equipment, difficult weather, and lack of regulation commonly caused crashes and deaths.

Military flying also added a host of new risks to the existing hazards of aviation. For instance, without pressurized cabins or oxygen available on many training planes, pilots were instructed not to fly above ten thousand feet, even though most bad weather occurred below that ceiling. The regulation forced aviators to choose between flying through a rough storm below ten thousand feet or getting above the clouds and passing out, as Miller had done on at least one occasion.

Some of the challenges proved less treacherous, but tricky in their own way. On one occasion, Miller was called into El Paso to help a fellow WAFS with some plane trouble. She arrived after the woman had been sitting on the runway for several hours in the hot summer sun. It turned out that she needed a change of pants: bathrooms were not available aboard most planes, and the Army Air Forces had not considered how a woman might relieve herself midflight. "If you weren't worried about crashing an airplane, you were worried about going to the bathroom on a long flight," said Miller. She gave the woman a clean pair of slacks and went on her way.

This unique predicament was also compounded by the fact

that the WAFS always had to travel light. They had to be prepared to fly any aircraft at any time, thereby restricting them to packing only the essentials. This included their flight suits, nicknamed zoot suits, since they were often borrowed from the men and produced comically large silhouettes on the women; a change of uniform; and a small bathroom bag. And, while there was no solution to the lack of bathrooms, Miller did find some extra room for a spare set of slacks, as well as other less essential items: "I got the right kind of screwdriver," she recalled, "crawled out on the wing, opened the ammunition box, and I could get a pair of heels in there."

Cochran, concerned as she was with optics, would probably have appreciated Miller's tactics, but she remained a skeptic of the WAFS program. Her misgivings were a result of two slights. First, Love and ATC regularly challenged her hold on the overall program for women pilots, and, second, the WAFS' narrow mandate stood in direct contradiction to Cochran's own approach to organizing women pilots.

Fortunately, Cochran's more expansive vision of a corps of women pilots, trained from scratch and conducting a wide range of domestic missions, finally had the green light. She wasted no time getting to work assembling recruits. Like Love, Cochran initially assembled a core group of women pilots from her personal network. She sent out the solicitation to hundreds of women, pulled from a list of over three thousand licensed pilots.

Cochran's standards were lower than Love's, but for good reason: she thought that women with basic flying experience could be trained to fly military aircraft, and to fly them well. If the Army Air Forces could train men with no prior flight experience as pilots, she reasoned, then she and the WFTD could certainly succeed with women who had spent dozens of hours in a cockpit. The initial standard—two hundred hours—would eventually be lowered to thirty-five hours as the war went on, but the standard always remained higher for women than for men.

The announcement of WFTD's creation spurred an emphatic response in the first several months of its existence. By one estimate, applications quickly topped twenty-five thousand. Women all over the country rushed to get the baseline level of flying experience necessary to apply to the WFTD, and Cochran personally interviewed and selected just over one thousand of them for her corps.

By then, Ann Baumgartner, now almost three years removed from her fateful summer trip to Europe in 1940, had become a very talented aviator. Having received her pilot's license in the early days of the war, she was exactly the sort of woman Cochran hoped would join the program: a talented flier with an admirable pedigree, and she was among the first women to apply.

Even so, Baumgartner felt intimidated on the day of her interview with Cochran. It was hard not to be, passing by the row of Harmon flying trophies arrayed in the hallway outside of Cochran's Manhattan apartment. But intimidation, and inspiration, was probably the point of the display. Above all else, Cochran wanted her pilots to be confident in themselves and in their flying skills, and she probably hoped the trophies reminded the recruits of the high bar she measured them against. Baumgartner remembered that the rest of the day was a blur, and spent most of it in awe of Cochran. Three weeks later, she was on her way to training camp.

Training for the WFTD started in November 1942, shortly after that of the WAFS. The training facilities were initially housed at a contractor facility in Houston, but Cochran soon moved WFTD training to Avenger Field in Sweetwater, Texas, an underutilized base that the Army Air Forces had recently renovated. The weather there was better than in Houston, and the dusty town soon acclimated to the influx of women pilots arriving every few weeks.

Since the WFTD trained more inexperienced fliers for a wider variety of tasks than the WAFS, its orientation program started at twenty-three weeks and eventually increased to thirty. The women received a minimum of 115 hours of flight-school training and almost 200 hours of ground-school instruction. Except for formation flying, the curriculum for the WFTD mirrored, almost exactly, that of the Army Air Forces and included navigation, aerobatics, and recoveries.

Nearly thirty percent of women who enrolled in the training failed to complete it. But the standards were high for a reason. Though the WFTD women had less experience than the WAFS, Cochran still expected them to do some risky flying, and to do it flawlessly. Within a year of the WFTD's founding, its pilots were performing diverse tasks such as testing new aircraft, training searchlight ground crews, training bomber crews, and, arguably the most difficult and dangerous task, towing gliders and targets for live antiaircraft artillery training. The latter was particularly hazardous work. "The engineer would release the target from the back of the bomb bay," recalled Mary Ellen Keil of her days towing targets in B-26 bombers for antiaircraft crews, adding, "It was a tremendous load, which included the weight of the target and the long length of cable. I remember how it would snap the plane up into a stall position and you had to be so careful."

Stalling, however, was just one of the risks. Madeline Sullivan, another woman pilot who flew antiaircraft artillery training missions, remembered that the squadron leader would sometimes fail to communicate the cease-fire order to ground crews firing live munitions. "You'd see these puffs coming at you," she remembered, adding that at least once, "we had an engine shot out and had to make an emergency landing, because they were still shooting at us when they were not supposed to be." Given the real risks the women faced during these training missions, the frequent levity of their male colleagues on the ground was not always welcome. "There was always a funny guy," Marge Gilbert recalled, "who'd call up and say, 'I see the target out there but what's that in back of it?'"

The humor was also sometimes indicative of more dangerous prejudicial attitudes that were widespread in the Army Air Forces. For instance, the maintenance crews serving the women's planes gained a reputation for notorious and egregious errors that frequently placed the women in danger. On one occasion, Baumgartner remembered being assigned as a tow-target pilot at Camp Davis, North Carolina, as a replacement for one of two women who had been killed in a series of suspicious accidents that were attributed to the lax maintenance practices for the women's planes. She recalled that the women pilots on base learned to take their safety into their own hands: "They began to check the airplanes they were to fly themselves," she remembered, adding that "they befriended the mechanics" in hopes that the men would take better care of their aircraft.

But these informal safety measures often failed. The accidents that resulted provided stark reminders of the dangers faced by women pilots on bases around the country. "Our first test," remembered Baumgartner about her arrival at Camp Davis, "was to acclimate ourselves to our bare barracks rooms so recently occupied by women like ourselves, but now dead."

Without question, the women pilots of the WFTD and WAFS faced extraordinary risks to their safety. Over three dozen women of the thousand pilots Cochran selected died on duty, including eleven women who died during training. But for all the risks they were taking for the Army, the WFTD and WAFS were not actually part of it.

Militarization for the women pilots proved to be a thorny question for Cochran. At the beginning of the war, the WAAC and Army leadership had proposed subsuming the women pilots into their program, but Cochran simply could not countenance such an arrangement. She argued that women pilots were a particular breed and that they required a wholly different type of organization and leader than what the WAAC offered.

Cochran was also not shy about her dislike for the WAAC. According to one historian, she thought they were "a sorry lot—untidy, ill-disciplined, and badly behaved" and, by some accounts, she had a special dislike for Hobby. So, in 1943, when the initial offer was made to integrate the WFTD into the WAAC, Cochran firmly opposed it.

When Cochran finally met Hobby about the proposal, she arrived staunchly opposed to the idea, and armed with the Army Air Forces' backing. When the meeting finally started, Hobby began by saying exactly the wrong thing: "I don't know one end of an airplane from another." Cochran, coat on her lap, pulled no punches with her response: "Look Mrs. Hobby, you've bitched up your own outfit. You are not going to bitch up mine." She then got up to leave, but not before adding, "If you think I'd work for a woman who doesn't know one end of an airplane from another, we are a different breed of cat." With that, the meeting was over.

General Arnold, commander of the Army Air Forces, supported Cochran's position, if not her tactics. He shared Cochran's belief that, while the Air Force and Army should always be tightly linked, pilots deserved their own organization. He had, in fact, been waging his own campaign for Army Air Forces' independence from the Army, trying to place his organization on equal footing with the ground forces, and sympathized with Cochran's view. Arnold laid out his and Cochran's logic to Marshall in a 1943 memo, making the case for women pilots to be militarized in a corps separate from the WAAC. Subsuming the women pilots into the WAAC, he argued, "would result in confusion, conflict, and inefficiency."

Hobby and the WAAC, however, were not the only obstacles to Cochran's attempt to create—and control—an independent military outfit for women pilots. She also remained deeply engaged in the process of consolidating her control within the Army Air Forces itself, since Love and the WAFS pilots continued to frustrate Cochran's efforts. Not only were WAFS commanders trying to siphon off pilots from the pool of generalists that Cochran was training, circumventing her carefully constructed allotment schemes, but they also contested Cochran's attempts to enforce corps-wide regulations among ferrying pilots, insisting that the ferry pilots were under the authority of the transport command.

By 1943, the tension between Cochran and ATC hit a boiling point. Cochran asked Arnold for control over all the women aviators, ferrying pilots included. In June, she got it. Arnold finally appointed Cochran director of Women's Flying Training, allowing her to determine how many pilots were needed, how they would be used, what their qualifications would be, how they would be trained, where they would be assigned, how they would be allocated, and which regulations would govern their conduct, regardless of whether they were ferrying pilots in Love's unit or generalists already under Cochran's authority. Two months later, Arnold completed the consolidation of the women pilots under Cochran's command, combining the ferrying pilots of the WAFS and the WFTD trainees already under her authority into one organization. They were named the Women's Airforce Service Pilots, known by the clever acronym WASPs.

With the creation of the WASP, women in uniform occupied every corner of the military establishment. But just as the first women's units were beginning to undertake the vital support tasks they had been recruited to perform, a string of unwelcome controversies lurked close behind.

As military leaders had feared, members of the media and the public initiated a smear campaign maligning the character of servicewomen almost immediately. Though few of these accusations were grounded in truth, they threatened to condemn the programs to failure in the eyes of the public. The directors of the women's programs watched apprehensively as their meticulous work to prevent such allegations clashed with the harsh reality of the times: women in uniform—regardless of their necessity and effectiveness—were, by their very nature, destined for controversy.

# 14

# "SOMEONE TALKED!"

## RUMORS

JOHN O'DONNELL SAT COMFORTABLY IN HIS OFFICE in 1943, tapping away at his typewriter, putting the finishing touches on the latest scoop for his syndicated column, Capitol Stuff.

The first line of O'Donnell's article got straight to the point: "Contraceptives and prophylactic equipment will be furnished to members of the WAACS, according to a super secret agreement reached by the high ranking officers of the War Department and the WAAC chieftain, Mrs. William Pettus Hobby." It continued with a not-so-subtle prod of the administration's support for women's equality, saying, "Mrs. Roosevelt wants all the young ladies to have the same overseas rights as their brothers and fathers." The article's thinly veiled implication was clear: women serving in the WAAC were being permitted or, worse, encouraged to have sex with Army soldiers.

Although untrue, the scandalous accusation caused exactly the sort of major controversy the WAAC leadership had been warned against from the beginning. Hobby and her staff had worked hard to present an image, backed by reality, of military women as polished, respectable, and patriotic. And they had worked even harder to preempt the gratuitous and unfair association of WAACs with sex workers sometimes found around bases. But O'Donnell's ac-

## By JOHN O'DONNELL.

Washington, D. C., June 8.—Contraceptives and prophylactic equipment will be furnished to members of the WAACS, according to a super secret agreement reached by the high ranking officers of the War Department and the WAAC chieftain, Mrs. William Pettus Hobby, wife of the former Governor of Texas and Publisher of the Houston (Tex.) Post.

The decision was made only after hours had been spent in discussing the many violent reactions which the decision was expected to bring. The discussion pivoted on the issues of religion, politics and medicine.

Health of the girls in uniform and a determined feminine punch to smash through any out-moded double standards won the day.

All in all, the decision must be marked down as a defeat for the males who think they have sole responsibility for winning the war.

It was a victory for the New Deal ladies who produced the cold turkey argument that the girls who want to go into uniform and fight what men have called the "total war" have the same right here and abroad to indulge their passing fancies. We quote from a lady lawmaker:

"Women have the same right to indulge their affections and emotions, whether married or single, here or overseas, just exactly as do the men in the same uniform. It is high time that the Army should pay as much attention to the women wearing their uniform when it comes to their sex relations as the Army has already done to the men. After all, we're more vulnerable.

"You men think that there is nothing wrong if a soldier sleeps with a girl so long as he keeps his health. Well, the same argument goes both ways."

Now all the present uproar applies to the WAACS and not to the gals who have enlisted in the WAVES, SPARS or Marines. The WAACS have gone overseas. The others have not. Mrs. Roosevelt wants all the young ladies to have the same overseas rights as their brothers and fathers

Now there is a bill pending before the Congress which may break or make the WAACS. At the present they are not really in the army —they are auxiliaries, with but not of. And the army like any long-established group, doesn't like a Johnny-come-lately in war time (which all auxiliaries are.)

The result is that the auxiliary gets kicked in the pants—witness the fate of the army specalist corps, built up by Dwight F. Davis, which was washed out after eight months of existence.

* * *

John O'Donnell's Capitol Stuff article.

cusations quickly undid their hard work, and as soon as the article hit newsstands, the damage was done.

The impact of the piece was, at least in part, a product of the reality that O'Donnell's libelous article amplified an already growing undercurrent of rumors, jokes, and smears that had plagued the WAAC from the start, rooted in longstanding American frustrations about the costs of war. Indeed, the demands of World War II threw into stark relief a difficult truth for many Americans: only twenty years after the United States sent men to fight and die on European battlefields during World War I, Americans were again being asked to send their brothers, fathers, husbands, and sons into another violent, traumatizing conflict. In this environment, the truth was that many men, and especially those burdened by the anguish of their families, did not want to go to the front lines and breathed a sigh of relief when they were assigned to noncombat duties. Then, in 1942, just as the scope of the war had become apparent, the WAAC had arrived in communities around the country and began recruiting women under the banner "Release a Man to Fight!" The slogan made the Corps' purpose unambiguous: women would be filling jobs at home so men could be sent to the front lines.

And that is, in fact, exactly the logic that senior military officials were counting on to win the war. At bases around the country, detailed records of the one-to-one replacements of men for WAACs were being collected and sent back to headquarters. According to a report from the 28th Base Headquarters and Air Base Squadron, a chart detailed which women were releasing which men, and to where: "Hanlon, Anna, Mailing Section" released "Fowler, Alfous to Lakeland AAFld," while "O'Neill, Elizabeth A., Photo Lab Tech" released "Long, William N. to the 500th Service Group."

Against this backdrop, the O'Donnell accusation breathed life into a simmering undercurrent of frustration. Despite having never encountered a WAAC, men were writing home to their families disparaging their work and, in many cases, lying about the roles they were playing in the war effort. For those soldiers whose wives, sisters, or mothers were considering joining the WAAC, some reacted with contempt and outrage:

> "Get that damn divorce. I don't want no damn WA[A]C for a wife."

> "I am stopping all allotments to her and am breaking off all contact with her."

> "Are you going to the WA[A]Cs, mother? If you did or do, I will disown you."

> "The service is no place for a woman. The woman's place is in the home."

While most of the rumors that circulated in the early days of the WAAC were simply mean-spirited, some were more damaging. WAAC headquarters learned of rumors in Virginia and Florida that claimed ninety percent of WAACs were prostitutes, openly soliciting men and engaging in sex acts in public places. Other widespread rumors implied that the WAACs were employed by the Army for "morale purposes." These were difficult to tamp down, and were often amplified by Army men in camp newspapers and comics. One soldier wrote home, "You join the WA[A]C and you are automatically a prostitute in my opinion," while another implied as much in a note to his wife: "Darling for my sake don't join them. I can't write my reasons because the censors won't let it through."

Equally disappointing was the silence and quiet whispering among men in uniform that proved just as damaging as the outspoken detractors. One civilian woman, a staunch supporter of the women's programs, wrote to Hobby, "I have been in gatherings where perhaps a total of 25 to 50 army men have been asked, at different times, their opinion of the WA[A]C," she stated, adding:

"Without a single exception, Colonel Hobby, their answers have been derogatory, defamatory, and calumniatory. I have not heard one single word of praise for any member of the WA[A]C." It was a disappointing and demeaning response to the efforts of so many women in uniform who answered the call of duty.

In addition to this wave of animosity from male soldiers, the WAAC also faced criticism from other segments of society: disgruntled civilians who had been pushed out of their jobs, or their favorite restaurants, by WAACs starting to arrive by the hundreds in base communities; begrudging women who had been denied admittance into the Corps; and conservative politicians who could not abide women serving in uniform. All contributed to the swell of public hostility toward the WAACs, and this slow accumulation of ill will in segments of the public provided fertile ground for O'Donnell's salacious column on the WAAC. For many Americans, his column confirmed publicly the private accusations they had already heard, or made, since the program was announced.

O'Donnell's claims could not have been further from the truth. The WAACs were not prostitutes, of course. On the charge of supplying contraceptives to the WAAC, Hobby had gone to great lengths to ensure that no such policy would be necessary, let alone enacted. The "super secret" memo he referred to was, in fact, a pamphlet on women's health that senior Army leaders, including several male commanders, had seen and approved.

The article, however, did contain one small element of truth. Despite protests by Hobby, the standards for admission into the WAAC had been lowered in early 1943 to meet the ballooning demands for women in uniform. The stringent background and credit checks and the high educational and training standards that had been instituted during the initial recruiting push had been temporarily lowered or removed. This resulted in a very slight uptick—"less than one half of one percent"—of women with "vice records" being inadvertently admitted to the Corps. O'Donnell exploited and inflated this misstep in his article. Though the backlash prompted by his article provided Hobby with evidence proving why the original recruiting standards should be maintained, it did far more harm than help.

Washington's reaction to O'Donnell's article was swift and forceful. The president himself responded to the controversy in a press conference that month, calling the article "a shameful thing." The First Lady, secretary of war, and several senior commanders and members of congress piled on, releasing statements unequivocally denying O'Donnell's claims and reiterating their support for the Corps. "The Secretary of War has already stated in forcible terms the views of the War Department in the matter," wrote Marshall in a private letter to Hobby, "but I wish to assure you personally of my complete confidence in the quality and value of the organization." He added, "I wish you would assure your subordinates of the confidence and high respect in which they are held by the Army."

Even some civilians rallied to the cause of defending the WAACs. JW Mathews, of Atlanta, Michigan, wrote directly to Eleanor Roosevelt questioning the validity of the accusations, which had been reprinted in a religious magazine. He promised that "if this report can be proven false, then we will ask the management of this magazine to make a retraction as quickly as possible." Vida Williamson wrote in the *Carroll County Democrat* that the best response to the rumors was to reply, "Yes, we've heard; and yes, we know what they say." Williamson continued: "We also know that all such sayings and rumors should correctly close with a click of the heels, an outstretched arm and a guttural 'Heil!'"—implying that the salacious article was Axis propaganda.

Thinking along the same lines, the Army directed the FBI to investigate whether the rumors were tied to an Axis plot. But the investigation's findings proved far more damning; the rumors had emerged from a purely American source, "a line of rumors widely circulated by Army personnel, Navy personnel, Coast Guard personnel, businessmen, women, factory workers and others."

Within the WAAC, the slander campaign was devastating. In the days after the article was published, calls flooded into units across the country from concerned parents, friends, and husbands. Amelia Madrak, an enlisted WAAC, returned home after the article appeared to reassure her family that the accusation was false, but she remembered the embarrassment viscerally, even years later: "When I went through the streets, I held up my head because I imagined everyone was talking about me, but when I was at last safe inside our front door, I couldn't say a word." Tucked inside the entryway of her home, she relented to the swell of humiliation and broke down in tears: "I couldn't understand how my eagerness to serve our country could have brought such shame on us all."

For those senior leaders committed to women serving in uniform, however, this first scandal was as motivating as it was upsetting. In the shadow of this controversy, the WAAC felt an urgent need to repair the damage done by O'Donnell, and seeing the negative impact of the article, the directors of the other services wanted to avoid a similar fate. Hobby and her counterparts knew the best way to leave this all behind them was simple: the women needed to do their jobs.

PART II

# THE SOLUTION

15

# "GOING WHERE WE'RE
NEEDED MOST!"

## NORTH AFRICA

**"NONE OF US WILL EVER COMPLAIN ABOUT ANY-
THING AGAIN."**

Miriam Stehlik, nicknamed Sunny for her light auburn hair, joined the WAAC in August 1942, in one of the first classes of women to join the Corps. With her prior experience as a bank stenographer in New York, the Army quickly found ways to make use of her clerical talent and sent her with the first wave of WAACs to staff Eisenhower's Allied headquarters in North Africa in early 1943.

Soon after her arrival, Stehlik lay in bed, eyes wide open, startled awake in the middle of the night by the peculiar chorus of air raid sirens—one, then another, and another—a circular sort of rhythm intended to get everyone who was outside to go inside. As Stehlik and her fellow WAACs were already inside their barracks, however, the siren only served to alert them to the surrounding terror.

Stehlik, like every woman in her unit, had volunteered for overseas duty. She had been overjoyed when she was selected, regarding it as a privilege to have been assigned to General Dwight Eisenhower's headquarters staff during the invasion of North Africa. "We know that this is something that no one will ever be able to take away from us," Stehlik recalled thinking at the time.

Stehlik arrived at the headquarters just one month after the initial invasion. From the start, the posting had exceeded every one of her expectations. She found herself at the heart of the campaign to retake North Africa from the German and Italian forces, and the WAACs had, more or less, become a part of the team. After deflecting some pointed curiosity from the soldiers—"What work are you girls doing here? Were you sent over to boost our morale?"—they had been left to do their work.

But serving in a combat theater came with its hardships. In the confidence of letters written to her fellow WAACs, Stehlik confessed there were considerable difficulties. "We have gone without a lot articles that we thought were absolutely necessary when we were home," she remarked, unable to mask her longing for the creature comforts of home, adding: "Give me a nice cold glass of milk, or a nice chocolate fudge sundae, topped with whipped cream and nuts and a maraschino cherry."

Despite the challenges, however, Stehlik and her colleagues understood the stakes. The women had been sent there by Army leadership as a sort of experiment to see if they could hack it in North Africa. If they passed the test, then maybe women could be used elsewhere overseas. There was no time for milkshakes.

Eisenhower, originally a skeptic of women serving in uniform in a combat theater, had started to see the wisdom of the idea while on a tour of British women's units with Eleanor Roosevelt and Hobby in late 1942. The trip was, in many respects, a calculated public relations move, packed with photos of Roosevelt and Hobby alongside the king and queen of England, but it also provided an opportunity to convince American commanders of the utility of women serving in combat theaters. Although the WAAC had the legislative authority to send women overseas, they knew they needed the backing of senior military officials to make any such assignments a success. No one was more important to convince than Eisenhower, who ran a considerable portion of US combat operations in the early days of the war, since he could help persuade even the senior-most holdouts of the efficacy of putting American women in uniform overseas.

Fortunately, Eisenhower's initial skepticism of women serving overseas faded quickly during his visit to England, where he was easily convinced of the practical rationale for allowing women abroad. After all, he needed any help he could get. Eisenhower's bruising campaign to recapture British and French territory in North Africa from the hands of Rommel, one of Germany's most adept ground commanders, had gotten off to a rocky start. By the end of 1942, Eisenhower had been bogged down by poor communications, stretched supply lines, and lack of integration both within the US commands and between the Allies. The Americans eventually turned the tide, but not before a grueling set of failures sapped their morale. In the wake of one particularly bad defeat by the Germans at the Battle of Kasserine Pass in February 1943, a senior general remarked that it "was probably the worst performance of the US Army troops in their whole proud history."

Shortly after the campaign began, the Americans realized they had made several miscalculations. First, enemy resistance proved far more proficient than the Americans had expected. Rommel, though considered a bit of a maverick in Germany, was an extremely capable tactician and had been fighting in the North African desert for several years by the time the Americans arrived. When it came to experience, the American forces were outmatched.

Second, North Africa was a desert, which meant there would be a great deal of sand, dirt, and mud to reckon with. The mechanized and motorized forces that American manufacturing had been churning out for the green fields and packed-dirt roads of Europe now needed to make their way across the massive expanses of slippery dunes, their machinery clogged with sand and mud.

Third, the desert was massive. From the start of the offensive, this strained the supply and communications lines that were necessary to link the front line with higher headquarters. Eisenhower struggled to get a clear picture of the battlefield and to provide real-time guidance, and, without strong supply lines, frontline units lacked what they needed to implement the instructions they received. Logistics units worked mightily to keep up with the pace of the advance, but it took time for them to adapt to the difficulties of the expansive desert battlefield.

Compounding these challenges, Eisenhower soon recognized that his staff was ill-prepared to manage the deluge of information about each of these battlefield problems flooding into his headquarters. He needed to assemble a staff that could keep up with the vital administrative work necessary to ensure he was apprised of and connected to developments on the front lines. Realizing that the WAACs were being trained precisely for the sort of clerical work that his staff desperately needed, Eisenhower put in an urgent request for a detachment of typists.

The planning for the North Africa invasion had been protracted. Though the Allies, for the most part, had been resolute in their "Germany first" position, the Americans and British held very different visions of how the march to Hitler's doorstep would unfold. At its core, the disagreement between the Americans and the British boiled down to when the Allies should invade Europe. On the American side, military planners felt that their best chance at defeating Hitler hung on an immediate and rapid offensive in France. The British planners, however, were rightly skeptical of the American ability to marshal forces of the necessary quality in the required numbers. They worried that attacking the Germans head-on in Europe before the United States was ready would lead to, at best, a stalemate or, at worst, costly defeat.

Given their apprehension, the British proposed an alternative route to Europe. Noting they had made little progress against Rommel's formidable Afrika Korps in their nearly yearlong battle with German and Italian forces in North Africa, they forcefully argued that the Americans should join them in the Mediterranean fray.

While this route to Europe was circuitous, the British pushed hard for its strategic benefits. Not only would it secure an important base of operations from which to expand future operations into Europe, but, they argued, it would also weaken the Germans

Oveta Culp Hobby posing in front of the Great Pyramid in Giza, Egypt.
Courtesy National Archives, photo no. 111-SC-241144.

by forcing them to divert more resources to North Africa from their ongoing assault in the East. It also seemed to be a winnable fight for the Allies. The British noted that their biggest handicap in the earlier battles had been the limits on the materiel they could deliver across the long battle and supply lines stretching across the desert. They believed their American ally was uniquely positioned to solve that problem.

For the most part, American military commanders remained unconvinced of the wisdom of this plan. They saw the Mediterranean as a distraction from the real effort, which they felt should be a direct assault against Germany, and perhaps Japan, but certainly not against some distant backwater theater that they felt held zero strategic value for the United States. Over the next several months, American military commanders persisted in pushing for a more immediate invasion of the continent, rejecting the British proposal.

Ultimately, however, President Roosevelt made the decisions about American strategy in the war. Although he understood the concerns raised by his military commanders, he was also a brilliant politician. With the campaigns in the Pacific starting to turn the tide against the Japanese, he reasoned that a quick win against the Germans, anywhere, would boost the national mood, and decided the British plan offered the best chance at such a victory.

With Roosevelt's decision made, the US military began preparations for an assault on the North African coast.

Ruth Haskell, a second lieutenant in the Army Nurse Corps, and her motley crew of four were lined up in formation, about to take the first step on their journey across the Atlantic. The group felt excited, of course, but also a bit apprehensive. They had received little information about their destination other than the cryptic orders authorizing the issue of "cold weather gear" and the whispers they heard while they waited for their transport. They could not help feeling the low buzz of their collective nerves.

The assistant chief nurse, who had been assigned to watch over the women for only a few hours while they waited that morning, still felt a responsibility for the assembled group. She gave them all a quick once-over. Decked out in their winter gear, with gas masks, musette bags, and bedding rolls hanging from every available strap, they were sweating under the weight of their wool uniforms in the late fall sun. They did not look like much, but they were her charges, and she felt obliged to give them a parting pep talk. "Remember that you live in the finest nation on this earth. Be a credit to that nation, the uniform that you wear, and most of all to yourselves. May God watch over and keep you, one and all," she said. With that, she smiled, turned on her heel, and left the women standing in a row.

Servicewomen traveling to overseas theaters got there almost exclusively by ship, and almost always on a troop transport filled with other soldiers. The trip was never particularly comfortable. "Sea sickness, like love, isn't at all particular where it strikes," wrote Haskell, speaking for many of the women bound for Europe and the Pacific.

Adding to the physical discomforts of the journey by ship, the women also suffered the discomfort of standing out. These relatively small units of women appeared as oddities among hundreds, sometimes thousands, of men headed overseas, and they were alternately the subjects of great interest, derision, or some combination of both. "We passed slowly into the dining room," Haskell remembered in her memoir, "well aware of the fact that some three hundred men had their eyes on us, and for that matter there weren't many of us missing a thing as far as they were concerned."

Midway through the journey, Haskell and the rest of her unit were finally informed of their destination: North Africa. Like their male counterparts, they were issued additional items tailored to the theater: "mosquito cream, head nets, netting for our cots, tablets to chlorinate water with, atabrine tablets for malaria, salt tablets"—and, of course, "tiny American flags to be sewn upon the sleeves of our jackets when we went ashore." They were told they would follow the advance of the first wave of American soldiers invading along the coast and provide medical care for the injured troops just behind the front line.

The appointed morning of the invasion, November 8, 1942, greeted the Army nurses with the sound of punishing naval gunfire before dawn. Breakfast that morning was quick and mostly uneaten. Everyone was in battle dress: "leggings, cartridge belts, canteens of water, gas masks, steel helmets—the whole works." The nurses were instructed to be ready to disembark at any time after 11 a.m., just hours after the first infantry had hit the beaches. Like the men, they would be packed into Higgins boats, the famous shallow-water boat that allowed troops to unload through the front, instead of over the sides, and would have to wade to shore when delivered.

None of the nurses knew what awaited them on land, mostly because they could not see it. The Allies masked the invasion with a literal smoke screen, a plume of titanium tetrachloride and white phosphorous that produced a curtain of white smoke to obscure the movement of the invasion forces.

But what the nurses could not see, they heard. The deafening sound of exploding shells had been nonstop since the start of the invasion. The German forces were putting up a fight.

By two thirty that afternoon, the nurses' moment had arrived. In addition to twenty enlisted men, each Higgins carried five nurses and two medical officers. The chief nurse, having assembled Haskell and the other women, told them that she would be going with the first group. Just before she climbed into her transport, she turned to the assembled women and said, "Chins up," and with all the confidence she could muster, "I'll see you on shore." And then, in a moment, she disappeared over the side of the ship.

As was the case with the rest of the American military at the start of the war, the Army and Navy Nurse Corps grew abruptly and exponentially in 1942 and 1943. On the day of the Pearl Harbor bombing, fewer than 1,000 nurses served in the Army. Six months later, 12,000 were serving in uniform, and by June 1943 over 36,000 Army nurses were serving worldwide. The Navy Nurse Corps grew from an active-duty force of about 800 in December 1941 to just over 11,000 in the final year of the war. The demand continued unabated for the duration of the war, and by its conclusion 57,000 Army nurses and 14,000 Navy nurses served on active duty.

Despite the essential role of military nurses and their increased presence within the ranks, however, their gender left them at a disadvantage, and the military often failed to provide them with the rank, authority, and benefits commensurate with their skills and indispensability. At the start of the war, for instance, neither Army nor Navy nurses were entitled to a full commission. The Army had outdone the low bar set by the Navy when it gave its nurses relative rank, but the move proved to be an empty gesture. Like the WAAC, the nurses' status meant that they had the title and duties of full rank but lacked nearly all the benefits that came with it. For example, Army nurses were not entitled to equal pay and an Army nurse with the relative rank of second lieutenant made $88.60 per month, according to one estimate, while a male officer of the same rank received more than double that figure. The Army's nurses may have been wearing the uniform and doing the job of an officer, but they were not getting the commensurate authority or compensation.

By 1942, the debates over and discrepancies between the status of the WAAC and WAVES threw into harsh relief the absurdity of the Army and Navy's approach to commissioning their nurses. The unequal pay ranked among one of the key insults of the nurses' inferior status, and in July 1942, on the heels of the WAVES' legislation authorizing women as a part of the naval reserve, the Navy had little choice but to provide the same pay for its nurses. However, rather than giving them a full commission, naval leadership opted to pass two pieces of legislation: the first authorizing equal pay for Navy nurses, and the second providing them with relative rank akin to the WAAC and Army Nurse Corps. The Army, for its part, authorized equal pay six months later.

Both moves were a step forward but failed to provide the nurses with other benefits, such as retirement and burial rights, granted to commissioned officers in the Army and Navy. Given that many nurses had died, and even more were in captivity, the compromise was disappointing and demoralizing. It was also not entirely unexpected. Men had always bristled at the notion of women in uniform, even when they were providing the lifesaving care that they depended on, literally, to survive. As a result, in a conflict that killed over four hundred thousand Americans and injured hundreds of thousands more, the women of the Army and Navy Nurse Corps received only partial benefits for military service. As nurses like Haskell dodged enemy fire and waded onto the North African coast, it was hard to reconcile their inferior status with the reality that now confronted them.

"Hi, Ho, Silver!"

The phrase was uttered in a whisper, but the unmistakable reference to the popular fictional American hero, the Lone Ranger, was the code that the Army guard needed to hear. Lifting the makeshift gate to the crude battalion headquarters, he replied, "Away," to the passengers in the waiting car.

With that, the engine rose, and the guard watched the jeep

lumber down the road toward the three-story battalion aid station, a tall black building sitting on the dark horizon. The jeep held three soldiers sitting close between the sharpshooters guarding the front and rear tires. Had it not been for their small stature and curled hair peeking out from under their caps, no one would have guessed they were nurses.

Haskell's first night on the beaches of North Africa turned out to be one of her longest and most haunting. With casualties pouring in from the front lines at Oran, Algeria, the shoestring medical staff based at the battalion aid station were overwhelmed, so Haskell and two others were sent under the cover of darkness to help triage casualties.

Upon arriving at the battalion aid station, Haskell noticed "the unmistakable odor of filth and dirt, mixed with the odor of old blood and stale ether"—an unshakable, visceral reminder that death was close. When the soldier escorting her team flicked on a small blue light, she quickly understood the stench was coming from the floor. Injured soldiers were laid out in rows on the ground, "pools of blood beside some of them, where the dressings had not been changed since the first shock dressing was applied." Kneeling down to each man, Haskell and the two other nurses began to triage the scene, assessing each man's wounds and deciding who needed surgery first.

"It was positively heartbreaking," remembered Haskell.

Having evaluated the situation, Haskell then ran upstairs to the makeshift, bare-bones surgical ward. A small table, with a twenty-watt bulb hanging limply above it, occupied the middle of the room. To one side of the table sat a small basin and tap, but the water had been cut off and the last drops dribbled slowly into the drain. A large piece of luggage had been set up as a stool for the anesthetist, but no one trained in the specialty was at the base. A small alcohol-burning sterilizer sat nearby, which would be used to clean the only available tools: a scalpel, clamps, and surgical scissors. Dark drapes shrouded every window, preventing any light from seeping out and revealing their location to the enemy sniper waiting just outside the aid station's perimeter.

For the surgery to proceed, the team needed to find an anesthetist. Although Haskell had not administered ether in years, she was still the best-qualified person in the group. She watched as the doctors washed their hands in a basin of alcohol and took her seat on the piece of luggage next to the operating table. There, she spent the next several hours putting injured young men to sleep, whispering a comforting word as they closed their eyes. Haskell was interrupted only once by a sniper taking a potshot at the window. It missed her head by inches.

Days later, Haskell and her unit of Army nurses established a makeshift hospital near the North African front. She spent the next several months following the Allied forces as they moved through the desert, reaching their final objective in the spring of 1943. Having achieved a victory in North Africa, the Allies, and the nurses supporting them, turned their attention deeper into the Mediterranean.

# 16

# "DON'T MISS YOUR GREAT OPPORTUNITY"

## ITALY

HELEN HAYDEN WAS BY TITLE, IF NOT BY TRAINING, an engineer. She had just started work at a Boston-area broadcasting station, WEEI, as a radio engineer, filling in as local men enlisted. Despite her title, the role was not that technical. She focused on the operational side of the house, putting shows on the air and setting up studios. "I'd be at master control, controlling all of the studios," she remembered during our interview, "but if an amplifier blew, I wouldn't know how to replace it."

Although Hayden's assignment as a radio engineer was unusual for the time, her colleagues were unbothered by her new assignment, and she did not remember any resentment at the office. Everyone adjusted to the arrangement rather quickly, and she remembered that five unionized stations in the Boston area had kept up with the changing times by voting to allow women members in their ranks. *Broadcasting* magazine even wrote up a short article on the two women at WEEI then working as engineers.

The International Brotherhood of Electrical Workers (IBEW), however, felt differently. Despite the reality that young men with experience working in radio had left the industry in droves, the IBEW disliked the idea of women stepping into their former positions. The IBEW argued that if there was even one unemployed unionized radio engineer in the country, that man should fill a vacancy at WEEI before a woman was allowed to take it. The situation left Hayden in a precarious spot, and IBEW soon found two men in the Midwest looking for work, forcing the station to reassign her to radio production.

But it was a hot labor market for anyone with radio experience, man or woman, and WEEI was not the only organization looking to fill slots. The Office of War Information (OWI) was also hunting for personnel. OWI, a civilian organization responsible for "information programs to promote, in the United States and abroad, understanding of the status and progress of the war effort and of war policies, activities, and aims of the US government"—in other words, propaganda—was strapped for talent. The Signal Corps had snatched up many of the male radio engineers in the country, and OWI was willing to consider anyone with the right skill set. The OWI recruiter, visiting Wellesley, Massachusetts, from his office in New York, saw the article on Hayden in *Broadcasting* magazine and came looking for her. Hayden instantly liked the sound of the OWI work and was especially pleased when the recruiter told her she would have her choice of international assignments. "The whole field is open," she remembered him saying, then adding, "You can go to Europe, the Pacific—wherever you want."

As a civilian agency, OWI was not technically a part of the Army, but Hayden's status, much like the early auxiliary status of the WAAC, was Army adjacent. Hayden was granted an officer-equivalent rank—second lieutenant—along with a uniform. She received the same series of shots as military women, and she was expected to adhere to Army regulations while abroad. Like thousands of other civilian women, she was going into a combat zone as a US government official, and, civilian or not, the Army kept a watchful eye.

Given the stakes, OWI ensured Hayden's training for her overseas deployment was extensive. Six weeks in New York, with one week of technical training on radio equipment and transmission on a private estate in Long Island, plus some superficial training in self-defense. Hayden loved it. Having never been to college, the evening lectures were a special highlight—it felt to her like a university campus.

After completing her training, Hayden discovered she had been assigned to a post in North Africa, and the RMS *Mauritania* would get her there. The *Mauritania* was a fast ship—twenty-three knots on average from New York to Liverpool—and it only had an air escort for half of the trip. Once on the open ocean, Hayden remembered, it zigzagged its way across the Atlantic, pausing only for the occasional depth-charge detonation to scare off any lurking German submarines.

When Hayden finally arrived in Algiers, OWI billeted her in a local hotel with one roommate and a common toilet shared by all twelve occupants on the floor, including several men with little sense of cleanliness. A pipe connected the sink basin in the corner of her room to the ones above her, and at night the large African cockroaches would use it as a highway to get into Hayden's quarters. When the air raid evacuation sirens went off and the city went into blackout, Hayden and her roommate sheltered in place rather than put their feet into cockroach-infested shoes.

While the accommodations left something to be desired, Hayden had not come to North Africa for a five-star-hotel stay, and she remained singularly focused on work. OWI had initially assigned Hayden to radio transmission, where she was going to be responsible for putting American propaganda translated into dozens of languages onto European wavelengths. The Allies hoped the broadcasts would inform civilians and demoralize enemy soldiers in occupied areas.

Transmission, however, was a dangerous assignment. The enemy commanders knew about the radio stations and, being masters of propaganda themselves, wanted it off the air. They hunted for the hidden stations relentlessly, searching for the signals that broadcasters were forced to beam out from fixed locations around the continent. Once they found a station, they pounded it with munitions.

At the last minute, OWI pulled Hayden from transmission duty. Between their worries about Hayden's safety and the Army commander's need for more administrative help, she was reassigned to clerical duty. The change left Hayden heartbroken, but there was little time to dwell. Even behind a desk, she knew that the work at hand was urgent and important, and that was enough.

By 1944, as Hayden settled into her new role in Algiers, the Allies finally had the Germans in North Africa on their heels. A year earlier, the German commander, Rommel, had failed to exploit his gains in the wake of the Battle of Kasserine Pass and was hopelessly overstretched. He lacked both the necessary reinforcements and the wherewithal to adapt his strategy to his materiel and personnel constraints.

With victory in North Africa assured, the Allies finally had good reason for optimism. The US forces had improved tactically from months of sustained combat, and senior commanders had adapted doctrine based on real battlefield experience. The Americans had finally hit their stride, and the Allies started planning for the next phase of the offensive.

Even with progress in North Africa, however, British and American commanders remained at odds about the wisdom of deploying more resources to the Mediterranean. American commanders again weighed several divergent strategies. On the one hand, US Navy commanders, led by Admiral Ernest J. King, argued that the entire operation in North Africa distracted from the Pacific campaign, which they believed should have been the main effort. Marshall, on the other hand, pushed for a ground invasion of the European continent as soon as possible. British commanders, meanwhile, presented a wholly different strategy. They argued for the continuation of operations in North Africa, followed by the invasion of Sicily and Italy and, in the distant future, an invasion of France. They made the case that the Allies needed to secure bases in North Africa, Sicily, and Italy before "tightening the ring" around the Germans. Doing so, they believed, would also force Hitler to divert more troops from the eastern front in Russia for the defense of his key Italian ally.

The British anticipated American resistance to their plan and came to strategic negotiations in May 1943 prepared. Their case for the Mediterranean approach looked seamless, especially when compared to American infighting over whether to focus on Europe or the Pacific. The Americans proved incapable of generating a coherent alternative to the British plan and soon acquiesced to the more organized British planners. As one US war planner at the meetings put it, "We came, we listened, and we were conquered."

Churchill and Roosevelt, having heard the competing proposals, agreed that an invasion of the island of Sicily would be next, and directed their commanders to prepare for the attack. Two months later, against the predawn darkness, Allied paratroopers dropped from the sky onto the Sicilian coast. Following on their heels came eight divisions—delivered by almost three thousand ships in heavy surf—which deposited eighty thousand troops on the shoreline.

In a preview of the invasion of Normandy a year later, the Allies succeeded in taking the Axis by surprise with an elaborate deception campaign, which left the Axis defenders flat-footed against the enormous Allied landing force. The Axis forces, convinced that Allied strategy—and the storm that was battering the coast—meant they were secure for the evening, were startled by the sudden appearance of thousands of ships on the horizon. They unexpectedly found themselves facing down a hail of naval gunfire, airstrikes, and, not long after, armor and infantry fires from the landing forces. With ground reinforcements too far away to be much help against the initial invasion, the combined German and Italian forces attempted to delay the invading forces, with some success, until the better-trained and better-equipped German units arrived. While their efforts succeeded in temporarily stalling the Allied advance, it proved insufficient. By August 1943, the Axis troops were forced to retreat in Sicily.

In both scale and strategy, the Sicilian invasion and the Italian offensive that followed soon after were harbingers of the invasion of France that was on the horizon. They also portended the violent end of the Italian regime. Benito Mussolini was deposed only days after the invasion of Sicily, and three months later, in September 1943, the Italian government—facing near-certain defeat—capitulated to the Allies. Sicily may not have been the invasion the Americans preferred, but it served to eliminate a symbolic pillar of

American tanks awaiting transport to Sicily. **Courtesy National Archives, photo no. 540074.**

the Axis alliance and set the stage for the next, final phase in the European theater.


As the Allies advanced, propaganda elements like OWI were a key part of maintaining a strong foothold in the Mediterranean theater. While the Allies had succeeded in the initial invasion, they now found themselves conducting precarious exploitation and stabilization operations in the rear areas. During this critical phase, Hayden and her colleagues supplied information to the local population that helped maintain support for the Allies in recently liberated zones and freed up resources for use at the front lines.

When the time came for OWI to move its operations into Italian territory, they told Hayden she was coming with them. Again, Hayden traveled to her assignment by ship, sailing to Italy on the *Ville d'Oran*. The vessel had certainly seen better days. As Hayden warily approached the dock, she found the peeling paint and rust off-putting but, as she watched the stream of Allied forces climb aboard, realized there was no other option.

When she safely arrived at the dock in Naples, she saw the wreckage that the invasion of Italy had left in its wake. The port had been heavily bombed in the preceding months, and the remnants of violence were everywhere. Ships were capsized, lying on their sides or partially submerged. With so much damage everywhere, the *Ville d'Oran*, finding no room at the port to offload its passengers, sidled up to a bombed-out ship that was still attached to a demolished dock and instructed its passengers to disembark.

Hayden slid over the side of the ship and went directly from the port to the office, where the first order of business was the switchboard. The board had been left unattended and flashed nonstop. Hayden's boss took one look at it and, baffled, demanded: "Helen, take care of that switchboard."

As luck would have it, the machine looked familiar to Hayden. She had occasionally manned a switchboard of the same make and model at WEEI. But Hayden did not speak Italian. She grabbed a local employee and made him write down a single phrase in Italian that she repeated for the rest of the afternoon: "I don't speak Italian, call back later."

As she had done in Algiers, Hayden focused on her work in Italy. After seven months in Naples, she again proved herself essential in supporting OWI's mission to broadcast positive news into occupied areas with leaflets, newspapers, and radio programs. When a call from Rome came down asking for Hayden to be transferred, her boss replied that losing her would leave a major void on the team. Higher headquarters responded, simply, "I didn't ask if you could spare her. I told you to send her up here."

The next day, Hayden climbed onto a British lorry, lined with benches on either side, and began the daylong journey from Naples to Rome. When Hayden arrived that evening, a local staffer again took her directly to the office. There was no electricity, so he led Hayden up the five flights of stairs by flashlight. She sat down at a typewriter and began to work on correspondence by candlelight. The British sergeant standing watch got her a bite to eat and, when she finished, led her to the bedroom of an OWI employee who had been hospitalized after suffering a nervous breakdown.

Hayden fared better than the room's previous occupant. Experienced in the work she was assigned and no longer put off by the rough living conditions, Hayden settled in well. She recognized it was all a matter of perspective. Only months earlier, her professional aspirations had been contingent on the whims of the IBEW. Now, she was a valued member of the team charged with loosening the Axis grip on the hearts and minds of the Italian population.

Hayden rarely saw other American women in Italy, but when she did, they were often wearing nurses' uniforms. American nurses and Red Cross volunteers, after all, were among the most numerous groups of women in theaters abroad and were hard to miss in their slick outfits. Among the most experienced nurses in Italy were the women of the 807th Medical Air Evacuation Squadron, composed of the flight nurses responsible for the troops on medical air-evacuation flights.

On a drizzly November morning in 1943 on the southern coast of Italy, thirteen nurses of this skilled unit, and one of their colleagues from the 802nd, planned to hitch a ride on a C-53 that was going to Bari, Italy. When they arrived at the airfield, however, the nurses soon found themselves stuck waiting on the tarmac due to a weather delay.

The women were all frustrated. They had been on enough trips to know that capricious weather in the south of Italy was common and, often, overblown. The flight to Bari had already been rescheduled twice for weather, and the nurses waiting at the airfield were sick of waking up early for a flight that never departed.

The nurses were relieved when, later that morning, the pilot reported that the storm coming in from the north would not arrive until the afternoon, well after their projected landing in Bari. By this point, the nurses knew the drill. They climbed aboard the transport, exchanged a quick hello with the pilots and flight crew, buckled in, and grabbed a magazine from their musette bag for the ride.

As the women climbed aboard, Agnes Jensen—Jens, as she was known—found herself at the front of the line. She settled into the second bucket seat behind the cockpit, opened her magazine, and enjoyed the familiar sensation of the plane detaching from the earth and roaring into the sky. But as the plane ascended high above the Mediterranean, Jensen glanced out the window and noticed something was off. "The usually brilliant blue water was an ominous dark green, flecked everywhere with frothy white" and, worse yet, she recalled, "ugly dark clouds loomed off to the left." It looked as if they were flying into a storm.

Jensen and the other flight nurses quickly realized the plane was in trouble. The weather and the accompanying turbulence were worse than most of them had experienced in months of bumpy flying. Within minutes after takeoff, the plane was violently jumping up and down, with shards of ice flying off the wing, smacking against the fuselage, jolting the passengers around in their seats. As the cold air descended around them, Jensen tried to stay warm by placing two magazines between her and the seat and tucking her feet up under her coat. More concerning than the turbulence, however, was the amount of time they had been in the air. Hours into what should have been a short flight, the nurses understood that the trip was taking far too long and that they were probably running low on fuel.

Soon after the plane had taken off, First Lieutenant Charles B. Thrasher, the captain, had been instructed to break off from the other aircraft in their formation, hoping to find smoother air at a lower altitude. But Thrasher found no such thing. By the time he had completed the maneuver and descended to a safer altitude, he was over three miles from the nearest plane in the formation. Alone, and still in the middle of a vicious storm, Thrasher did his best to contact the airfield at Bari. By noon, hours after takeoff, the plane had fallen out of communication for good.

In any combat theater, being on a plane that has veered significantly off course is a nerve-racking experience. In Italy in 1943, where the Germans still occupied most of the northern part of the country, being low on fuel and possibly miles into Axis-held territory was an especially sobering reality. But the nurses aboard were used to masking their true feelings from creeping onto their faces. Years of experience hiding grimaces from their patients helped them to project a stoic calm as they stared straight ahead, trying to ignore the worsening flight conditions. The pilots, keenly aware of the dwindling fuel supplies, attempted but failed to land the plane once, before they realized that a crash landing remained the only option. As they looked down for a clearing, Thrasher told the passengers to buckle up.

Jensen, terrified but projecting only calm, resigned herself to her fate. Her unit had never been issued parachutes. She noticed ten life jackets in the plane, twenty fewer than needed for all the passengers, and she realized she was helpless to do anything. Reconciled to whatever came next, Jensen simply "smoothed out some musette bags next to her, loosened her seatbelt, slid down in her seat," thinking to herself, "'What the hell, I'd rather be sleeping.'"

When Jensen jolted awake, she found herself crash-landing in a shrub-filled field on the east coast of the Adriatic Sea, in Albania, the tiny nation that had been mired in a civil conflict since Italy began its occupation of the country at the start of the war. All the passengers, amazingly, survived the crash with relatively minor injuries, and frantically exited the wreckage of the plane. Jensen guessed that the dramatic crash landing would have been spotted by observers on the ground and expected her fate would come down to whoever found them first: the German-backed partisans or those backed by the British.

Much to Jensen's relief, the men who emerged from the edge of the woods fell into the latter category, with their leader appropriately riding a white horse. Under his care, the group spent the next few months traveling on foot through treacherous terrain, and eventually rendezvoused with the British. Along the way, they survived a harrowing escape from German strafing, a round of Italian potshots, and a trek over Albania's second-highest mountain peak during a snowstorm. Finally, three months after they departed for Bari, the nurses arrived back in Italy.

All things considered, Jensen and the other nurses were fortunate. Although they had endured a dangerous escape with much hardship along the way, they had evaded capture, or worse. The women knew that luck had been with them from the moment their plane bounced across the empty field in Albania and they walked away from the crash relatively unscathed, only to be greeted by sympathetic partisans.

They also knew others had met worse fates than theirs. Every American nurse had heard the story of their friends and colleagues

The flight nurses who escaped from Albania on foot display their worn-out shoes. **Courtesy National Archives, photo no. 204882478.**

still trapped in captivity in the Santo Tomas internment camp in the Philippines after almost two and a half years. There, almost one hundred Army and Navy nurses had been held captive by the Japanese since the summer of 1942. They faced difficult and dehumanizing conditions at Santo Tomas and the surrounding camps. "Dead bodies piled up for days, and footlong rats ate their toes off," wrote Madeline Ullum, an Army nurse.

Dorothy Still, for example, was a far cry from the pastel sunsets and weekend dances that she remembered so fondly, and was still waiting in the Philippines for a rescue months after she entered captivity. Even so, she made do. Still remembered her camp's bathroom even made light of the bleak circumstances: "It was wall-to-wall women and there was a deafening chicken-yard cacophony," she wrote, adding that "several women shivered under the cold-water showerheads attached to a jerry-rigged pipe extending across the length of the room. Under a frosted window hung a sign: If You Want Privacy, Close Your Eyes."

As American military leaders had predicted, medical units composed of nurses like Jensen and Still proved to be a vital support element that enabled the steady advance of Allied forces. Indeed, by 1943, the rate and nature of the injuries sustained on the firepower-intensive battlefields of World War II required medical professionals to quickly move large numbers of injured soldiers away from the front to locations where they could receive intensive care. This task required an unprecedented number of medical personnel, including flight nurses, like Jensen, who provided care to soldiers as they moved from the front lines to the hospitals in the rear areas. It was a complex and labor intensive process, but American commanders hoped the high quality of care would return men to the battlefield quickly and ease the insatiable demand for manpower in theaters abroad.

The complexity of caring for injured troops during World War II stemmed, in large part, from the unique terrain on which battles were being fought. During World War II, combat rarely occurred in open fields and easy-to-reach locations. Rather, frontline forces were most often located in remote and exceedingly difficult places to access, deep in Pacific jungles or European forests or mountainous Mediterranean terrain. Sending fully equipped medical units to the front lines was considered too risky since their presence would bog down advancing forces, and locating hospitals in permanent facilities close to the front lines was ruled out given the units' inherently limited ability to defend themselves. As a consequence, the medical establishment had to find a way to do the impossible: move hundreds, if not thousands, of critically injured men from remote battlefields to medical facilities located far enough from the front lines to minimize the risk of attack.

In response to this daunting logistical challenge, the US medical corps developed a "chain of evacuation" that incrementally moved injured forces back from the front, providing more advanced care as they went. The system consisted of five primary nodes: battalion aid stations, field hospitals, evacuation hospitals, station hospitals, and general hospitals. Nurses were posted at four of them.

Concurrent with the medical corps' efforts, the Army Air Forces were working to identify ways to supplement this extensive chain of evacuation on the ground. To do so, they developed a system of air evacuation that removed injured soldiers quickly and efficiently from airfields near the front lines to rear areas where they received treatment.

In the early 1940s, the concept of medical air evacuation was groundbreaking. Though air evacuation from battlefields had been used in isolated instances during World War I, and the concept of "air ambulances" had grown in popularity between the wars, the use of aircraft for evacuation remained a new frontier for the American military.

Given its novelty, air evacuation caused no shortage of controversy. The main problem, as in most cases in World War II, was finite resources. A limited number of planes and people were available in each theater, and the notion of diverting those resources toward an untested and complex method of evacuating battlefield casualties was viewed with great skepticism.

Some of this concern was well placed. Medical air evacuation was manpower intensive. For instance, the C-47 Skytrain, nicknamed the Gooney Bird by American pilots in the Pacific, proved the workhorse of medical evacuation flights, and it required nearly fifty people just to function. Medical air evacuation, as innovative and effective as it would prove to be, demanded enormous resources at a time when American forces were already stretched to the limit.

The military also faced a harsh reality about the challenges of airpower in World War II. Flying planes to airfields just behind the front lines was extremely dangerous. Flight crews regularly disappeared on routine flights, and combat, of course, heightened the already high stakes for American fliers. On every sortie, they faced a litany of threats: antiaircraft artillery, weather, pilot error, and mechanical failure, among others, all of which were persistent and commonplace culprits in downing American planes. Although difficult to stomach, the reality for evacuation flights was abundantly clear—some flight crews and patients would not come back.

In the end, military planners reached a compromise. The Army Air Forces decided to equip C-46, C-47, C-53, and C-54 transport planes with convertible litters that would swing down from the sides of the planes. This design would allow the air force to efficiently use the same aircraft for dual purposes: the inbound flight transported supplies into the theater, and, after the plane was converted on the tarmac, the outbound flight evacuated up to twenty-five patients. One nurse, assisted by an enlisted soldier trained in basic medical care, oversaw treatment for the evacuated patients during the flight.

This arrangement, however, did have a distinct downside. While the first leg of the trip, bringing supplies, weapons, and other support equipment to the front lines, was classified as a combat mission, the second leg was a noncombat medical mission. The dual purpose meant that the transport planes could not be painted with red crosses on either leg of the trip, and without that to safeguard them, medical air-evacuation flights became fair game for German and Japanese pilots.

Even with all the inherent risks, however, air evacuation proved essential to providing lifesaving medical care for American men and to returning them to combat. It epitomized the importance of combat support units in sustaining frontline forces and enabling success on the battlefield. By the end of the war, over thirty air-evacuation squadrons were deployed around the world, and more than one million patients were evacuated by air—over five hundred flight nurses served on these vital flights.

* * *

As women in uniform set up camp in the muddy plains of North Africa and escaped German Stukas in the mountains of Albania, the case for militarizing the WAAC grew considerably. Not only had WAACs performed well in the field, but WAAC recruiting had outperformed early expectations, and commanders were requesting that thousands more women be added to the program.

The case for militarizing the WAAC was helped, perhaps more than anything else, by the stark reality that, even in 1943, two years after the United States had entered the war, there was still much fighting to be done. The string of victories in North Africa and Italy and the Allied success in stopping the Japanese advance were certainly welcome developments for American military commanders, as was the Russian success in rebuffing the Germans in the East.

But these successes were a far cry from facing off against the still formidable German and Japanese forces near and within their home territory. US leaders understood that some of the worst, most vicious battles of the war lay ahead, as they set their sights on France and Germany in the west and the Philippines and Japan in the east. The United States would need to marshal enough personnel to undertake several near-simultaneous and enormous amphibious landings—and then exploit those operations with sustained overland combat.

At the same time, Marshall was consumed by the need to balance the demands of the battlefield with the ongoing and equally important demands of the American manufacturing industry. As the Allies advanced deeper into combat against the Japanese and German defenders, the demands for materiel were only increasing. By the end of 1943, Marshall and his advisors recognized that their personnel requirements were rapidly approaching the limits of what the American population could sustain. The manpower spigot would soon turn off, and both manufacturing and military planners would need to use what they had more efficiently.

"For a long time there has been a great deal of discussion regarding the problem of manpower," wrote Marshall, "which daily grows more acute with the necessity for an increase in the production of war materiel and the urgent requirements for farm labor." The solution, he added, lay in finding efficiencies wherever they existed. "The women are daily playing a more and more important part in our war effort," and making these women full-fledged members of the Army, he argued, was a key part of solving the manpower puzzle.

Hobby had been lobbying for the change from the very start, both for the sake of the women in the Corps and to bolster her own authority. The issue took on more urgency, however, when the Army began to use its authorization to send women to overseas theaters. Deploying women abroad exposed them to much greater risks of accident, injury, and even death than they encountered in stateside service, and, by not conferring full status on the WAACs, the Army faced the serious dilemma of ordering women to go into a combat zone with few of the protections they guaranteed to Army men.

Ultimately it was General Eisenhower's enthusiasm for the women that forced the issue. Eisenhower's request for a detachment of WAACs during the North Africa invasion had worried Hobby, and for good reason, since the handful of women posted abroad had already faced some harrowing situations.

In fact, some of the first WAACs to be shipped overseas, five executive secretaries assigned to Eisenhower's headquarters, had just arrived on the beaches of Algiers—but only after their troop-transport ship had been torpedoed by a German U-boat. The WAACs had escaped the listing ship on a life raft, only to spend the next several hours pulling wounded and drowning soldiers out of the frigid Atlantic and into their raft, while the able-bodied men sharing their lifeboat became violently ill from the tumultuous seas.

After being rescued by a British destroyer, the women arrived at the Algiers port, filthy and freezing, having only narrowly escaped with their lives.

The ordeal was so harrowing that Roosevelt had been briefed on it, and soon after conveyed the story in a press conference. Despite his professed admiration for the women, however, the official transcript of his remarks reveals Roosevelt's surprisingly belittling tone: "The ship was torpedoed . . . and finally all five of them were safely landed in Africa without any clothes whatsoever (slight pause here, on purpose). They had nothing except what they had on their backs . . . (loud laughter)."

Hobby, on the other hand, found nothing funny about the WAAC's ordeal. As she began planning to assemble a company to be shipped overseas to join the small contingent already abroad, she remembered these women. In response to Eisenhower's request, Hobby insisted that the unit be composed entirely of volunteers, apprised fully of the risks of their undertaking. She traveled to the WAAC training center in Daytona Beach to personally inform the prospective units of the request. Hobby, a commander of great integrity, wanted to convey directly to the women the dangers of serving in a combat zone without full military protection.

When she entered the room, three hundred WAACs awaited her, ramrod straight in their chairs. The women soldiers revered Hobby and knew that her personal presence presaged something important. She told the crowd only what she could, that a request had been made for personnel to serve in "an unnamed but dangerous combat theater." She reminded them in the strongest terms that they lacked military status and would not have the full protection of the Army should anything happen to them. If the women died, they would not receive a military burial, and they were not eligible for military life insurance. If they were injured, they would not be eligible for a military pension or access to the subsidized veterans' medical care. If the disability was permanent, they would be discharged from the military hospital and told to leave the base. After Hobby finished her remarks, with all its warnings, she asked volunteers to step forward. Without pause, the entire room stood up.

By the end of June 1943, Congress had taken notice of the complications and contradictions that Hobby laid out in her speech, and it passed legislation changing the WAAC to the WAC, the Women's Army Corps. Hobby and her corps were finally an Army unit with the same protections and benefits conferred on male soldiers. On July 5, Hobby repeated her oath of office and became a colonel in the US Army. By the end of September, every woman in the Army was given the opportunity to leave the service or retake her oath. Despite months of inequities, disparagement, indignities, and defamation, eighty percent of the women chose to stay on for the duration of the war.

WAC leaders, having finally secured protection for their units, breathed a sigh of relief and directed the women to return to their essential work.

# 17

# "WHICH ONE OF THESE JOBS WOULD YOU LIKE?"

## STATESIDE SERVICE

BY THE END OF 1943, THE US MILITARY AND THE women serving in it were finally in the fight. The United States was simultaneously engaged in combat in several theaters, including campaigns in North Africa, Italy, and the Pacific, and it appeared the Allies were winning. But the extent of these campaigns, and especially the operations in North Africa and Italy, had placed even more demands on American commanders' manpower calculations. Senior American military planners had been surprised by the difficulty of the fighting in both theaters, and both the German and Japanese forces had proved to be formidable, experienced, and committed, even on territory far from their homelands. Their entrenched defense against Allied attempts to reclaim territory in far-flung theaters did not bode well for American offensives on Axis soil, including the future and much larger invasions of France, Germany, and Japan. With some of the largest, most difficult Allied operations still months if not years away, American commanders worried about their ability to meet their future personnel demands.

Moreover, even if the US military could outfit the front lines with enough combat forces, that did not solve the equally vexing question of how to train all of them. Already, training millions of men how to fight, particularly given the requirements of the new equipment and doctrines, proved to be a lengthy and resource-intensive enterprise. The result was a massive bottleneck: in 1943, it took divisions so long to move overseas that the War Department had to slow down the activation schedule.

For military planners, answering the question of how to secure available and suitable personnel to train all the divisions stacking up stateside became paramount. While taking experienced men off the front lines to teach green troops was considered, planners rejected the idea in order to keep the most skilled forces on the battlefield. Women in uniform, on the other hand, were not needed on the front lines and could learn the essential skills required to train troops during a short instruction course. The military turned, again, to them.

Susan Ahn grew up straddling two cultures. As the oldest daughter of Ahn Changho, one of the leading Korean activists in California opposing the Japanese occupation of Korea, she reveled in both the American habits and hobbies of her hometown of San Francisco and the Korean customs of her parents' homeland, from which they had emigrated in 1902.

On one hand, Ahn loved the close-knit community of Korean American families that animated her childhood. But Ahn was also an American kid. She grew up going to American schools and, from an early age, was taught that the Korean struggle for independence shared a great deal with the American struggle to shake off British colonialism. Most of all, she loved baseball and played pickup games with her friends behind her house. "I was the oldest of the kids playing," she remembered, adding that "I always got my way, it seemed."

Given Ahn Changho's history as a renowned Korean dissident, there was little question about whether the Ahn family would contribute to the war effort when the Japanese struck Pearl Harbor. The Japanese had attacked their home twice, first in Korea and now in the United States, and all of the Ahn children wanted to participate in the fight against Japan's aggression.

And, so, after signing up for the WAVES, Ahn found herself eating a breakfast of pancakes, eggs, toast, and coffee on an old railcar on her way to Cedar Falls, Iowa, one of the early training facilities that preceded the Navy's move to Hunter College. Like many women who had signed up for the WAVES, she had assumed her training would take place on the coast or, at least, within driving distance of the water. But the Navy, strapped for resources and real estate, had decided the WAVES, who would never serve on a ship, did not need to be anywhere near the ocean to be trained for their jobs.

Ahn had graduated from San Diego State College in 1942. Had she been White, her educational and family background almost certainly would have led to a commission in the WAVES officer corps. Instead, the WAVES rejected her officer application on the grounds of lack of experience, although a friend later told her it was likely due to her ethnicity. But Ahn persisted. She wanted to serve, in whatever capacity was available to her at the time, and so she reapplied to the WAVES' enlisted ranks. She was among the first group of WAVES to enlist, and among an even smaller cadre of Asian American women who would serve in the war.

Ahn took naturally to the Navy. She excelled at boot camp and found the transition to the military routine unremarkable. "This is the life," she wrote in a letter to her little brother, Ralph. She continued: "We never do anything until we are told to and we never speak until spoken to. It's an easy way to live." She liked her uniform and made fast friends with another woman, a friend of her brother's, and the two spent most of their time studying and writing notes home. Ahn stuck out among the group of young, mostly

White women—"I still seem to be an oddity here," she wrote to her sister, "they get me mixed up with a gal from Hawaii"—but she was generally too focused on her training to be fazed much by the casual racism she experienced.

During training, Ahn had initially hoped to specialize in aerology, which she found interesting and which offered the best prospects for overseas service. Since she had done well during boot camp, Ahn figured that she had a decent shot at getting selected for the competitive role monitoring the weather. To her surprise, however, Ahn learned that she had been assigned to an even rarer specialty. She was selected as one of seventy-five women, chosen from over a thousand, to receive advanced schooling as an aviation-training instructor, specializing in the "Link Trainer."

The Link Trainer was a peculiar but widely employed device that was, essentially, the predecessor of modern-day flight simulators. The contraptions did not look like much: a stubby wooden box, painted blue and accented with a bright yellow tail and wings and lofted up on a small lift, but it could mimic the movement of a plane and had just enough room for a pilot to sit comfortably. Inside, the pilot would find a replica of the instrumentation found in the cockpits of Navy and Army Air Force planes. Link Trainers intentionally had no windows, meaning that the pilot would have to rely on the instruments alone to maneuver the machine, allowing it to simulate key scenarios like night and instrument flying, but while safely on the ground and under the watchful eye of an instructor.

The technology was simple but effective. Celestial navigation was replicated with small bulbs installed on the roof dome, imitating night-sky conditions. Ground-attack training was conducted with enlarged photos of enemy terrain moving below the feet of the pilot and "landmarks he would detect if he were flying over the country at an altitude of 10,000 feet." The pilots may not have spent a minute over Italy, France, Germany, or Japan, but if the

Link Trainers worked, the stars and the landscape would look familiar when they did.

Crucially, from a manpower and training perspective, the airmen and sailors in charge of Link training did not actually need to be trained fliers themselves; they simply had to learn how to correctly use the device. It was a brilliant workaround, since pilots could get the training they needed without tying up the time and skills of more experienced aviators. Women were especially well suited to the work.

Many of the women who performed best in these training roles had been teachers in their civilian lives. They were used to learning about complex topics with which they had no direct experience, distilling them down to discernible bits, and then walking others through the task. Other women may not have been teachers but came from exactly the sort of mechanical or mathematical

A Coast Guard Link Trainer. **Courtesy National Archives, photo no. 205576754.**

backgrounds that made them adept at learning the complicated commands and calculations necessary for teaching difficult aerial maneuvers. And others, like Ahn, were just extremely bright. Whether they were teachers, tinkerers, or intelligent women, military planners reasoned they would make perfect Link training instructors. Ahn and her fellow trainers' newly acquired skills were quickly applied in the Navy's push to get trained aviators to the Pacific.

The Japanese, even more so than the Germans, understood that time was not on their side. If they were going to take on the American behemoth, which dwarfed them in both manufacturing and military might, the Japanese recognized it would require surprise and speed at every turn. As a result, their strategy was predicated on inflicting a massive series of rapid, consecutive blows to key American holdings in the Pacific, pushing the Allies out of the region and buying them time to dig in.

With this strategy guiding them, the Japanese moved to quickly expand their defensive perimeter. Following the attacks on Pearl Harbor and the Philippines with a series of brutally efficient assaults in 1942, the Japanese extended their position deep into the western Pacific and the South China Sea, dislodging and killing thousands of Americans along the way. The US Marines stationed on Wake Island, for instance, totaling just under five hundred men, managed to forestall the Japanese offensive for several days, until the Japanese returned with two aircraft carriers and forced a surrender. Near simultaneously, the Japanese extended their reach into Guam, making quick work of the small Marine Corps outfit posted there. By the spring of 1942, the Japanese had arrived at the doorstep of Australia and New Zealand, leaving American commanders reeling and furious as they surveyed the damage.

Facing this onslaught, American naval leadership, headed by Admiral King, the commander in chief of the US Fleet and chief of naval operations, pushed forcefully for an emphasis on retaking the initiative in the Pacific in 1942 and 1943. The United States needed to answer Japanese aggression, he argued, before it crept any farther out into the Pacific and cut off American access to key allies and supply routes in the region.

Roosevelt, in part, was inclined to agree with King. He knew that there needed to be some response in the Pacific, but his rationale was as much based on political calculation as it was on military strategy. The longstanding Allied strategy may have been "Germany first," but Roosevelt knew the Japanese could not be left untouched in the aftermath of Pearl Harbor—the American public would not stand for it. In response, Roosevelt had approved a targeted attempt to reverse the Japanese progress in the Pacific in 1942 and 1943. The Navy quickly began preparing to mount a series of campaigns, jointly with the Marine Corps and Army, to stop the Japanese advance and retake the initiative.

First, and most important, the Americans had to slow the steady momentum that the Japanese had gained in the first half of 1942. In May and June of 1942, the United States did just that. At the Battle of Coral Sea, one of the first carrier battles of the war, the Allies successfully defended against the Japanese attempt to take Port Moresby in New Guinea. Then, in a widely publicized and rousing reversal, the Allies rebuffed the Japanese at the Battle of Midway, marking a defeat from which the Japanese struggled to recover.

With these two naval victories under their belt, the Allies had recaptured the momentum—and public support—for a long-awaited counterattack. Wanting to capitalize on this shift, American commanders proposed a series of joint campaigns to retake the holdings that they had lost in the opening months of the war. Under the command of Admiral Bill Halsey, the Navy and Marine Corps pursued retaking several key islands in the Solomons—Tulagi, Florida, and Guadalcanal—while, near simultaneously, under the leadership of General MacArthur, the Army began an assault against New Guinea en route to retaking Rabaul and, eventually, the Philippines.

For the Navy, the Solomons campaign held a particular importance. Midway had stopped the Japanese advance, but a strong showing in a Pacific offensive would exploit the momentum they had gained and provide a critical boost to morale. It would also be the first time that the Marine Corps would employ its new and largely untested amphibious assault doctrine, on which they had staked much of their strategy for retaking the Pacific.

The Solomons offensive started off well enough, with American forces taking most of their objectives within days. But the success proved short-lived. Once the Japanese understood the full scope of the attack, they responded by strengthening their deployment on Guadalcanal, creating a stalemate. Both sides reinforced their embattled units as the casualty numbers rose steadily, as much from combat as from disease. It took over six months for the United States to dislodge the Japanese and involved seven fleet engagements, three major ground battles, the loss of twenty-four warships, and near-constant air engagement. It was the first of many hard-won victories in the Pacific.

The aftermath of the Battle of Guadalcanal provided the US military—and the Navy in particular—with a newfound understanding of the state of the war in the Pacific. First, new doctrines, including amphibious assault and carrier warfare operations, were put into practice by inexperienced men with admittedly mixed results, but they had prevailed. "The myth of Japanese invincibility," reads one history of the campaign, "died in the Solomons." But second, and just as important, the Navy now understood that the Japanese would not go quietly. The US military needed to be fully committed to a lengthy, ruthless, and costly fight, stretched across thousands of miles of tenuous supply lines in unfamiliar and unfriendly climates, to defeat this entrenched adversary. By 1943, the Navy believed they could win in the Pacific, but knew it would be a dogged effort and would require hundreds of thousands of personnel.

In this environment, assignments for Navy women at bases around the United States ballooned as men were being pulled from support units and sent to the front lines. Many women, like Ahn, were finding themselves in high demand for nontraditional roles, especially in fields like naval aviation. Of the two thousand women assigned to the Bureau of Aeronautics, for instance, over six hundred were assigned to receive specialized training at MIT, UCLA, the University of Chicago, and other elite institutions. With their new credentials in hand, these women found themselves filling roles like celestial navigation instructors, air-combat information specialists, photo interpreters, aviation-gunnery instructors, and air-transport officers.

Their impact was immediate and extensive. "During the war's two final years, every naval aviator going into combat had received some part of his training from a WAVE," estimates one historian of Navy women, further noting that "1,000 WAVES taught instrument flying in Link trainers to 4,000 men a day." Thousands of women, like Ahn, were training naval aviators to succeed in the skies over the Pacific, and the Navy soon came to depend on the women it had once dismissed as unnecessary.

There is a story that WAVES liked to tell about a pilot coming in for a landing at Naval Air Station Jacksonville. The pilot, having just radioed to the control tower in preparation for landing, received the standard reply from the control tower: "266271. This is Navy, Jacksonville. Over."

But, as the legend goes, the pilot was puzzled by the voice of the control tower operator. He thought it sounded like a woman. Confused, the pilot continued his dialogue with the control tower. "Five miles north of field, would like permission to enter traffic circle, and landing instructions."

The same control tower operator responded: "Clear to land on the mat to the right of the circle. The course is one eight zero degrees. 266271, Roger, out."

This time it was indisputable. The pilot was sure that a woman was guiding him in for landing. Emboldened, he responded by confirming the details of his descent but decided to add at the end, "That's a mighty pretty voice you've got. What are you doing later?" Before she responded, the control tower operator looked to her partner for the day, a junior enlisted man who had overheard the entire exchange. With a smirk, the man responded, "Navy, Jacksonville, what was that sir?"

The control tower operator was not the only woman at Naval Air Station Jacksonville that day. Like their counterparts supporting naval aviation, many Navy women proved especially adept at taking over the stateside maintenance and repair roles at places like NAS Jacksonville, and with the war in full swing, these rolls were steadily growing in importance. According to one estimate, for example, the Army alone spent one billion dollars a month on maintenance between 1942 and 1944. The Navy was not far behind: by 1945, they produced over eighty thousand landing craft and ships, in addition to more than a thousand combatant vessels, all of which needed to be maintained, fixed, and sent back to combat theaters around the world. Ensuring that this equipment could be kept in service meant developing an equally large and efficient maintenance operation that stretched from the United States to the Mediterranean, Europe, and the Pacific. American military leaders were faced with a now familiar dilemma, finding uniformed personnel who had the patience and skill to conduct these tasks without robbing the services of much-needed frontline manpower.

The solution to this problem came in the form of women like Czsława Kontrabecki. Kontrabecki was born on a kitchen table in Niagara Falls, New York. Her parents had both arrived from Poland in 1912, and she was the tenth child of eleven, six of whom died of malnutrition before she was born. Her mother was the youngest of three and shared a three-story apartment building with her sisters, each on a different floor. Her father fixed train engines for the railroad and, according to family legend, was strong enough to lift a railroad tie over his head unassisted.

Her father's strength, however, was not a blessing. "As far as I was told, he turned out to be quite a bad man," she remembered when we spoke. An alcoholic, he played the fiddle at a local dance hall and came home drunk most nights. He wasted the family's money on alcohol, the children suffered from persistent hunger, and their mother suffered terrible abuse. When Kontrabecki was three years old, she recalled, her father hit her mother over the head with a chair, causing her to fall down the stairs. "That's the first time I remember having a mother and a father," she recalled.

Child services eventually intervened, arrested her father, committed her mother, and placed Kontrabecki and one of her sisters in the Wyndham Lawn Home in Lockport, New York. When Kontrabecki arrived at the home, she was given a milkshake every day to improve her weight. Her polish name, Czsława, was Americanized into Jessie, which she would go by for the rest of her life.

After graduating from Nardin Academy in Buffalo, an elite women's Catholic school where she was accepted as a "charity case," Kontrabecki started work at a shredded wheat plant in Niagara Falls. The factory put the new girls at the end of a conveyor belt that pulled the biscuits along and, in a scene straight out of *I Love Lucy*, Kontrabecki found that the piles of shredded wheat accumulated much faster than she was able to pack them. She left two weeks later.

After a short stint scooping ice cream at the local deli and another at the Bell Aircraft Corporation changing the oil in F-4 Corsair fighter-bomber planes, she started to consider military service. "I thought there was more to all this than just that," she said of working at the aircraft plant. In August 1943, Kontrabecki joined the class of enlisted women at Hunter College.

The Navy quickly took notice of Kontrabecki's aptitude with her hands and assigned her to aviation repair. After three months, she, along with the other mechanics in her class assigned to the role, made their way to Chicago for advanced training in aviation instrumentation. She thought it was an amusing coincidence that the training facility was in a repurposed brassiere factory.

Once trained, Kontrabecki was sent to Naval Air Station Jacksonville, one of the largest air bases in the United States and the maintenance hub for repairing whole swaths of the Navy's air fleet, where she was assigned to the Overhaul and Repair (O&R) division. She had earned the rating of AMMI2, aviation machinist's mate (instrument mechanic), and was assigned to fixing damaged plane parts and aviation instruments—altimeters, oil gauges, pressure gauges, and the like—that had returned to NAS Jacksonville from the battlefield and needed to get back into working order.

Kontrabecki remembered the arrival of her unit made a bit of a stir, since the men at NAS Jacksonville weren't used to seeing many women in uniform, let alone women assigned to do repair work of the type Kontrabecki had been assigned. "They looked at us like we were something out of this world," she recalled.

But Kontrabecki and the WAVES were extremely skilled, and the men soon adjusted to their presence. "I had to be very efficient at the work," said Kontrabecki, who remembered taking the delicate instruments apart; cleaning them with the prescribed chemicals, benzene and tetrachloride; repairing them; and then putting them all back together again. The work was particularly well suited to small hands, and the men started to take notice of the WAVES' efficiency at the task. "They came over to see," she told me, adding, "They had to watch me to figure out how they should be doing it."

As Kontrabecki and her counterparts filled increasingly diverse positions in the maintenance functions that had become so vital,

WAVES perform maintenance on the engine of an SNJ at NAS Jacksonville.
Courtesy National Archives, photo no. 520608.

the WAVES' sister services experienced similar expansion in the breadth and depth of available positions. The Marine aviation branch alone requested over nine thousand women to serve at naval air stations and, by the end of the war, a full third of Marine women served in aviation-related roles. Serving as motor transport drivers also proved to be one of the most popular roles for Marine women, and they eventually ran, with a perfect safety record, the entire motor transport section at Pearl Harbor. In the WAAC, women filled over 400 of 628 military occupational specialties.

The SPARS found themselves equally in demand, with one unit, Unit 21, manning the top-secret Long Range Aid to Navigation (LORAN) station in Chatham, Massachusetts.

The enthusiasm for women among senior commanders making personnel allocations, however, was not as common at lower echelons. While senior commanders could see the bigger manpower picture and how women could lessen the strains on it, sailors on bases around the country often did not. At the working level, it took time and exposure to convert many men to the benefits of having women in uniform, particularly in nonclerical roles.

In most cases, opponents to women serving in nontraditional roles quickly revealed their backward logic. One base commander, for instance, refused to let a group of women trained as aviation machinist's mates—the sailors responsible for operating, repairing, and maintaining equipment on the Navy's planes—do their jobs because separate bathrooms were not available for the women. After some cajoling, and a reminder that the cost of adding bathrooms paled in comparison to the sunk cost of the women's advanced training, the commander admitted his reluctance was based on his feeling that "women couldn't do the job properly," and that he had never worked with women before. Eventually, he agreed to give them a chance and, in the end, he found a simple (and economical) solution to his initial concern: "Put a peg outside the door of the head, and when a man goes in he hangs his hat on the peg and no women go in. When a WAVE goes in, let her hang her hat on the peg and the men will stay out."

Moreover, even in the face of more malicious efforts to undermine the effectiveness of women in newly expanded roles, the women found clever ways to prove themselves. McAfee often told the story of two women who were sent to a base to replace two men who wanted to stay put. The men worked in a warehouse and, in an effort to prove their indispensability, greeted the women with an impossible task on their first day: moving a set of truck tires up to the top storage shelf. Knowing the women did not have the strength to lift the tires, the men simply wished them luck, and went to get lunch. But when they returned to check on the women, they found, much to their surprise, all of the tires in their spot high above the warehouse floor.

"How on earth did you do it?" they asked, incredulously.

"We rigged a pulley, of course."

# 18

# "HAVE YOU GOT WHAT IT TAKES TO FILL AN IMPORTANT JOB LIKE THIS?"

## DISAPPOINTMENT AND DISILLUSIONMENT

AS THE US MILITARY SENT TRAINED WOMEN TO bases around the country and the world, the critics of women in uniform began to quiet. Seeing the essential work that the women were doing to end the war, which entered its fourth year in 1944, the public began to appreciate the wisdom of releasing men to serve on the front lines by placing women in support roles. This was especially true on bases and at headquarters where uniformed women performed critical administrative tasks that kept the bureaucratic machinery of the military running.

Indeed, the reality is that most women in uniform served their country as secretaries, typists, stenographers, and other administrative support staff. For instance, in one request for 120 WACs, assigned to Palm Springs, California, 110 were requests for clerical workers—primarily clerks, typists, and stenographers. Similarly, at the peak of the WAC's enrollment, fifty percent of the women assigned to the Army Air Forces held administrative or office jobs. In a table compiled by the Army Service Forces of almost three thousand assignments for WACs, nearly half were allotted to "Typist" and "Clerk—non-typist." In the Army Ground Forces, seventy-two percent of women were assigned to administrative and clerical roles.

Many of the women who served in these clerical roles thrived. Women like Christine Shanklin, who served as one of Eisenhower's most trusted secretaries and staffed him during peace negotiations—earning her the nickname "Ike's Little Carrier Pigeon"—were indispensable in their administrative positions. These women, unlike many of the men they replaced, were also excellent at their jobs and happy to do them. "The boys, many of them, had no interest in being yeomen from the point of view of running a typewriter," remembered McAfee, "and when these girls came in knowing there wasn't any better action than this for them, they did a perfectly stunning job."

World War II created an explosion of bureaucratic and administrative demands on the military. The sheer size of the enterprise, simply the number of personnel and equipment that needed to be accounted for at all times, is difficult to fathom. "The simple headquarters of a Grant or a Lee were gone forever. An army of filing clerks, stenographers, office managers, telephone operators, and chauffeurs had become essential," remarked Eisenhower years later.

At the most basic level, the magnitude of forces in the United States generated an extraordinary amount of paperwork—paperwork for commissions, paperwork for orders, paperwork for transportation, paperwork for uniforms, paperwork for leave, paperwork for every step of the journey from hometown hero to duty station, and then some. Add to this the records, memos, transcripts, letters, and calls that could be generated by a single individual or office, compounded over millions of personnel, and it becomes clear why an army of administrative staff in every corner of the world was needed to keep track of it.

What's more, the individuals assigned to this work needed to be learned and practiced in the skills necessary for their jobs. Fortunately, many of the women who served in these positions had undergone years of formal training at business schools across the country before they joined the military. Others had spent equal or more time working professionally in exactly the type of role for which they were now needed in the military. Women, it seemed, had precisely the experience required to tame the mountains of paperwork that the military generated daily.

Given the importance of the work, however, even the experienced women received training for administrative and clerical duties. One worksheet, the "Simple Rules of Tabulation," outlined the settings for font, spacing, margins, and paper size: "Underwood–narrow carriage Elite type: paper always in at 0, Left margin at 12, Middle point of paper at 48, Right margin 84, Right end of paper 96, Also applies to L.C. Smith and Royal Narrow Carriage." Another, "Principles of Alphabetic Filing," listed twenty-five guidelines, including how to deal with hyphenation and name changes, with the "Principles for Dividing Words" consisting of thirteen guidelines. Spelling rules, a seven-page review of English grammar, and seven additional pages on the use of question marks, quotation marks, colons, semicolons, capital letters, and dashes were also included.

The work demanded great speed, organization, efficiency, and laser focus on details. The rules of formatting, spelling, grammar, and—most important from the military perspective—indexing had to be followed to the letter. In the deluge of paper that flooded headquarters and staffs around the country and abroad, there was no time for administrative and clerical errors. If documents were misfiled, lost, or unreadable, they were useless. An errant hyphen, a misspelled name, or a misfiled report could result in hours of delays as staff searched for the correct information, and mistakes on even a small portion of these tasks, executed millions of times a day, quickly added up. Administrative personnel functioned as the backbone of the American military bureaucracy, holding in the balance the efficiency of thousands of offices around the world. It may not have been frontline combat, but clerical work made or broke the efficiency of a headquarters and, in turn, the units it commanded.

Among the many women trained in administrative tasks was Millie Corbett, the WAC who had made her way from Tulsa to Fort Des Moines. By 1943, she was posted at Fort McClellan, Alabama, where she was the second in command to Corrie Sherrard, with whom she got along beautifully. It was fortunate that they did,

Black WACs are taught the post switchboard schedule by enlisted men at Fort Huachuca, Arizona. **Courtesy National Archives, photo no. 266694430.**

since the segregation on base required that they be housed to-gether in a bungalow. The house, spacious and well appointed for the two women, had been outfitted with new furniture and re-quired them to call a car to bring them to the office each day. It was an expensive and labor-intensive arrangement, but necessi-tated by the Army's policy. "All of that," Corbett told me in our interview, "just to keep us segregated."

Nonetheless, Corbett settled in nicely, and she and Sherrard often found ways to enjoy themselves in their limited downtime. On one memorable evening, the two had been watching a movie at the base theater and, when the lights went up, received a call to report to the back of the theater. Worried that something had happened to one of their soldiers, they hurried back to the pro-jection booth. Standing there was Joe Louis and Sugar Ray Rob-inson, two of the most famous professional boxers in the world. They had traveled to the base as part of their participation in the Army's recruiting and morale campaign, and they asked Corbett and Sherrard about their plans for the evening.

The night turned out to be uneventful, all things considered. The men came back to their house and played a few games of cards, gambling for pennies. They all got along well, enjoying the novelty of each other's company. But while the company may have been good, Corbett's cards were not. To her dismay, she found herself losing over and over again. Looking across the table, Louis smiled at Corbett and said, "Don't gamble with anyone else until you learn to play better," and, returning the handful of pennies he had won from her, added, "I was cheating you."

After McClellan, where Corbett received a commendation for "excellent character, spirit, and disposition," the Army sent her to Fort Benning, Georgia, to command a Black unit there. Not sur-prisingly, she performed well, and when a slot opened at Adjutant General School at Fort Sam Houston, Texas, she was at the top of the list for the advanced training.

Despite its seemingly dull name, the Adjutant General Department in World War II, as now, sits at the center of the manpower and personnel equation of the Army. While its closest corollary in the civilian world is human resources, its tasks in combat are often far more complex and impactful than the comparison would imply. Not only did the adjutant general oversee recordkeeping on virtually all administrative elements of each individual soldier's experience—including testing, processing, allotment, deployment, reintegration, and casualty and death management—it was also responsible for maintaining a strategic sense of how and where Army personnel were deployed around the world and, critically, for filling any readiness gaps where they existed.

With several million personnel serving in World War II, the Army's Adjutant General Department faced the staggering enterprise of compiling, recording, and interpreting that data on an enormous scale. In fact, the task was so demanding that the department developed one of the first mobile electronic-accounting machines, a predecessor to modern computer technology, to keep track of millions of people coming through training centers, bases, and combat theaters. Compiling and maintaining these records required a cohort of over fifteen thousand personnel, composed primarily of individuals with a knack for detail and a great deal of forbearance—two traits that Corbett possessed in spades.

As Corbett rode the train down from Georgia to Texas to attend Adjutant General School, she wasn't paying much attention to the other passengers. She was headed down to her first advanced-training course and instead focused on being rested and ready for whatever awaited her. The train was segregated, which meant that when Corbett went to get her meals, she was expected to sit in a separate part of the dining car, shielded behind a small curtain. The limited space available in the dining car, however, meant that the segregated area was also the area where VIPs would be seated, shielded from prying eyes. In this case, that VIP was General James Ulio, adjutant general of the Army, on his way to address the class that Corbett would be attending.

With Ulio in her seat, Corbett was out of luck. After the waiter apologized for the inconvenience of not being able to segregate her, Corbett started to make her way back to her cabin. A White major, however, had overheard the commotion and asked her to join him for the meal. Corbett was grateful for the invitation and for the major's kindness.

Just as she and the major were finishing their meal, Ulio came out from behind the curtain. Seeing the pair, he stopped to talk with the two of them, asking where they were headed. Corbett, recognizing the stars on his uniform, obligingly told Ulio that she would be attending the Adjutant General School course—to which he responded that he would see her there since he was the keynote speaker.

Corbett returned to her seat for the remainder of the ride, and when the time came to disembark, she collected her things and headed to the nearest exit. She noticed a group of dignitaries and senior officers assembling on the platform, surely there to greet Ulio. As the four-star general in charge of personnel, he was considered one of the most important officers in the fight.

Lined up and ready to disembark, Corbett felt the train come to a stop and stepped into the vestibule. Then Ulio appeared. Upon seeing the general, Corbett and the other passengers around her paused to allow him off the train first, as was the military custom. But Ulio, knowing where Corbett was headed and understanding, perhaps better than anyone else, the necessity of getting trained adjutants into the field—no matter their color—realized she had somewhere to be. Without skipping a beat, he looked at her and said, "After you, Lieutenant."

The crowd on the platform, who had been waiting for Ulio to step off the train, were shocked to be greeted by a one-hundred-pound, five-foot-two Black woman in an Army uniform. Smiling, Corbett continued on her way.

\* \* \*

While Corbett thrived as a Black woman assigned to the Adjutant General Department, her experience was not always shared by other women in her shoes. Some women, Black and White alike, felt disappointment at being assigned to clerical roles. Many women had joined the military both because of a patriotic impulse and because of their disaffection with their lives as teachers, housewives, and telephone operators at home. The recruiters had promised them an exciting new life. "You can ask for the job you'd like to do," advertised one recruiting pamphlet. Instead, many women had gotten the same life in a uniform.

Women assigned to administrative roles for which they were overqualified felt especially disgruntled. They soon became bored of the work, and morale plummeted. "Morale stayed high wherever the work was hard and the hours long," wrote Hobby, "and dropped only when the WAC women were allowed to feel useless or unwanted by some military commander." McAfee, director of the WAVES, agreed: "I never worry when the women have too much work," she wrote, adding that "I worry only when they don't have enough work to do."

From the start, all the directors had objected to overpromising and underdelivering to recruits when it came to the jobs they would do, but McAfee was particularly adamant in her stance. In fact, one of the few occasions she appealed to Admiral Jacobs, the Navy's chief of personnel, was to override a decision to release a recruiting film, which Navy public relations had tried to push through, that promised "an adventure that we couldn't possibly guarantee." McAfee foresaw that the women would be used to fill many boring, drab jobs. She wanted volunteers to have a realistic sense of what their contributions would be, particularly since many of them would be leaving behind promising careers and lives to do so. "We cannot have this thing which will make them think they're coming in to get their man and to have a thrill," she remembered thinking, "because we can't come through with it, and we'll soon ruin their career."

Unlike Corbett, many Black women also became disillusioned by their military experiences, particularly since they were disproportionately assigned to the very service tasks they sought to escape by joining the Army. Despite being trained for high-skilled jobs, Black women, often at the whim of their base commanders, frequently faced instances of blatant discrimination and were forced to perform unskilled work in uniform. While Army leaders were well aware of the egregious waste of talent caused by these prejudiced behaviors, they took little action to curb them, and their failure to do so led to a deep well of resentment among many Black WACs.

The dissatisfaction that many Black women felt on base only intensified when compounded by the treatment that they often received off base. As many Black WACs discovered, dangerous consequences sometimes existed for them being seen off base in uniform, particularly in towns adjacent to bases in the South. Some White Americans were galled to see Black women donning military uniforms, and, for them, such a sight hit a nerve.

This anger was not new—it had been directed at Black men in uniform for decades—and often contained a violent undercurrent. As Brenda Moore notes in her history of Black servicewomen, "Less than a year after World War I, seventy African American men were lynched in the United States," adding, "Ten were soldiers in uniform." In World War II, Black women were not spared this brutality; rather, their uniforms often intensified their mistreatment. To some, the women were doubly infuriating: not only were they women in uniform, but they were also Black. In a few cases, this was enough to warrant violence.

In one instance, two Black WACs stationed in Alabama refused to give up their seats in the segregated section of a bus filling up with White passengers. When they disregarded the bus driver's order to stand, civilian police called to the scene pulled one of the WACs from the bus, while the other WAC protested, correctly, that the women fell under the authority of the military police. Her admonitions ignored, the police also dragged the second woman from her seat, as White passengers chanted "Kill 'em." The civilian policemen violently beat the two women, leaving one in the hospital for over a week. In another instance, civilian police officers beat three Black WACs for failing to move to the segregated waiting room of a bus station in Elizabethtown, Kentucky.

Over time, the indignities faced by Black WACs on and off base became known within the Black community, which seriously tarnished the Corps' reputation and made maintaining a steady stream of Black women difficult. The reasons were manifold, predictable, and well known: lack of enthusiasm for Black units among many senior Army leaders, base commanders' rampant misassignment of Black units, segregation of Black units and facilities, and violent incidents of racial attacks on uniformed women.

All these reasons reflected the stark reality of the times for Black women in uniform. With no meaningful Army response, little support, a great deal of mistreatment, and more plentiful options for employment in the industrial sector, the WAC struggled to recruit and keep Black women in the Army.

For its part, the Navy did not fare much better in its treatment of Black women, having resisted mightily the integration of any Black sailors—man or woman—from the start of the war. By the time that the WAVES legislation was signed into law in 1942, the naval leadership, and especially the secretary of the Navy, Frank Knox, had successfully circumvented integration mandates by relegating the Black men who had signed up for the Navy to only the most undesirable jobs, assigning them to roles as stewards, cooks, cleaners, and other service jobs. According to the Navy's official history, at the start of 1943, over two-thirds of the 26,909 Black men serving in the Navy were messmen, and it took the Navy until March 1944, just one year before the capitulation of Hitler, to allow the commissioning of Black officers.

The story for Black women in the Navy, however, followed a

slightly different script. For the first several weeks of her tenure as director of the WAVES, McAfee professed she was unaware that Black women were not being recruited for the program. When informed by Black leaders about the discrimination, she replied that she "couldn't see any reason at all why there couldn't be," and then "began inquiring." But her inquiries led mainly to dead ends. Navy leaders, who were unenthusiastic about integrating the WAVES, argued that Black WAVES could only replace Black sailors. Since Black men were limited to service jobs and the Navy had enough recruits to fill those roles, they told McAfee, Black WAVES would be unnecessary.

But as time went on, and particularly as Black women started appearing in Army uniforms, the pressure increased on McAfee, the Navy, and, especially, Roosevelt to allow Black women into the WAVES. By 1944, the sudden death of Navy secretary Knox opened a window of opportunity. The new secretary, James Forrestal, was far more amenable to the idea of Black women serving in the Navy, and Roosevelt quickly directed him to begin the integration process. "With very little notice," remembered McAfee, "the Secretary's office called over to my office and said 'The President has ruled that beginning next week, we will admit Negro women.'"

The first two Black women chosen as WAVES officers, Harriet Pickens and Frances Wills, were hand selected. Pickens, a southerner who grew up in Alabama, was by all accounts brilliant. She was the daughter of the acclaimed writer and activist William Pickens and had attended Smith College, Columbia University, and Bennett College for Women. Wills was equally talented. A native of Philadelphia, she had attended Hunter College and the University of Pittsburgh and had been employed as a social worker for several years before joining the Navy. As polished, college-educated women, they perfectly fit the elite image that the WAVES had worked so hard to cultivate.

Pickens and Wills's initial entry into the WAVES, however, did not get off on the best foot. The timing of their admission and unexpected delays in their arrival for training at Smith College in Northampton resulted in them joining their officer training class three weeks late. They arrived at Smith during dinner and were escorted to the mess hall after receiving only one piece of their uniform, their hats. There, they were directed to their seats in the center of the room, packed with White WAVES decked out in their full uniforms. As Pickens and Wills uneasily made their way to their table, they felt as if they had arrived from another planet: "two brown skinned women," remembered Wills, "one a head taller and a little darker than the other, in city suits and Navy hats."

Aside from their awkward reception, however, Pickens and Wills had no time to dwell on reactions to their presence. Instead, they focused on catching up from arriving three weeks late by spending most of their free time doing makeup courses. "We knew the score," remembered Wills in her memoir, "and we knew that the only way we could win the game was to continue to break out the books at every possible opportunity." If succeeding meant studying in the bathrooms after lights-out, which it often did, then Pickens and Wills did it.

The officers they joined offered a mixed reception. Some women in the WAVES had long felt that integration of Black women was overdue and warmly welcomed them. Laura Rapaport Borsten remembered that she had been "troubled by the absence of Black women among the younger candidates" and delighted in the assignment of Black women to integrated units.

Others were less sanguine about their presence. One woman, responsible for assigning Wills to her barracks on her first duty assignment, refused to provide the standard "Welcome Aboard" greeting when Wills arrived at her posting. At the time, Wills thought little of it. But, later, she found out that the woman had protested all the way up the chain of command about Wills's presence on the staff, stating that if Wills so much as sat next to her, "she would get up and walk out." The commander, to her credit, responded that if the woman started walking, she should continue directly to the commander's office, where she should submit her resignation.

But Wills had far less to say about the mistreatment that she received on account of her race than she did about what her position as an officer meant to the other Black sailors who she encountered in uniform. She found this was especially, and surprisingly, the case with Black enlisted men. Having been relegated almost exclusively to service roles, they were often stunned to see Wills, not just because she was a Black woman in uniform, but because she was a Black officer. In fact, Wills once found herself, mid-meal, to be the subject of much scrutiny. "I became aware," she remembered of her visit to a New York navy yard, "of a brown face, staring, wide eyed from the galley opening." Trying to act naturally, she couldn't help noticing that the moment the sailor disappeared, "another brown one took [his] place immediately, equally wide eyed." The men, having just returned from their tour overseas, had never seen a Black officer before.

Though Wills knew she was doing something exceptional, she never viewed her presence in the Navy as a political act. "When the Navy said it was ready for me," she recalled, "and I said, 'Take me,' I was not consciously making a statement about race relations."

On the day of their commissioning, Wills and Pickens agreed to a request to pose for photographs. One of the photos captured them in an "entirely fictional" pose, pushing down on a packed suitcase. It became one of the most famous images of the women, published proudly with the news that the Navy had fully integrated its women's services before the close of the war. Wills fondly remembered the photo and the genuine pride it captured on their faces: "It was not difficult to smile a happy smile."

For many women, like Pickens and Wills, the difficulties of military service were outweighed by its professional benefits. But not all the advantages of military service were strictly professional. For some, joining the military also offered a new and exciting environment for personal growth. After all, the services had created the perfect backdrop for a lively social scene when they brought together hundreds of thousands of young women from across the country, and gave them shared quarters, disposable income, and a

Harriet Pickens and Frances Wills, the first Black WAVES officers, pose for a photograph. **Courtesy National Archives, photo no. 520670.**

few hours of free time. However, as many women enjoyed the vibrancy of their new environment—almost always harmlessly and without incident—salacious and unfounded rumors about their behavior continued to hound the programs.

# 19

# "MAKE A DATE WITH UNCLE SAM"

## CONTROVERSY

THE LEAVE PASS WAS ANYTHING BUT SUBTLE.

Ethel Becker, posted to Mitchel Airfield on Long Island in 1943, had been given the pass to show any military authorities who might inquire about her status off base. On the front was an illustrated woman in uniform, with a halo above her military cap, angel wings sprouting from her epaulettes, and a delicate finger placed on her chin. She was glancing coyly at her shoulder, where a small devil was perched, smiling invitingly with its arm wrapped around the woman. Printed below the image was a single line, SGT BECKER, ON PASS. It was an oddly provocative image, especially given that its intended message to Becker, and any woman in the military during this period, was not to encourage improper behavior but to reduce it.

Becker, who spent most of her leave visiting family who lived in Brooklyn, did not need this advice. Moreover, she had an interest in making sure all the women in her unit were on their best behavior, as she oversaw the distribution of passes for the 909th headquarters WAC detachment assigned to the airfield. She had a good reputation as being strict but fair in her role, and the base paper even made up a jingle in her honor:

*Ethel Becker handles the passes*
*So watch your step and cut out the razzes*
*For she's the gal who can say no, no*
*And make it stick when you'd like to go.*

Becker had been in one of the early classes of Army women, joining in September 1942, only a few months after the inau-

Ethel Becker's leave pass. **Courtesy Fred and Laurie Iskowitz.**

gural group arrived at Fort Des Moines, and she had then been assigned to the Army Air Forces. Her work at Mitchel Airfield included filling in on clerk duties, checking pilots in and out, performing secretarial tasks with classified material, and, occasionally, working in the aircraft plotting room, moving miniature models of American and German aircraft across a table to provide real-time tracking of planes for the senior commanders looking on.

Although the work may have seemed unexceptional, it was serious. For years following the attack on Pearl Harbor, the military had persistent and very real concerns about another attack on the American coasts and it considered New York to be a key target, with its many ports and shipyards, and populous city. Mitchel Airfield was home to the Army Air Forces keeping watch, monitoring for enemy planes and submarines that got too close to the shoreline.

Given the stakes, it is not surprising that Becker and her colleagues were held to a high standard of conduct both on and off base. The women knew that when they put on their uniforms, no matter where they ended up, they had a duty to wear them with the honor, dignity, and respect that they commanded. "You are no longer individuals," Hobby counseled her soldiers. "You wear the uniform of the Army of the United States. Respect that uniform. Respect all that it stands for. Then the world will respect all that the Corps stands for. Make the adjustment from civilian to military life without faltering, and without complaint," she said.

But these women were also in the prime of their lives, experiencing a once-in-a-lifetime adventure, and they were living through a period of rapidly changing norms. How to balance the women's conduct with the shifting social standards of the time became one of the most essential tasks faced by the women's programs.

\* \* \*

The recruits arriving at military training centers and bases around the country reflected an unusual cross section of American women at the time. For the most part, the women had been drawn, quite intentionally, from a conservative demographic. "The WACs themselves expected higher standards of behavior from women," wrote Hobby, noting "that they could not work well and remain happy if they had to share barracks with women of coarse behavior—drunkenness, cursing, fighting, et al." In that respect, the conservative selection bias in the recruiting process had paid off, since the women were generally well behaved by the standards of the time. Many military women spent their free time participating in uncontroversial activities: writing letters home, going to base movies and dances, and attending religious services.

But, at the same time, some of the women who signed up to be members of the armed forces during this period—an atypical choice for a woman of the time—also had a personality that predisposed them to seek out more adventurous forms of entertainment. In cities and base towns teeming with young people, most of whom had a steady paycheck and few expenses, some women, perhaps for the first time in their lives, were going to have a little fun.

As a result, military leaders faced the challenge of managing the plentiful opportunities available to young women for less conservative pastimes, including drinking and meeting dates. "Parties just happened," remembered Helen Gilbert, a WAVE: "By night time, we usually ended up with ten or twenty of us in one room. We drank rum and cokes as well as beer, ate lots of food, and had great fun." Since women in uniform were often the lone group of women on base, dates were easy to come by. "There were so many cadets that we referred to them as our 'hot and cold running cadets,'" recalled Gilbert, adding with her delightfully biting wit, "on tap at any time."

For some women, serving during the war also provided their first exposure to consensual sex—sometimes before marriage and sometimes with more than one partner. These encounters often occurred in a private place, including hotel rooms and homes, but, at times, particularly given the many restrictions on who could be in military barracks, they happened in cars or parks or even alleys. In at least one case, a WAVES member assigned to air-traffic control recalled becoming a member of the "mile high club" during a nighttime joyride in a PBY Catalina plane, "one of my more prestigious accomplishments," she remembered. In this new environment, many women in uniform had their first and most liberating experiences with drinking, dating, and sex.

In truth, the directors of the women's programs were aware of the impossible standards facing women in uniform, and knew that women under their command regularly flouted them. After all, most of the women leading the women's military organizations had come from college campuses and knew full well that young women could follow rules and break them in equal measure. They also understood that male commanders tended to go easy on the women in their units and that strict regulations needed to be in place to moderate their conduct. "I looked at the girls as human beings and not just as little cuties," remembered McAfee, adding that "I know out of experience they were as different and as varied as any boys, and that they need to be held to certain standards or they would soon run off with the place."

Acknowledging this reality, military leaders did their best to minimize ill-regarded behaviors and to reassure the public that they were isolated instances if they became the subject of gossip. Numerous recommendations for solving these alleged slips of character were proposed. Women were provided with accommodations on base for hosting dates and, where possible, moved from hotel billets to on-base billets. Recruiting standards were updated and improved. Smaller changes were also implemented; for example, the receipt of overdue uniforms was sped up to encourage a stronger esprit de corps—and an attendant sense of accountability to the unit—and to make the identification of offenders easier.

But, at the same time, military leaders recognized their limitations in trying to restrict the behavior of young women. They had two options, either to ignore this reality or help their women navigate it. For the most part, they chose the latter, accepting that some level of behavioral boundary pushing needed to be expected—and tolerated.

As a result, even as the women's services erred on the side of social conservatism, they did not hesitate to provide women with material that could help them make informed decisions about their well-being, particularly when it came to sexual health. They recognized that education provided a baseline of knowledge that helped prevent unexpected outcomes, especially since the women in their ranks arrived with differing attitudes toward and knowledge of sex. To do so, military leaders approved the issuance of a joint manual, aptly titled *Sex Hygiene for Women Officers and Women Officer Candidates of the Armed Forces*. The pamphlet provided women in the service with a shared, basic understanding of sexual and reproductive health. "One of the main purposes of instruction in sex hygiene," the pamphlet stated, "is to help those who have not had access to the facts to recognize their problems, and to know how they may obtain information they require from competent sources." It was an extraordinarily modern document, and it provided women with the facts necessary to make informed choices about their sexual and physical well-being, often for the first time.

The manual provided, first and foremost, an accurate and straightforward description of female anatomy, noting that "adequate sex education includes anatomy, physiology, and pathology of the reproductive system, the function and hygiene of menstruation and menopause, the significance of cysts and tumors, and the prevention of venereal disease." It included a description of the female reproductive system, providing accurate names and descriptions and dispelling common myths, including a note that the hymen has "always been the object of more attention than it deserves." It also included a discussion of exactly how a woman becomes pregnant, the typical functioning of the menstrual cycle, the process of menopause, and the identification of abnormalities. For the time, it was a remarkably frank primer, which had the genuine aim of protecting women of all backgrounds from the unanticipated consequences of sex.

But even the most explicit counsel could not protect the women from the choices of others, and especially from men who felt entitled to harass and assault women in uniform. Then, as now, many men wrongly assumed that women's professional and sexual empowerment provided justification for overtures and attacks, and the historical record is strewn with references to women in uniform being the objects of unwanted attention. Many of the reported comments and actions bordered on, or were in fact, what we would now call harassment. For instance, men in uniform sometimes used their superior rank as a pretense to demand dates and attention from their subordinates, feeling entitled to romantic consideration from the women who worked for them. When the men were turned down, their reactions could be frighteningly aggressive. On one occasion, a WAC reported that a disappointed suitor followed her onto a train, shouting, "You goddam WACs. All you want to do is sleep with the officers." Some pilots flew over the women's showers to look at the naked women below, while others bragged about what they thought were clever nicknames for the women they dated: P-38 was the woman with "the best looking shafts"; B-24s were the women in Casablanca—"fat girls"; and a B-26 was simply "a whore," since they were "fast, with no visible means of support." The Navy, too, had its own disparaging expressions, including the slogan "Join the Navy to ride the WAVES!"

The women on the receiving end of the verbal abuse often had neither the language to name it nor the recourse to do anything about it. "The phrase 'sexual harassment' had not yet been invented," remembered one woman, "but WACs were certainly the victims of it." She added that wolf whistles followed her anywhere with GIs nearby. Overwhelmingly, the women recalled what we now consider workplace sexual harassment as just another day at work. "There was nothing we could do about that," said a former WAVE during our interview, adding, "We just took it for granted."

Many women also experienced sexual violence while serving during World War II. Given the institutional and cultural biases of the time, such cases were reported and discussed even more rarely than harassment. According to Leisa Meyer, in her comprehensive history of sexuality and gender in the Army women's program, there were just under one thousand rape convictions in the Army for the duration of the war, with only 273 occurring before the Allied victory, rates that are "fairly astounding given that over 12 million men served in the Army during the war." The low reporting rates were not because assault did not happen—it certainly did—but because the dictates and norms of the time often prevented any discussion, formal or otherwise, of sexual violence. One WAC, taking police reports at the provost marshal's office in France just before the invasion, remembered with disgust documenting allegations of GIs raping Englishwomen, reports that rarely resulted in any sort of investigation, reprimand, or consequence for the perpetrators.

As Meyer illustrates with a series of vivid examples, even when official reports of sexual violence were made, the victim's respectability—real or imagined—played a critical role in the outcome of the investigation. In one case, a woman's claims were dismissed based on her prior divorce and rumors that she had been "boy crazy." In another, the assault of a woman with "bruises, abrasions, and blood on her legs and underwear" was not investigated because a condom had been used, which the investigators argued implied consent, stating, "In a situation where a woman is resisting and struggling to the utmost of her ability it is decidedly unusual for the man to cease his attempted attack to secure and adjust the device."

Above all else, the military's own precautions against the threat of sexual violence provided the best evidence that men in uniform presented a danger to servicewomen. "One commander was so startled to have women on his base," wrote Hobby, "that he set up what could only be termed emergency rules: he put a barbed wire fence around their barracks, set guards at the gate, and announced that WACs were to use the post exchange and post movie on Tuesdays and Thursdays while the men—with careful segregation—would use them only on the other days." In another instance, military police kept WACs under their constant escort for several weeks. The women "would be locked within their barbed wire compound at all times except when escorted to work or to approved group recreation by armed guards. No leaves, or passes, or one-couple dates were allowed at any time," writes Meyer.

Whether or not the actual threat of sexual violence warranted such extreme measures was, in some ways, beside the point. Without question, women were expected to meet a standard of conduct that far exceeded the expectation of men in the service. While senior women commanders wrung their hands over women drinking in public or kissing in a park, senior male commanders knew of and prepared for the possibility of men committing violent felonies against women wearing the same uniform. The contrast was extraordinary.

But the contradictions of policing of women's social behavior were not limited to drinking and sex. It soon became clear that many of the conservative dictates of the time also proved harmful when applied to the romantic relationships that sometimes emerged between women in the military.

# 20

# "NOW IS THE TIME
# TO INVESTIGATE
# THE OPPORTUNITIES
# OFFERED"

## COURT-MARTIALS

WHEN MILITARY COMMANDERS IN THE OFFICE OF
the Judge Advocate General received a complaint from Mrs. Josephine Churchill, the mother of Private Virginia Churchill, they
took it very seriously. Enraged and horrified, Mrs. Churchill reported that while her daughter was on leave, she had discovered
letters between Private Churchill and Sergeant Mildred Loos.
They were, as she put it, "some of the most shocking letters I have
ever read in my life."

She alleged that Loos had been the ringleader of several lesbians who had preyed on young women at the WAC training center
at Fort Oglethorpe, Georgia. "My little girl who I know was clean
of heart and mind," she wrote, had confessed to a sexual and romantic relationship with Loos. Private Churchill, though almost
certainly lying under the pressure of her mother's interrogation,
alleged that Loos was equipped with a nefarious ability to convince women to sleep with her. As Mrs. Churchill reported, "My

daughter says she hypnotizes them in some manner and that she is afraid of her. Her letters show that a timid girl would fear her."

Worse yet, Mrs. Churchill continued, Loos was not alone in her alleged predatory behavior. She went on to indict a handful of other women on the base who, she claimed, had formed a ring of lesbians that took advantage of unsuspecting young women. She named each of them, along with their rank and location. "Instead of rehabilitation camps," she concluded, "our gov[ernmen]t will need to build more asylums after this war." She then suggested Loos be court-martialed.

The Army conducted a comprehensive investigation of the allegation. The investigators—led by Lieutenant Colonel Birge Holt and Captain Ruby Herman—concluded that "the general allegation of extensive homosexual practices was found to be an exaggeration and not substantiated in fact." Even if the allegations were true, they argued, the concern was likely overblown, noting that the handful of women identified as part of the alleged ring were only a minuscule proportion of the thousands of women that processed through Fort Oglethorpe. Moreover, the investigators added, the actual extent of the problem was likely overblown, rooted as it was in "rumor and surmise" among the women.

Even with these caveats, however, the investigation noted that considerable evidence did exist both in letters and in testimony from the women themselves that the allegations of "homosexual conduct" were true. In the case of Loos and Churchill, the letters included in the appendix of the official report confirmed the two women were very much in love. Contradicting Private Churchill's allegation that she was hypnotized by Loos, the two women professed a mutual affection for each other. The correspondence was, even by the standards of today, fairly explicit—detailing in code various sexual acts, fantasies, and requests between the two women—but reflected little more than two young people in the throes of a romance. "Honey, if I had you here right now I would just take you in my arms and love you and kiss you until you fell flat on my bed," wrote Loos, later receiving Churchill's reply: "Darling, I miss you so terribly, I need you and want you so much. My whole body aches for the want of you. You know what I mean, don't you sweetness?"

Other women under investigation also endured the humiliation of having their personal correspondence entered into the official Army record and retained in the National Archives of the United States for time eternal. The intimate correspondence between two WACs, Patricia Warren and Ruth Kellogg, was also included in the investigation, and was no less affectionate: "I love you. I love you so much that I get mad at myself for not being able to find words to express what I am feeling," wrote Kellogg, adding, "I can feel your arms around me—I can feel your lips covering mine."

For some women in uniform, the nature of the military environment provided an opportunity to explore and experience relationships with other women. Not all the women who did so considered themselves lesbian or queer—or had the language to label their romantic and sexual preferences—but, like the population from which the women were drawn, the range of their experiences was wide.

Some women joined the military expressly because it provided them an opportunity to meet women. Pat Bond, a WAC, remembered that many of her lesbian friends applied for the Corps in attire that, by her recollection, clearly indicated their sexuality by the standards of the time: "argyle socks and pinstripe suits and the hair cut just like a man's with sideburns shaved over the ears—the whole bit." Even as they were dressed in conspicuously masculine attire, Bond recalled, the women responded to the standard vetting question about previous "homosexual conduct" with a simple "of course not!" and were admitted.

At the same time, other women found themselves unexpectedly in romantic relationships with women, or in relationships that skirted the line between friendship and romance. Even in the highest ranks, the nature of many relationships between women was difficult to decipher. For instance, Gildersleeve, the leader of the Navy's advisory council, shared a home for several years with Elizabeth Reynard, a senior-ranking WAVES officer, and the two were rumored to have had a romantic relationship. Stratton, too, moved in with her former deputy, Helen Schleman, late in life, raising questions about the nature of their partnership. Some historians have persuasively argued that both sets of companions were simply the product of career-focused women in deeply supportive—if celibate—relationships. But even without speculating on the nature of specific relationships, the historical record is clear that many women found the full range of connections in the military: deep and abiding friendship, romantic love, sex, and everything in between.

Regardless of the true character of these relationships, the consequences for women accused of engaging in same-sex romance could be harsh and unforgiving, since the military's official policy was to punish convicted women with dishonorable discharges. "Individuals guilty of homosexual acts while in the service were presented with appropriate charges and specifications for trial," wrote the Marine Corps, "or were given the alternative of accepting an undesirable discharge for the good of the service and to escape trial by a general court-martial."

Despite its official policy, however, the military faced several challenges in investigating and proving such claims to make a formal conviction. First, the investigation itself was difficult to undertake without damaging morale. "All commanding officers hated to find them," reads one report on cases of alleged same-sex relationships, "because of the inadequacy of most evidence and the very real danger of doing a serious injustice to persons who had behaved foolishly but were not confirmed homosexuals."

Second, finding evidence of romance or sex between two people—evidence that is often private—proved challenging. This was especially true since women who did have relationships with each other were well aware of the taboo surrounding them and were quite adept at concealing their affections. Although it came with personal costs, many women made the difficult choice to hide their personal relationships and to protect themselves from the negative professional consequences.

Third, even in instances where women publicly flaunted their relationships with other women, bias complicated the issue. People tended to see in women's relationships what they wanted to see. Some observers misinterpreted ambiguous evidence of women's affection toward each other like hugging, linking arms, and holding hands, and dismissed more obvious displays of romance as the product of a close friendship.

Finally, institutional and public relations concerns existed that impeded the military's efforts to prevent and punish same-sex relationships in the women's programs. With their fixation on presenting an image of polished, respectable women to the public, military leaders in World War II had created a dilemma. Discharging women based on an official conviction of "homosexual conduct" raised questions, sometimes publicly, about the type of women enrolled in the armed forces.

These factors made prosecuting women for their sexuality and relationships not only difficult but also sometimes harmful to the military's goals. As a result, despite agreeing with the social norms of the day, military leaders often found their hands tied in prosecuting and enforcing punishments when it came to alleged lesbian conduct.

The Fort Oglethorpe investigation prompted by Josephine Churchill's letter epitomized the military's muddled approach to formal prosecution of same-sex relationships. After a weeks-long investigation of the allegation, including interviews with dozens of women, psychological exams, and a detailed review of the private correspondence between the accused women, the report's conclusions were surprisingly mild. In their review of the written letters, the investigators concluded that "clearly the language and references in the letters are vulgar and obscene," but, they reasoned, the written romantic overtures were not evidence of activity, and some of the language could be considered an "expression of grotesque and fanciful imagination." As dismissive and insulting as it may have been to relegate these relationships to nothing more than the overactive imaginations of young women, the lenient interpretation undermined the case for a strict punishment.

Similarly, the findings of the psychological examination undergone by the women were equally dismissive. When it came to Loos and Churchill, the psychological evaluator concluded: "I think these [women] slid more or less into an accidental relationship and that they are not very likely to repeat it." And, given the glowing endorsements of their superiors, the evaluator noted that it would be a shame to discharge the women on what she chalked up to an error of judgment. Citing a recent Army medical bulletin, the investigators added that Army policy on individual instances of same-sex relationships had evolved and that "the latest circular letter, particularly for soldiers overseas, stressed that homosexual relationships should be tolerated as long as no violation of private rights is concerned, as long as no force is used, and as long as it does not impair the morale of the group." In other words, the report concluded that under certain circumstances, the Army was willing to turn a blind eye to same-sex relationships.

Nonetheless, the investigation itself was degrading and humiliating. After subjecting all the named women to an embarrassing series of interviews and psychological assessments, the investigators recommended that "the interests of the Service would be best served by a discreet and careful inquiry" regarding five of the women identified in the investigation. Since they were considered first-time offenders and were serving at bases around the country, the investigators began by asking their commanding officers whether the women had generated any further complaints or concerns. In the meantime, the investigators recommended that the women be hospitalized for psychiatric treatment.

The report recommended that only one woman, Patricia Warren, be given the maximum punishment. Since Warren had testified honestly about her record of previous relationships with women, the investigators felt she should be discharged. First, however, they gave her the opportunity to resign "for the good of the service."

Warren did resign, but not for the service. Before submitting her resignation, she confirmed with the investigators that, in doing so, she would spare her partner—Kellogg—from any repercussions. "About the only thing I want to do," she testified, "is take all the blame for this and clear the kid." After the investigators assured Warren that Kellogg was safe, she left the WAC.

While estimates suggest a strikingly small percentage of men and women were formally discharged from the military for homosexual conduct in World War II—totaling around nine thousand personnel in a force of millions—countless more men and women probably submitted preemptive resignations as Warren had done. For those affected by these investigations, the outcome was often personally distressing and professionally devastating. Moreover, the focus on punishing same-sex relationships in the women's programs proved to be a red herring. Evidence of lesbian and queer relationships was just one of many possible scandals that stalked the women's programs, and, as the war dragged on, far more damaging controversies awaited them.

# 21

# "GIVE US MORE P-47'S"

## WASPS IN THE FIELD

MARJORIE KUMLER HAD JUST PULLED OFF A TRICKY landing. Putting the AT-6 Texan down on a dirt runway at Yoakum Field, two hours from Houston, Texas, had been a bit bumpy, but Kumler knew what she was doing. She had beat the rest of the women pilots who were flying with her to the base, including her control officer, and was waiting under the wing of her plane until they arrived.

A few minutes later, a young Army Air Forces pilot landed his own AT-6 and taxied over to Kumler. Descending from the cockpit, he walked over and asked if she was guarding the plane. When she replied yes, he couldn't hide his confusion:

"Where's the pilot?" he asked.

"I'm the pilot," responded Kumler.

Dressed in civilian clothing, Kumler knew that she didn't necessarily look like a military aviator, but she felt the source of his confusion was more likely a product of her gender than her attire. When her control officer finally arrived, Kumler explained that the young man did not believe she was the pilot of the plane, and therefore responsible for it. The control officer, no doubt amused, walked over to the young man and informed him that not only was Kumler indeed the pilot but that a group of women were soon to follow in landing their own AT-6 Texans. The Army Air Forces pilot, still skeptical, informed the control officer that he was also waiting on the rest of his unit to arrive with their Texans. Then, feeling cocky, the incredulous pilot proposed a wager: "I'll match my boys against your girls," he said, adding, "If it's a girl, I bet she bounces the landing."

Kumler's control officer not only took the bet, but agreed to pay the pilot a dollar for every woman who bounced. But he also upped the ante and demanded a dollar for each man who did the same. It turned out to be a lucrative wager for him: almost all of the men bounced their way to a stop on the dirt runway, while every single woman nailed the landing, without as much as a wobble.

The WASPs were, to the woman, excellent fliers. Even those who signed on during the later part of the war, subject to less stringent entry requirements than those who joined in the early classes, still proved to be skillful pilots. Their safety and crash records were as good as, and often better than, those of male pilots in comparable roles: about nine percent of the overall WASP force died in fatal accidents, whereas the Army Air Forces fatality rates in similar assignments were closer to eleven percent during the same period.

These rates were especially impressive given that they did not reflect two risks unique to the women fliers. First, the WASPs faced issues of safety in the maintenance of their training and ferry-ing planes. While it is difficult to find direct evidence of explicit negligence, many women pilots, including Cochran herself, often worried that the women's aircraft did not receive the same careful attention as their male counterparts'. They suspected that some Army Air Forces maintainers, reluctantly pulled from their jobs supporting male pilots or reassigned because they could be easily spared, were not of the highest caliber. If the widespread rumors were true, then the WASPs were flying planes with sketchier safety records than their male counterparts.

Second, Army Air Forces instructors and commanders who did appreciate the WASPs for their skill and professionalism had a habit of using them to make a point. Recognizing that no man wanted to be upstaged in the air, and certainly not by a woman, many Army Air Forces officers assigned the women to untested and dangerous planes to prod male pilots unwilling to fly them. It proved to be a highly effective strategy, but it often placed WASPs in dangerous situations, as in the case of the B-26 Marauder.

Known as the "widow maker" among Army Air Forces pilots, the B-26 was a difficult plane to fly, and especially to land. The flight manual instructed pilots to descend the aircraft at extremely fast airspeeds, with little margin for error. If landed too slowly, the plane would stall and crash before it made it to the runway. Many pilots, distrusting the instructions and overconfident in their skills, followed their instincts and slowed the plane too much and too far from the airfield, crashing and killing most of the crew.

To solve the problem, crews needed to be retrained to ensure the pilots would follow the instructions rather than their instincts. But getting them to do so was difficult, since the plane had developed a dangerous reputation. Army Air Force leadership had to find a solution. The planes were expensive, solid pieces of equipment, and, when flown correctly, they proved to be one of the safest bombers in the United States air fleet. They just needed to find pilots willing to fly them.

The instructors at the Army Air Forces Training Command, being pilots themselves, knew how to get men back into the B-26 cockpit. They understood that many young male fliers were motivated to perform, chiefly, by pride, and the instructors devised a solution to the B-26 issue with this in mind. On a warm fall day in Alabama, Air Force instructors assembled men training at the airfield to "watch a spectacular air show by two B-26 pilots." When the performance concluded, four WASPs emerged from the planes.

Not to be outdone by these willing, capable women safely at

the helm of the B-26s, the men soon returned to the cockpit. Delighted at the success of their airshow, the instructors repeated the performance several times over in a range of aircraft deemed too risky to fly by the male aviators. The strategy worked near flawlessly.

As a result, by the end of the war, over one hundred WASPs had qualified on the B-26s, without a single crash. The women attributed their success not to skill or daring but to something much more powerful: they followed the instructions.

Given the high risk of injury and death in the WASP, it seemed a particularly cruel irony that they still lacked the protections and benefits of military status three years into the war. This was, in part, by design. Cochran had spent much of the war defending the independence of the WASP, first as director of the WFTD and then as director of the consolidated program, and she was not shy about her unwillingness to merge with the WAC. For better and worse, Cochran had remained uncompromising.

By early 1944, however, Cochran began to realize that she might have miscalculated. Her stubborn stance left the WASPs exposed, depriving the women of official military rank and the benefits of uniformed service in the case of accident or death. The civilian status forced the WASPs to raise funds themselves for transport and burial when one of their colleagues died, and required them to pay hospitalization and recovery costs resulting from accidents. With the dangerous tasks WASPs were now performing, the situation was unsustainable. Though Cochran refused to make the WASPs a part of another women's military unit, she knew they needed to acquire some level of military standing to defer the risks and costs the women took on when they signed up.

Cochran and Army Air Forces leadership decided to make a formal request to Congress in 1944 to authorize that a corps of women pilots be attached directly to the Air Force. This arrangement would allow the WASP to retain its independence from the other services while still conferring their pilots with military benefits. In preceding months, a similar precedent had been established when Congress approved legislation for medical officers to be attached to the Army Medical Corps, and, of course, the authorization of WACs, WAVES, SPARS, MCWR, and the Army and Navy Nurse Corps had also paved the way. Cochran and her allies assumed these precedents would assure passage of their request.

But Cochran and her chief supporter, General Arnold, the commander of the Army Air Forces, failed to anticipate one key factor in their plan to militarize the WASP in 1944: public mood. Congressional and public attitudes toward the war had changed a great deal since the legislation authorizing the other women's services had passed. The nation had been at war for almost three years, and in some corners questions were growing about whether and when the Allied strategy would succeed. For several months, it seemed that Allied victory was all but assured as American forces made steady battlefield progress in North Africa and Italy. Yet the end of the war was still not in sight.

In this context, the patriotic impulses that had motivated the authorization of women's programs at the start of the war were quickly waning. In 1944, Congress and the public more closely scrutinized even routine authorizations that, years earlier, sailed through Congress—and legislation that authorized a corps of women to pilot military aircraft was anything but routine.

By 1944, the successes in North Africa and Italy had been a boon for the Allied forces, but the invasion of France and its many materiel and manpower demands rapidly approached. At the same time, naval leaders had only begun to reverse Japanese gains in the Pacific and knew some of the most grueling and bloody combat of the war would take place in its final gasps. This left Marshall preparing for a long, harrowing offensive through most of Europe and a massive joint invasion in the Pacific, just as popular support for the war was starting to fray at the seams.

Even so, Marshall's priorities had not changed: he still needed a lot of people—mostly infantrymen—to do all this fighting. The result, however, was that as the American public was starting to tire of the war, military leaders were starting to ask for more men, not to fill stateside jobs, but to fight overseas against the last, most entrenched remnants of the German and Japanese militaries.

For the male pilots of the Civilian Aeronautics Administration (CAA), this news was particularly alarming. These men had spent most of the war conducting domestic transport missions alongside the WASPs as contract pilots for the Army Air Forces. During the early phases of the war, they had declined to join the Army Air Forces, using their status as civilian transport pilots to secure an exemption. In 1944, however, the Army took a second look at the men who had been excused from military service and, no longer in dire need of military pilots, they were directing new draftees into the infantry, regardless of their flying ability. The CAA pilots, therefore, faced the prospect of being drafted into the infantry— with several major ground invasions still in the offing—unless they could prove their continued necessity at home.

When the Army Air Forces decided to introduce legislation militarizing the WASPs in 1944, the CAA saw an opportunity to push for their continued necessity in the United States. They launched a media blitz aimed at tanking the proposal for militarization, hoping to convince the public and Congress that the women were redundant and then scoop up their jobs. CAA SAYS WASPS TAKE JOBS FROM ABLE MEN FLIERS, reported the *Buffalo Evening News* in March 1944, describing the dispute as "a modern battle of the sexes" and "a Washington gossip-monger's dreams."

The CAA wasted no time portraying the women as being unqualified and unnecessary in the press. ARMY PASSES UP JOB-LESS PILOTS TO TRAIN WASPS: PREFERS WOMEN TO OLDER,

EXPERIENCED FLYERS, announced one paper, adding, "With 5,000 experienced airplane pilots looking for jobs, the government is training more than 1,000 young women, at an estimated cost of 6 million dollars, as ferry pilots for the Army." The women were driving qualified civilian male pilots out of their jobs, the argument went, and forcing the men to be sent overseas to fight and die. "'I guess we'll be drafted and become infantrymen' one of the CAA pilots said today," reported the *Chicago Tribune*.

The articles also accused the program of extreme mismanagement and attacked Cochran viciously, even alluding that she had seduced Arnold into buying her snake oil program. "The fact is that the government has spent more than $21,000,000 training lady fliers," reported a Tennessee paper, "primarily at the behest of vivacious aviatrix Jacquelin[e] Cochran," adding, "Magnetic Miss Cochran seems to have quite a drag with the Brass Hats." The *Des Moines Tribune* put a finer point on it—only after reveling in alleged infighting between Cochran, Love, and Hobby— adding the allegation that "WASP training has been unnecessary, far more expensive than is justified, and . . . outside congressional authorization."

Arnold pushed back hard against the CAA's attempts at misinformation and false accusations. He forcefully deconstructed their argument by stating the facts: the women were more qualified than most of the men entering the Army Air Forces, and their transport and training jobs could not, and would not, be filled by men if the women were fired. He argued that the critical shortage was overseas, not at home, and whether or not the WASP was militarized, men would not be spared from serving abroad to fulfill ferrying duties stateside.

The WASP leadership also did its best to defend the work of the women. In one letter, Hazel Taylor, in WASP public relations, pleaded the WASP's case to an associate editor of *National Aeronautics*: "While lack of men is not imminent today, it might be tomorrow," she wrote, adding that training women pilots for noncombat duties was, actually, a sign of the Army's farsightedness. Costing little and presenting no threat to the men, she argued, the WASP was just part of sound campaign planning.

In defending the WASP, public relations officials supplemented their practical arguments with other, more patriotic arguments. As Taylor wrote, "Young American women with an aptitude for flying have just as much a right to donate their best skill to the war effort as have young men." Plus, she argued, there was also the issue of precedent: "Certainly Wasps have a justification of existence equal to that of the WACs, Waves, the Spars, and the Women Marines. Industry as well as the armed services are trying to recruit more and more young women. The President and the Secretary of War, among others, have called for a national service act to include women as well as men." Women were being recruited everywhere, proponents replied to the skeptics; why should aviation be any different?

But then, as now, the truth of an accusation often matters little in Congress. The purpose of the CAA's argument was not to generate an inquiry into the reality of the situation. Instead, its purpose was to distract. With women out of the picture, they reasoned, the military's logic might change.

Despite the high-level support from both the Army Air Forces and War Department, the CAA strategy worked like a charm. Congressmen flocked to the CAA's cause and began an inquiry into the WASP program. Their conclusions mirrored the unfounded criticism lodged by the CAA: the WASP was a wasteful program, taking stateside jobs from qualified men. In the end, the truth of the allegation did not matter. The inquiry generated a level of scrutiny that the WASP was unprepared to handle, and the harm was done.

Cochran's attempts to counter with positive WASP messaging could not keep up with the negative publicity, and the media story soon became one-sided. The military, to its credit, attempted to combat the misinformation with reasoned logic and appeals to the facts. It sent its representatives to Congress to testify and responded to inquiries about the WASP with glowing praise.

Although some were convinced by the arguments put forth by

General Hap Arnold with Jacqueline Cochran on the flight line during the last WASP graduation. **Courtesy of WASP Archive, Texas Woman's University, Denton, Texas.**

Arnold, Cochran, and others, it did little to influence the outcome. The public's mood had shifted, as had its opinion of the hitherto unknown WASPs. The women had been cast as job-stealing, unqualified seductresses, instead of the patriotic pilots that they were.

In June 1944, the House voted down WASP militarization. Facing this setback and unwilling to devote more resources to the political fight, the Army Air Force leadership pulled their support. Arnold calculated that it was easier to drop the women's program entirely than continue to invite more controversy.

Four months later, Cochran received a memo from Arnold formally requesting the deactivation of the WASP. He stipulated that the changing wartime demands "make it evident that the WASP will soon become pilot material in excess of its needs," adding, "The time has arrived to plan the program's deactivation."

And so Cochran's stubborn insistence on preserving the independence of the WASP proved to be a miscalculation that doomed her beloved program. The following week, Cochran broke the news to the class of cadets training for the WASP. She conveyed that the disbandment had been ordered due to overall low combat losses, not WASP performance. She reminded the women to feel proud of their work. "I felt sure when this organization was in its infancy that, given an opportunity, women could prove themselves capable in any situation they might be called upon to face," she said, adding, "You girls have corroborated my statement many times over."

The women trainees were devastated. Many of them had dreamed of becoming WASPs, and just as they had begun to realize that dream, it was abruptly snatched away. For the women already in the air, the news was equally disappointing. "To have our service terminated before the war's end made us feel incomplete," wrote one WASP, adding, "After honing our skills and dedicating our lives to the war effort, we were now surplus." Feeling especially jilted, the final training class at Avenger Field memorialized the moment in a song. The lyrics got straight to the point: "They taught us how to fly / Now they send us home to cry / 'Cause they don't want us anymore / We earned our wings now they'll clip the darned thing / How will they ever win the war?" The women pilots had taken extraordinary risks for their country, endured long hours and terrible conditions, and sent friends home in body bags. But when they asked to be recognized for their service, they were denied.

It was a stinging defeat, but the women of the WASP were not then, nor had they ever been, easily discouraged. Geraldine Masinter, who had signed up for one of the first classes of WASPs using money from her stenographer's salary, put it best: "It will take a long time for women to win a definite place in the Air Corps. But if America ever needs them, they'll make grand fighters," adding, "Women always have."

Two weeks after Arnold had formalized the cancellation of the WASP, and days after Cochran confirmed its deactivation internally, Ann Baumgartner walked up to the side of a gray-green test plane at Wright Field in Ohio. After she spent several months towing artillery targets for male recruits in North Carolina, the Army Air Forces had transferred Baumgartner to its elite testing and training hub in the Midwest. Baumgartner was delighted to be relieved of the dangerous training duty and loved her new assignment. Flying beside some of the best pilots in the Army Air Forces, she spent her days putting the newest American planes through their paces, spinning, stalling, and generally pushing them to the brink.

On that fall day in 1944, Baumgartner remembered that the latest plane to arrive at Wright Field looked like most other testers she had flown over the past few months. But it did have some peculiar features. First, there was an armed guard posted just under the wing, an unusual sight even on a base responsible for some of the most advanced aircraft in the US inventory. Even more odd, however, was the propeller. It was fake. Attached as a decoy, the nose gear was purely ornamental, affixed there to help the plane blend in with the surrounding fighters. In reality, the plane did not need a propeller to fly. Instead, sitting below each wing was a cavernous turbojet that would power it through the sky. This was the XP-59A, the first jet-powered aircraft in the United States arsenal.

Baumgartner and her fellow test pilots had anticipated the delivery of the first jet plane for weeks. Although their duties regularly offered access to planes and equipment on the cutting edge of aviation, the jet was especially impressive. This was not simply an upgrade to navigation or the airframe; this plane fundamentally altered the nature of flying.

Baumgartner's turn finally came after lunch. She received a brief from the commanding officer and then, she remembered, "I was alone with the jet." In moments, she was in the air—the scream of the engines now behind her—focused, climbing, and "the only jet over the United States that day."

The flight itself was uneventful, and the landing even less so. Baumgartner registered her first impressions in the evaluation report and continued on with her day. All things considered, it was a fairly routine day of flying. Even so, she remembered, "the step had been made into the jet age"—and, just like that, Baumgartner was the first-ever American woman to fly a jet plane.

Two months later, she and the rest of the WASPs packed their things and went home.

# 22

# "WACS ARE GOING PLACES!"

## FRANCE

ON A HUMID NIGHT IN LATE 1943, KATHERINE KEENE sat, sweltering, in a bunk in Memphis, Tennessee. The heat had started to break some days, but most days it was still almost too hot to bear. As was her custom, she composed a letter to her parents, updating them on the events of her day and making special note of the oppressive heat. Toward the end of this particular letter, however, Keene mentioned an unusual piece of news she had received from a friend: "Doris wrote that she was interviewed by an Army intelligence man about me," continuing, "It was an investigation to see if I qualify to handle confidential and secret papers."

Keene's offhand comment was the first of a series of increasingly vague references to her work with the WAC. Soon, her letters contained only opaque mentions to her duties, and then her return address changed to an official Army forwarding service. By 1944, Keene's letters contained few of the details they once included, her parents knowing only that she was in Europe, doing something important.

Keene enlisted in the WAC in December 1942, signing up in a Los Angeles county building and making weight only by taking the ubiquitous banana advice. By the end of January 1943, she was in training at Fort Des Moines. She remembered her uniform and shots more than anything else, except perhaps the visit from Eleanor Roosevelt, which had necessitated extra drill practice and a deep cleaning of the barracks, inside and out, since the soot from the coal heaters had dirtied the exterior of the buildings. "Of course," she wrote, "Mrs. Roosevelt came nowhere near our barracks."

From Des Moines, she had been sent to the Operations Section (G-3) of the Second Army headquarters on the former Tri-State Fair Grounds in Memphis, Tennessee. She found her work as a typist to be interesting, but mostly she remembered it being so warm that even the flies could not survive. "We'd find their little bodies at the head of the stairs, parboiled in the heat." While in Memphis, she put her name in for a transfer overseas, and Army intelligence began interviewing her friends. In September, once the heat had finally broken, Keene got the news that she would be transferred. She left for Fort Oglethorpe, Georgia, the next day, where she began overseas training.

Keene was slightly confused, however, since neither she nor her colleagues had ever heard of the department to which she was being assigned, the Office of Strategic Services (OSS). The colonel who signed off on Keene's transfer told her that the OSS must have been important since the Army was pulling personnel for high-priority work with the unit. When she got to Oglethorpe, Keene learned one additional piece of information: everyone assigned to the OSS unit spoke a foreign language.

Keene wasn't told her assignment until weeks after arriving at Oglethorpe, when a major from Washington summoned her to the dayroom. He told her that the OSS—or what we now call the Central Intelligence Agency—acted as the primary US intelligence agency responsible for collecting, surreptitiously, information about the enemy. He informed her that she was being posted in London and, should anyone ask about the assignment, instructed her to reply that she was going there to do clerical work.

In this role, Keene, like many women in Army and Navy uniforms—and some in no uniform at all—joined the ranks of American intelligence officers that helped inform Allied combat operations around the globe. The women who secured employment with the OSS, as well as those in Army and Navy intelligence more broadly, were, as a rule, exceptional. Like Keene, they possessed a unique set of skills that made them particularly well suited for intelligence work. Foreign language speakers translated reports from clandestine sources; expert mathematicians and puzzlers broke Axis codes; diplomatic wives entertained, charmed, and reported back on foreign military officers; and average-looking women with uncommonly calm demeanors rode their bikes down the streets of occupied France, couriering messages between meetings of the resistance.

The women of the American intelligence apparatus in World War II proved to be among the most effective personnel in the entire war effort. Women represented nearly one-third of the workforce assigned to the OSS during World War II and routinely engaged in critical assignments behind desks in Washington and behind enemy lines abroad. Their rosters were filled with many familiar names, including Julia Child, Marlene Dietrich, and Josephine Baker, but many less-familiar women contributed as well. Virginia Hall, known to the Germans as the "the Limping Lady"—a reference to her infamous prosthetic leg that she affectionately named "Cuthbert"—was notorious among German commanders. And Gertrude Sanford Legendre, a debutante turned spy, escaped six months of Nazi captivity with a sprint across the Swiss border. Many American women, unknown even to this day, did the critical intelligence work that gave the Allies a crucial advantage in the fight, and were among the most courageous and inspiring Americans produced by the war.

Keene, a member of this elite club, completed her overseas

training in early 1944 and was promptly sent to Washington, where she was assigned to the Secret Intelligence branch and became acquainted with the peculiarities of her new job. Once, she was asked to type a copy of a magazine article and then add SE-CRET to the top of the document. Confused about why an article in a popular magazine needed to be classified, she remembered, "I was told 'It's secret now because we have copied it.'"

Fortunately, her assignment in Washington was fleeting, and she was soon on her way to Camp Kilmer, New Jersey, where she would depart for London. Packed and ready, Keene and her unit stood in line waiting to board the ship, weighed down by overcoats, steel helmets, gas masks, pistol belts, canteens, first aid kits, stockings, socks, shoes, and gloves. Their bags were stuffed with extra shirts, coats, sleepwear, and fatigues, and another small backpack held their remaining belongings. Comically off balance but ready, they marched aboard.

The trip to London was circuitous: a train from Hoboken to the dock of the *Queen Mary*, four days by ship across the frigid Atlantic, a train ride from Scotland to Victoria Station, and a final, short drive to the town house on Upper Brook Street near Grosvenor Square where Keene would live for the next several months.

After arriving and unpacking, the unit quarantined for several days, giving them some time to get acquainted with the realities of the war in Europe. In the first few weeks, Keene and her unit were taken by taxi to see the damage from the aerial bombing. It was a sobering introduction to the field. Keene remembered being stunned by buildings with whole walls shorn off, revealing their once-private interior and "a beautiful stairway curved up to nothingness." They received air raid training, but were told not to worry since an antiaircraft battery was located nearby in Hyde Park. "Will we be able to hear the ack-ack there?" asked Keene, not realizing the battery was only a few blocks away. "Oh I think so," replied the warden.

Within a few days of her arrival, Keene learned that she

had been assigned to serve as a typist for the Secret Intelligence branch, and she would be responsible for typing the reports coming from agents in the field. As exciting as the detail may have sounded, however, it soon proved tedious. Keene needed to make eight carbon copies of each report, requiring her to type slowly and deliberately for the typeset to transfer through. Plus, most of the reports were in French, and Keene's language skills were rusty. She guessed at the meaning of what she was typing but was never sure of its content, making the work quite boring.

Keene's commanding officer, an unusually perceptive woman, took notice of her tedium and asked her if she would prefer a transfer. Keene protested, noting that she knew the work was important. The next day, however, she found herself sitting in front of Richard Ruggles, an economist, who had been assigned to the OSS to covertly gather information about the dwindling stockpiles of German equipment. Ruggles was looking for assistance in completing the demanding task he had undertaken in recent months.

For most of the war, proponents of the Air Force's strategic bombing doctrine had been adamant that destruction of Germany's production hubs would cripple its economy and undermine its ability to fight the war. The key question for the Allies, however, was whether the air campaign was having any meaningful effect on German stockpiles, since in 1944 the claims of the strategic bombing advocates looked vastly out of step with reality. While the campaign had certainly crippled parts of the German production and supply infrastructure, Nazi industry had proved extremely resilient. By one estimate, the Germans almost doubled their aircraft production in 1944 alone, suggesting German plants had found a way to adapt to the hail of bombs that greeted them near daily. At the same time, American and British costs rose. The American Eighth and Fifteenth Air Forces, responsible for strategic bombing, lost more than 29,000 men throughout the campaign, and the Army Air Forces lost close to 40,000 men in total.

In the face of this puzzling reality, the Allies needed to determine how much damage was actually being done by strategic bombing. This is where Ruggles came in. He conceived a rather simple strategy: locate the serial number on captured enemy equipment, either by inspecting it in person or looking at photos of it, as a means of deciphering the German accounting system for their equipment. These numbers, Keene was told in her job interview, would allow the OSS to estimate "where a particular item had been made and possibly to tell what the weekly or monthly rate of production was."

If Keene transferred to Ruggles's team in the OSS, she was told, she would be responsible for copying all the information on the equipment that came in from the field. Though Keene worried that the work might be just as boring as transcribing French agent reports, she figured she would at least be able to read what she was typing. She took the job with Ruggles.

From the start, Keene was sent out with her colleagues to inspect captured equipment and spent munitions, traversing England in a small truck with the license plate covered in canvas. Some days were boring and long, and she regularly worked at least twelve hours, but they were tempered by the thrill of day trips to equipment depots or additional field training in gas attacks and pistol firing. In June 1944, Keene's unit received a personal visit from General William "Wild Bill" Donovan, head of the OSS, in recognition of their vitally important work. But Keene missed the ceremony—she was out visiting a tire depot.

Keene woke up the next morning, June 6, 1944, to the roar of plane engines overhead. On any other day, this was not an unusual sight or sound in the sky. But "on this day," she remembered, "the roar never ceased."

It was D-Day.

\* \* \*

Two WACs in Normandy use a steel container to wash their hair. **Courtesy National Archives, photo no. 176888114.**

The Allies had taken a circuitous route to France. The summer 1943 invasion of Sicily, led by General Bernard Montgomery on the British side and American commander General George Patton, had gone well. Soon after, Montgomery and Patton's initial invasion of Italy, using the bases, supply lines, and airfields in Sicily, had also been a success. Almost a year later, however, the invasion of the Italian mainland, for which the British had so forcefully advocated, remained bogged down.

After the Italians had capitulated within weeks of the Allied invasion of Sicily, an armistice was quickly signed in September 1943 and, at first, it appeared that another speedy advance would be in the offing, delivering the Allies, and especially the British, the resounding victory against an Axis power they had been aiming to achieve for three years. But the Germans had seen Italy's surrender coming. The pressure from the Sicily defeat, along with internal attempts to unseat Mussolini in the days before the Italy invasion, tipped them off. Seeing that Mussolini was not long for command, the Germans developed plans to reinforce the Italian peninsula as soon as possible after his deposition, and did exactly that in the fall of 1943. The German defenders dug into the northern and central Italian terrain, notoriously difficult ground to take, and dashed the British hopes and plans for a quick, decisive victory.

In the wake of the Italy stalemate, the British strategic arguments in favor of a Mediterranean approach to the continent had lost much of their credibility. The Americans had been engaged militarily in the war for over a year and arrived at the next round of strategic negotiations, in late 1943, prepared to push for a cross-Channel invasion of the continent in 1944. This time, the cards were in their favor. First, the American military leadership had proved themselves worthy of serious consideration by racking up several victories in North Africa, Sicily, and Italy. Simultaneously, the share of American men, women, and materiel supporting combat operations around the world continued to increase rapidly. And the Russians, who had fought so impressively in 1943, supported the American proposal.

Despite British insistence on launching a new offensive to break through the deadlocked Italian front, the American proposal for an invasion of France in 1944 succeeded. The Allies decided to minimally reinforce the forces in Italy, but not at the expense of preparations for the cross-Channel invasion of the continent. Preparations quickly ramped up, but necessitated the utmost secrecy. Retaining the element of surprise was essential.

The element of surprise had been vital in many of the Allied landings during the war, but it was particularly important during the cross-Channel invasion. The reason was simple. The Allies were planning to mount a massive and complex amphibious assault against German defenders who had occupied the country for three years. Those defenders were entrenched in the local terrain, well supplied, and could be reinforced over land. The Allied force, on the other hand, had to traverse the English Channel, carrying all the troops, equipment, and supplies needed to fight their way into position. If the Germans quickly reinforced their forces at the landing site, the numerical advantage would shift away from the Allies. But "if the Germans did not redeploy before D-Day," estimates one history of the campaign, "the Allied invasion forces would face just six German divisions in Normandy, only two of which were first rate." Against this force, the Allies could win.

When the Normandy landing finally came, the Allies succeeded remarkably in their effort. They employed an extensive deception operation, including a varied suite of tactics such as "air attacks, dummy military installations and shipping, misleading radio communications, false agent reports, and other intelligence ploys." As additional insurance against German reinforcements, the Allied air forces spent months destroying French rail and road infrastructure in the interior, focusing the bulk of their efforts away from the landing site to maintain the illusion that the invasion would be farther north.

The deception involved thousands of personnel diverting German attention away from Normandy by engaging in activities that, while not directly a part of the invasion, significantly influenced its success. Among the forces that would enact this plan was a petite New Yorker with an eye for detail, Gertrude Pearson.

The Bronx of the 1930s, where Pearson grew up, then a country suburb consisting mainly of farmland speckled with cows, sheep, and horses, would be largely unfamiliar to contemporary New Yorkers. Pearson was enjoying her life in the Bronx but, on the day that the Japanese attacked Pearl Harbor, felt an instantaneous desire to contribute to fighting the war. Months later, when she learned that women would be allowed to serve in the military, she stopped into the Navy recruiting station to inquire whether they would be sending women to theaters abroad. When told no, she walked around the corner to the Army recruiting station, asked the same question, received the answer she had hoped for, and enlisted on the spot. She made sure the recruiter noted her desire to serve overseas at the very top of her application.

Despite her initial enthusiasm for the WAC, Pearson got off to a rough start. She arrived at the training center in Daytona Beach on an unusually cold night in January 1943 at three o'clock in the morning, bone-tired and freezing. Despite the hour and the cold, Pearson and her classmates were nonetheless given an aptitude test on arrival. The initial results suggested that Pearson would be ideal for administration, and, after basic training, she was sent to Maxwell Airfield in Montgomery, Alabama, to start her duties. When Pearson arrived, however, it became clear that "administrative work" was a loose interpretation of what she would be doing. She had, in fact, been assigned to a signals unit, where she trained as a cryptographic technician, better known as a coder.

After almost a year and a half of on-the-job training, Pearson was itching to go abroad. Stories of women going to North Africa, Italy, and Europe with the Army had been circulating in the WAC for months, and Pearson was eager to realize her dream of serving overseas. Finally, her day came. In May 1944, she was selected as one of five hundred WACs to go to Europe as part of a signals detachment. Just weeks later, she arrived in Scotland and received her assignment to the Allied Expeditionary Air Force's 385th Signal Service Company (Aviation), northwest of London. As part of the deception operation, the unit had been tasked with obfuscating Germany's ability to see the actual invasion coming, and they promptly got to work flooding the German forces with noise.

On June 6, 1944, Eisenhower, now the senior commander directing the invasion of Normandy, and the Allied planners were especially grateful for the work of Pearson and hundreds of thousands of others. Their efforts had succeeded in convincing Hitler that the Normandy invasion was not, in fact, the main attack. Hitler believed instead that the Allied invasion would occur elsewhere and, relying on this assumption, failed to quickly reinforce his divisions on the coast and allowed the Allied forces to land over one hundred thousand troops ashore on the first day of the assault.

The Allied losses were high, especially on Omaha Beach, where German defenders had dug in on the high ground above the coast, but with the help of relentless air and naval assaults, the Allied forces were able to establish a beachhead within days of their arrival on the shores of Normandy. What's more, the counterattack that the Allies had feared never came. Hitler continued to believe the assault was a diversion and refused requests for meaningful reinforcements for several weeks, a fatal error that allowed the Allies to gain a strong foothold along the coast.

But, as had been the case in Italy months earlier, the advance was soon slowed by dense, entrenched defenses that littered the unfavorable interior French terrain. The bucolic French countryside of hedgerows, stone walls, and open fields turned into a nightmarish disadvantage for the Allied invasion force that took time, resources, and persistence to overcome. Two months into the campaign, the Allied forces found themselves again bogged down and in desperate need of a breakthrough.

Eisenhower pushed his commanders to find a hole in the German defenses to exploit. In late July 1944, General Omar Bradley, commanding the US First Army, finally found one. Bradley launched a punishing combined-arms attack in the area around Saint-Lô, creating a gap in the German resistance, and allowing Patton's forces to exploit the gains from the initial assault. Hitler ordered reinforcements to the area, but the Allies, having cracked the German codes, knew what was coming. By September 1944, they had regained the initiative in France.

* * *

Just as the Allied forces were breaking out in France, Pearson arrived on Omaha Beach, now a rear area funneling supplies and support to the front lines farther south. After Pearson disembarked with twenty-one other WACs on the damp, sandy beaches of the French coast, the officer in charge told her to find a foxhole and get comfortable for the night. She was in the fight.

Like thousands of signals units, Pearson's had been ordered to land in Normandy as part of the increasingly strained mobile communications infrastructure responsible for getting orders and updates between the front lines and headquarters. It is hard to overstate the importance of signals units in World War II. Little known to the American public, these units were at the center of the rapidly evolving modern battlefield. Essentially communications units, the signals units in World War II provided links between the combat forces on the front line and higher headquarters in the rear, and they functioned as the eyes and ears of senior commanders. They made sure that dispersed forces had a shared picture of the battlefield and could communicate orders and information.

Doing this on a battlefield in the 1940s was an exceedingly complex and difficult enterprise. The Signal Corps was responsible for building "networks of wire lines and radio circuits over continents and oceans to reach the theaters of war . . . [weaving] vital nets over beaches, mountains, rivers, and plains so as to serve the troops in combat," and built a multifaceted web of communications equipment and personnel in order to collate and pass thousands of pieces of information from the front lines to the rear of the battlefield and back every day. They were exactly the type of combat support units that American commanders had rightly predicted would be critical to Allied victory, and, in 1944, they were literally and figuratively in the middle of the battlefield, including units composed entirely of women.

The Signal Corps was more progressive than most other branches when it came to assigning women to nontraditional roles. According to a 1944 estimate from the chief signal officer, nearly five percent of the WAC total strength had been assigned to signals units, with at least 1,700 in Europe alone. But even more striking than the numbers of women was their distribution into nonclerical assignments. Over sixty percent were trained as technical specialists, compared to only twenty-five percent assigned to administrative duties.

Pearson was among the technical specialists working to build and repair the communications infrastructure on which the commands relied, and she thrived in this challenging environment. By October 1944, her unit had made it to Vittel, about twenty-five miles from the front lines, and was so close that she heard the heavy artillery pounding in the hills around them. The barracks had little heat and only wooden slats as beds. Helmets were used for bathtubs, and K rations, a notoriously bad packaged meal meant to withstand the rigors of combat, were the primary food source.

Security concerns were paramount. Spies were everywhere this close to enemy territory. On one occasion, a woman arrived in Pearson's barracks claiming she had plane trouble and needed a place to stay for the night. The unit, trained in counterintelligence and predisposed by their signals work to notice small details, distrusted the woman. Pearson also spotted an especially peculiar feature of her outfit: the mystery woman claimed to be British but wore German shoes. Suspicious, the unit reported her to the military police on base, and she was quickly removed from the barracks. No one saw her again.

While Pearson was warily eyeing the German operative's shoes, Eisenhower also had concerns about the Germans. In the three months since the invasion, the Allied forces had successfully, if slowly, held counterattacks at bay. At this point in the campaign, however, Eisenhower anticipated that a major engagement lay ahead, and found himself anxiously examining his manpower tables, wondering how many personnel he could employ against a consolidated and determined German counterattack.

Dismayingly, Eisenhower found he had no combat forces to spare. In the fall of 1944, American military planners had decided to cap ground forces at ninety divisions and subsequently cut activation of new units. They had assumed that the twenty-four divisions available for deployment, composed of hundreds of thousands of men, would be sufficient for the remaining operations around the world. It was a gamble, and it put Eisenhower in a precarious position.

Without the ability to call up additional combat divisions, the Army's strategy shifted to redistribution. This required them to dig even deeper into their existing forces, again taking men from support units and putting them on the front lines. The redistribution at the end of 1944 meant that men would need to be taken not just from the home front, but from the rear areas of active battlefields, leaving gaping holes in the noncombat infrastructure at home and abroad. American commanders knew they needed to find personnel to take over for the men being shipped overseas. Once again, they found women in uniform ready to ship out.

## 23

# "I'D RATHER BE
# WITH THEM—
# THAN WAITING"

### EUROPE

AT THE END OF 1944, AS ALLIED TROOPS BEGAN TO stream into France following the Normandy invasion, American support needs ballooned almost overnight. With a foothold in Europe, the US forces massed ground and air forces on the continent, attempting to drive deep into German territory and to deliver a final, fatal blow to Hitler's diminished forces. It was an ambitious undertaking, which the Americans had pushed for since the start of the war. At the end of 1944, as the Army began to make its way through the continent, they took intrepid women like Evelyn Zahn along with them.

Growing up in northern New Jersey as an only child, Zahn had always found loyal and devoted friends everywhere she went, but was also happy on her own, sometimes becoming obsessed with her more solitary hobbies—puzzling, crosswords, cryptograms, sewing, and drawing. Zahn had dearly loved her mother, Adele, who doted on her as a girl, but, at fifteen, she died unexpectedly, leaving Zahn's home with little of the warmth and kindness her mother had brought to it. Her stepfather, who assumed her care, was by Zahn's account a cruel, abusive alcoholic. He had married Zahn's mother when Evelyn was only three years old and worked odd jobs in manufacturing, first at a pearl-button factory and then a silk mill, before briefly opening a tavern that became insolvent less than two years later. Before long, he began abusing Zahn, once chasing her around the kitchen table with a knife.

Between the loss of her mother and the abuse of her stepfather, Zahn was forced into being self-sufficient at a young age, a trait that animated the rest of her life. When, after high school, she saw a classified in the local paper: "Help Wanted—Female; ARTIST GIRL—Experience in textile designing. Steady work, good salary. Multitone Engraving Co., Fairview, N.J.," she jumped at the chance to put some distance between her and her hometown.

Zahn, an excellent artist, had been drawing most of her life and had a knack for sewing and textile work. She immediately took the job, painting designs on copper rollers used for fabric printing. Zahn enjoyed the work, and especially appreciated the steady paychecks that provided her with a degree of independence that she had never before experienced.

The distance, however, between her hometown and Fairview proved too close to keep her stepfather at bay. He still managed to hound her at work, often drunk, making an embarrassing scene. His public harassment mortified her, and she soon recognized she needed more than a few miles of space to escape his abuse. When the war necessitated that the copper used to print fabric be diverted to war production and upended the stability of Zahn's work, she, like so many women at the time, chose a life in the military over the difficulties of life in small-town America.

Artists like Zahn were in high demand at the time. Visual conveyance of critical military information in World War II, including signs, maps, pamphlets, posters, and propaganda, had to be hand drawn to create templates for printing. If men on the front lines needed updated maps, artists drew them. If bases needed signs, artists painted them. If the Army Air Forces wanted to warn civilians of an impending air raid, artists made the flyers. Civilians could do some of this work, but most of it involved sensitive and classified information that needed to be handled by military personnel. Finding skilled soldiers to do these jobs became an immediate and ongoing priority across the services. But identifying individuals suited to these roles was also difficult, since the work required people with several uniquely overlapping skills. They needed to have an artistic background, not mind doing repetitive and sometimes boring work, and not be deployed to front lines. Zahn met all the criteria.

When Zahn enlisted in the WAC, she had little idea of how in demand her skills would be. After completing basic training at Daytona Beach, Florida, she was asked to stay on at the publications office to help create the informational silk-screen posters that greeted women as they arrived at the base for processing, including illustrating the various Army insignia that the new troops needed to learn. But she didn't stay long since, by 1944, artists were critically needed abroad. As the Allies were making steady progress on the continent, they were desperate for maps and charts to help guide their way through the challenging landscapes in their path.

Zahn, like many other WACs, made her way to London on the *Queen Mary*, "the Grey Ghost," a massive, retrofitted ocean liner painted gray, and responsible for ferrying hundreds of thousands of Allied forces between New York and the United Kingdom. Like most WACs, Zahn found little to enjoy about crossing the Atlantic Ocean in early spring. It was frigid and dreary, and she soon developed a cold to accompany her seasickness, shivering in shower water pulled from the ocean. The food was hardly bearable, particularly the boiled potatoes and stewed fish for breakfast, and Zahn survived mainly off soda crackers and tea for most of the trip. By the time she arrived in the United Kingdom, she was grateful for the C rations that she ate on the darkened troop train to London.

Zahn's unit was first assigned to the Southern Base Station

headquarters in Salisbury, where she was embedded with the provost marshal's office. There, she began the essential, highly detailed work of making traffic maps for the military police. The job description, "pen and ink tracing map overlays, charts, marked installations, and the like on maps of Southern England," underplayed the importance of the job. Changing traffic patterns, long convoys, and blackouts, particularly when combined with the hazardous nature of driving in the 1940s, posed many challenges for the military police. Up-to-date maps were essential in making sure that traffic moved safely and steadily, especially given the wave of troops making their way across southern England to their embarkation points for the invasions of France and Germany.

In August 1944, just months after the invasion of Normandy,

WAC Evelyn Zahn with other GIs in Europe. **Courtesy Weidaw family.**

Zahn was moved to the WAC detachment, Northern Base Station, in Cherbourg, France, only miles from the front line. Zahn was again responsible for map overlays and charts, as well as the creation of graphs and other graphics that helped visually convey projects in the Control Section. Her unit was billeted in a barren barracks on rue Seconde decorated only with wooden bunk beds. Lacking hot water, the women improvised by heating helmets full of water over the fireplace.

But just as they settled in, it was again time to go: Zahn's unit moved with the front, and, within six months, their headquarters had traveled one hundred miles east to Deauville by truck. There, they found the conditions at the Bellevue Hotel, where they were billeted, vastly improved. The hotel offered several spaces for entertaining and dining, and beautiful views of the coast, although the women couldn't walk the beach because of the mines still buried in the sand. Zahn remembered fondly living at the Bellevue Hotel. The women shared rooms with only one or two other occupants and, most important, they had "hot and cold running water, steam heat, and hotel beds with linen." Zahn even had a real bathtub, an unheard-of luxury in the field—"Here was plush living," she remembered.

But the luxuries of the Bellevue stood in stark contrast to the serious work Zahn was doing in France. Assigned to the headquarters "war room," Zahn found maps lining the walls from floor to ceiling, layered so deep that they "turned like book pages." Even later she would report little about the content of the work—it was too sensitive—but her drawings lit the way for thousands of American troops trudging through Europe in the spring of 1944. Without Zahn's work, these forces were, quite literally, lost.

Although neither Zahn nor anyone else in the US forces knew it at the time, the maps that she was making would soon be needed to guide the American forces as they fought back against the final surprise attack of German forces at the Battle of the Bulge. In advance of this battle, however, two major problems still plagued the Allied forces. The first was one of their own making: American military commanders and political leaders consistently failed to accurately assess the military strength possessed by the remaining, most desperate, holdouts in both the German and Japanese militaries. They expected these forces to collapse under the steadily mounting attacks of the Allied advance in both theaters, and continued to underestimate the tremendous will of the depleted forces left to defend their homelands against the numerically superior Allied forces.

Second, the Allies faced extraordinary pressure on their rapidly expanding supply lines stretching around the globe and converging in the heart of Europe. At the same time, German supply lines were shrinking as they retreated closer and closer into the heart of their homeland. On the eve of the Battle of the Bulge, therefore, the Allies realized they had overestimated their comparative strengths and had profoundly overstretched their supply lines.

The result was that the Battle of the Bulge started off tipped in Germany's favor. The German counterattack surprised the Allies, and it concentrated the strongest remaining elements of the German military against the unsuspecting forces. In the first several weeks of combat, the offensive threatened to reverse many of the key gains that the Allies had worked so hard to achieve over the past six months.

Ultimately, however, the Germans were outnumbered. Despite the American supply challenges, the Germans lacked the necessary infrastructure to sustain combat operations of the scale and scope required to defeat the Allied forces streaming into the theater, and the Bulge proved to be a last, futile attempt to stave off Allied invasion of Germany. As the Germans retreated, the Allied forces continued their advance, guided by the freshly printed maps of the German countryside that Zahn had helped make.

With the Allied forces advancing through Germany in late 1944 and 1945, the WAC saw an opportunity. Support forces, like Zahn, in rear areas of the battlefield rarely saw combat but provided critical support to the battle-weary troops fighting at the front. This vital but overlooked element of military operations in Europe proved to be the perfect place for WACs.

Charity Adams boarded the train beaming. She had just been promoted to major, an unusual achievement for any WAC, but especially impressive for a Black woman in the service, and she was deservedly proud of the accomplishment. On learning the news, she had been moved to tears, and she proudly wore the major's oak leaves gleaming on her uniform.

Adams, used to passing the time on long train rides, was focused on the book on her lap. On this trip, however, Adams noticed a White woman sitting across the aisle who had been glaring at her, seemingly since the train departed. As Adams glanced up, she saw the woman stop the military policeman patrolling the train. Looking suspiciously over at Adams, the woman demanded that he "check on that negr[o] woman sitting over there."

"What do you mean check on her, ma'am?"

"The woman over there is wearing an officer's uniform and I'm sure she is an imposter. Why she's a negr[o]."

Adams kept her eyes on her book as she listened intently to the conversation. She had heard the stories of the Black WAC officers brutally beaten in waiting rooms and on sidewalks, and she waited for the MP to respond.

Finally, looking over at Adams and taking note of the shining brass on her lapels, he responded:

"I'm sorry ma'am but I have no reason to bother that officer."

The woman remained unsatisfied. "Aren't you going to ask her for her identification?"

The MP, impatient and aware that, Black or White, Adams significantly outranked him, responded matter-of-factly: "Ma'am

I am here in case of trouble or a problem of some kind. There is no problem here. If I check, to use your word, that officer and she is not an imposter, I might not be a sergeant tomorrow."

He concluded, "Besides, an imposter would not pick a rank that high; there are too few WAC Majors in the army."

With a salute to Adams, he continued his patrol.

The sight of Adams in a major's uniform continued to provoke confusion, disdain, or delight in equal measure. Other MPs, particularly when she traveled alone, insisted on checking Adams's rank, only to find themselves answering for the mistake later. But among the other Black women, the sight of Adams in her major's uniform was a source of endless pride and inspiration.

The promotion to major also provided Adams with opportunities available only to a handful of WAC officers and to an even smaller number of Black women. As the WAC footprint around the world grew, this included the opportunity to travel to overseas theaters. In mid-December 1944, as the Battle of the Bulge raged, Adams's commander asked how she felt about going abroad. She at first felt apprehensive, but then eagerly accepted the challenge. "The truth was," she remembered, "I had been involved in so many firsts that I did not want to be left out of any new venture." By the end of the month, she was assigned to be the first commander of the first Black WAC unit to serve abroad.

Adams and the group of nearly one thousand women assigned to the 6888th Central Postal Battalion received very little information about their destination. They knew it would be cold, since they had been given orders for winter uniforms, and assumed they were heading to Europe but didn't know for sure until they boarded a transport ship to cross the Atlantic. Only after the women arrived at their destination—Birmingham, England—were they finally briefed on their assignment.

The 6888th was responsible for the mail. On its face, the assignment may have seemed tedious to some. Sorting mail, whether in Europe or at home, was not what most soldiers envisioned when they imagined overseas service, and the notion of traveling hundreds of miles abroad to sort through stacks of mail in eight-hour shifts might not seem interesting or important.

But anyone who doubts the importance of this work, then or now, needs only to ask a soldier who has been deployed overseas how much they look forward to hearing news from home. It is an essential part of sustaining morale, and briefly restores a sense of normalcy in what can often feel like an endless cycle of violence, fear, and adrenaline. Personnel posted abroad during World War II regularly read mail aloud to their friends and units, knowing that news from home lifted the spirits of the entire group, particularly for those who had not received any word from their loved ones. For many soldiers, covered in grime and dirt, far from home, cold, and miserable, mail was one of the few bright spots during their deployment. It reminded them what they were fighting for and, most important, what was waiting for them when they came home. Mail was, in other words, a lifeline.

This was especially true in 1944, since the fastest way for military personnel to hear from home was through the mail. That is, if it could get delivered to the right person, in the right place, at the right time. With millions of people deployed overseas, over several operational theaters, in hundreds of locations, and constantly on the move, getting mail to its intended recipient was a daunting task. In a single month in 1943, for instance, over one hundred thousand pieces of mail had been dispatched to the Southwest Pacific theater alone, and in the same period in the United Kingdom, well over one hundred and fifty thousand pieces of mail were received.

When the Six Triple Eight, as they were known, arrived at the warehouse that stored the backlog of mail that awaited them, they were confronted with a shock. They found the mail in complete disarray, with little structure dictating how and where it had been stored. Adams estimated several thousand letters just for "Robert Smith" were found in the piles of mail that they were responsible for sorting and sending. The disgusting conditions of the warehouse—filthy, dark, and vermin infested—where millions of pieces of paper had been stored for months did not help matters.

Despite the challenging working conditions, the women of the Six Triple Eight knew the stakes. They understood not only how important it was to get mail delivered to the men at the front but also that their success or failure would influence any future consideration of sending Black women overseas. Compounding this pressure, Adams knew that other branches' experiments with sending similar deployments of Black women overseas had not gone well. Almost a year earlier, a detachment of Black nurses in the 25th Station Hospital had been deployed to Liberia, only to be recalled after several months. On arrival, the nurses had realized their assignment had been more of a savvy public relations move than an operational necessity, as their skills were duplicative of those of the units already there. With little to do, the women were sent home in a matter of weeks. Given this precedent, Adams worried that Black women were running out of chances at overseas service.

The Six Triple Eight got to work sorting, compiling, cleaning, repairing, and sending thousands of pieces of mail. They were immediately and undeniably good at their job. By one official account, "the unit broke all records for redirecting mail . . . [and each] eight-hour shift averaged more than 65,000 pieces of mail." Three months after they had arrived, the Six Triple Eight had cleared six months of backlog. One review of their work noted that the 6888th's "output of work averaged twice as many pieces of mail processed as had been done by enlisted men, and three to four times that handled by civilian employees." With each letter delivered in the field, the battle-weary American forces received a precious moment of relief as they pursued the Germans through the cold, bloody battlefields on the continent.

\* \* \*

Despite the difficulty and importance of their work and their demonstrated efficiency, the women of Six Triple Eight suffered some of the greatest indignities faced by women serving abroad during World War II. Adams, their beloved leader, experienced the worst of it.

Adams often found herself serving as a bulwark for the rest of the unit, taking the vilest, most racist fire to protect those in her command from experiencing the same abuse. As a child of the South, she understood that the segregation imposed by the Army was a blight on its record. She had railed against propositions to enforce the separation of the WACs at home and now found herself doing the same overseas.

When, for instance, the Red Cross told Adams that it insisted on setting up a segregated recreation facility for the Six Triple Eight, she refused to accept the equipment, telling the Special Services officer, "If our girls are not good enough to visit their club, then their equipment is not good enough for us to use." Weeks later, she refused to tolerate the suggestion that her unit stay in a segregated hotel while in London. On another occasion, she was forced to ask her soldiers to stay out until twelve-thirty at night to quell rumors among the local British population that Black women had tails that came out after midnight.

As the commander of her unit, Adams did not tolerate mistreatment in any situation, whether the stakes were low or incredibly high. In one case, a senior general in the European Theater of Operations (ETO), whom Adams refused to identify even years later, reviewed the 6888th in formation and remarked that the battalion was noticeably understrength. Adams explained that, as was the custom, the women who were on shift or sleeping after overnight duties were not assembled for review. The general, shouting at Adams, informed her that he was going to "send a white first lieutenant down here to show you how to run this unit." Adams, in an expression of pluck that surprised even her, looked the general dead in the eye and responded, "Over my dead body, Sir."

In early spring of 1945, as the Allies overran the Germans, the Six Triple Eight continued to outdo the high expectations placed on them with their exceptional performance. "The women of the 6888th had ventured into a service area where they were not really wanted," wrote Adams, recalling the many difficulties they had faced in the field: "They had assumed jobs that had normally been assigned to men; they had been and were performing in a valiant and praiseworthy manner; they had survived racial prejudice and discrimination with dignity."

"They were proud," she concluded, "and had every right to be."

At the end of 1944, the Battle of the Bulge had forced the Germans into a retreat, and shifted the pendulum of the war firmly back in the Allies' favor. With no escape routes, Hitler and the Nazi military found themselves wedged between the steadily advancing British and American forces in the west and the Russian army in the east. Many German cities were in tatters, crumbling under the near-constant assault of Allied airpower, which was a vindicating reversal from the earliest days of the war when German planes terrorized civilians across Europe. By the end of April 1945, the Red Army had encircled Berlin, the site of Hitler's last holdout, and the Nazi leader found himself increasingly isolated as his former acolytes fled or turned on him.

Against the backdrop of the closing Russian forces and incessant, massive bombing of Berlin, Hitler dictated his last will and testament to his secretary, appointed his successor—Admiral Karl Dönitz—and retreated with his wife to the bunker where he had spent the waning days of the war. The next day, April 30, 1945, Hitler placed a loaded gun to his head and pulled the trigger, all but ensuring the end to one of the darkest chapters in German history.

A week later, women and men around the world—some in uniform, many not—were glued to their radios. Hitler was dead, the remaining German leaders had surrendered, and the Allies controlled Germany. Only weeks earlier, Roosevelt had died suddenly, although not totally unexpectedly. The world awaited a statement declaring victory in Europe from Roosevelt's successor, Harry Truman, who had taken office a month earlier.

Truman did so on May 8, 1945. "This is a solemn but glorious hour. . . . The flags of freedom fly over all Europe," Truman stated. He knew, however, that the war was only partially won, and urged the American public to turn their sights on the Pacific: "The West is free, but the East is still in bondage," he remarked, adding, "I call on every American to stick to his post until the last battle is won."

In Barracks 438 at Ellington Air Force Base in Houston, Texas,

WACs of the 6888th Central Postal Battalion sort mail in Paris, France.
Courtesy National Archives, photo no. 175539203.

the radio was on, but the WACs assembled there were only half listening. Truman's momentous speech had been timed for the early morning, just as the women were getting ready for their day, so their attention was split between the radio and the mirror. But when the president made his proclamation, they all took a moment to pause. Shortly after, all base personnel—thousands of soldiers and airmen—were assembled on the parade ground for a formal announcement from the base commander. After his short speech and a prayer, the women at Ellington went back to work.

Aileen Kilgore, one of the WACs assigned to the photo lab on base, was among them. In the weeks after Victory in Europe Day, she grew frustrated with the apparent complacency of the troops on base who, it seemed, thought the war had been won. She was especially galled by the returning combat soldiers, who seemed particularly insubordinate, and she was bored by the lack of work on base. "Everybody sits around idle and trouble thrives," she wrote in a letter home. "It's getting on my nerves."

Even so, when, at the end of May 1945, Kilgore and her fellow WACs with a year of service were given the opportunity to be discharged, she wasn't interested.

"Me," she wrote, "I'd like to see a little more."

# 24

# "BLUEPRINT FOR VICTORY"

## THE PACIFIC

EVEN WITH THE NAZI SURRENDER IN EARLY MAY 1945, the war in the Pacific still raged. The Japanese, from the most senior commanders all the way down the ranks, had not been dissuaded by Germany's defeat, and were mounting a fierce defense of their homeland.

At the same time, the Allies had settled into an effective, if halting, strategy in the Pacific. By 1944, two years of hard-fought but steady victories against the Japanese had made clear that the Allies could retake the region. The only dilemma that remained was what strategy the US would employ for the final string of offensives. The Army and Navy initially took very different positions on where to place their emphasis. The Navy wanted to take a direct tack toward Tokyo via the Gilbert, Marshall, and Marianas Islands; while the Army, influenced heavily by MacArthur, wanted to focus the advance on the Philippines through New Guinea.

After weeks of infighting between their subordinates, Army and Navy leaders decided to do both. They divided the theater into separate but reinforcing campaigns that would converge around Japan, thereby strangling the Japanese from two directions, splitting their limited resources, and forcing them to defend against dual assault on their mainland.

The Navy forces in the Pacific took the direct route to Tokyo. Building on the success of the 1942 Solomons campaign, the Navy launched a series of attacks against Japanese holdings; first, the Gilbert and Marshall Islands, followed closely by the Carolines, and finally the Marianas, where the Navy planned to base the new B-29 Superfortress, which would provide vital support during the invasion of the Japanese mainland. The plan became known as the Central Pacific campaign.

Meanwhile, the Army, under the command of MacArthur, would take the southwestern route through the Pacific. MacArthur's longstanding commitment to retaking the Philippines had not waned since he had been forced to retreat in the opening salvos of the war. He would lead his forces through the southwestern Pacific—first recapturing New Guinea, then the strategic port of Rabaul, and finally the Philippines, where he would converge on Japan with the Navy's forces. If the strategy worked, the Japanese would find themselves overstretched and overwhelmed and facing defeat from two sides.

But for all its strategic and operational might, the campaign in the Pacific had a potential weakness: its reliance on the newly developed amphibious assault doctrine that had been employed successfully on only a handful of occasions during the war. The doctrine itself, the ship-to-shore movement of troops by amphibious landing craft, was simple enough, but the operational concept had not been employed widely prior to World War II. Even so, the Navy and Marine Corps were relying on this novel doctrine to put them directly ashore and establish strongholds at beaches across the Pacific.

In theory, amphibious assault promised an impressive fusion of naval and land power, enabled by a suite of technical advancements. These included the development of massive firepower aboard naval ships and amphibious landing crafts that could go from sea to shore, enabling masses of personnel to be delivered close enough to the coastline that they could wade onto the beach and continue their assault on land. But for this new doctrine to work, intelligence—particularly about landing sites—was critical. Landing craft were powerful tools but easily sunk on uneven ocean floor, on coral reefs, and by strong tides and currents. To successfully deliver their men to designated landing sites, naval officers needed to have a detailed understanding of the variable coastlines of the dozens of Pacific islands they planned to invade.

Against this backdrop, the Navy faced extremely tough odds. They were going into offensive combat thousands of miles away from American holdings and using new doctrine against an enemy that had occupied the terrain for four years. Success required, above all else, the best information they could find on the islands' coasts.

Twenty years before the Navy would make use of her extraordinary knowledge of the sea, Mary Sears was an undergraduate at Radcliffe College. There, she spent most days at Harvard's Museum of Comparative Zoology, studying marine invertebrates. Sears, then a short, bespectacled, and unassuming young woman of twenty-two, was enamored with the work she was doing. She was a born scientist, fascinated by amphibians—frogs and salamanders in particular—from a young age. In her youth, she frequently waded into Heard Pond of Wayland, Massachusetts, where she grew up, looking for critters.

By 1933, her childhood love of amphibians had blossomed into a career, culminating in a doctorate from Radcliffe, her third degree from the institution, with a dissertation titled "Migration of Pigment in Frogs' Eyes." While completing her doctoral work, she had studied under the most celebrated oceanographic scholars, including her advisor, Henry Bryant Bigelow, and other men who were building the oceanographic field from the ground up.

The field's growth was also being spurred by the Navy's interest in it, since the sea-based services realized they would be major beneficiaries of a deeper and more scientific understanding of the ocean, especially as the crisis in Europe and the Pacific unfolded.

By the time the Navy was deep into its planning for amphibious assaults in the Pacific, Sears had moved to the Woods Hole Oceanographic Institution (WHOI) in Cape Cod, Massachusetts, where she was working with a small but growing number of oceanographers. The "Harvard Yacht Club," as the WHOI team was known, was being propelled by a gifted, creative, and motivated band of scientists, of which Sears was a central figure. While there, she had made a name for herself, and the Navy took notice.

By the end of 1942, the Navy's Hydrographic Office (Hydro) had gutted WHOI of its most talented scientists to assist them in coordinating the expanding oceanographic research and in creating the maritime charts for the Pacific campaigns. Sears had been recruited from WHOI in December 1942 by the head of the Hydro, and by February she had been appointed as an officer in the WAVES and posted there.

The office was responsible for creating and distributing up-to-date navigational charts "to afford the maximum possible navigational safety and facilities to ships on the sea and to aircraft operating over sea routes." This special mission, which the office had been doing since 1866, had suddenly become much more urgent and demanding with the onset of hostilities. The uptick in Navy activity in the Pacific threatened to overwhelm Hydro as it struggled to keep up with the demand for new, detailed, and accurate navigational charts and memoranda to guide the transport and invasion forces scattered across the sea and sky.

By the time Sears arrived on the scene, Hydro had been moved under the Chief of Naval Operations, a reflection of its growing importance in the unfolding war in the Pacific. Personnel had grown somewhere between two hundred to five hundred percent for months, and 13 million charts and publications had been printed in 1942 alone. Most Hydro sections were working in two shifts to provide near-constant coverage, and where possible they had three. But the demands never ceased, and Hydro had trouble retaining personnel as their civil service staff was lured away by job opportunities in the military and industrial sectors. They began requesting the Navy's personnel and resources to fill the gap.

Midway through the war, however, nearly every Navy office was competing to fill personnel gaps. Hydro stood little chance of securing the complement of trained, low-ranking, enlisted men they had requested to help meet their requirements. Instead, the Navy offered them seven officers and ten enlisted women from the WAVES.

The WAVES quickly proved their worth. Within a month, Hydro's air navigation branch requested ten more WAVES; a year later, Hydro estimated it needed three hundred. The women worked as stenographers, draftsmen, IBM operators, lithographers, and multilith operators, and often trained on the job for more advanced tasks. Karen Berkey, for instance, was among the WAVES assigned to Hydro. She had been selected for her artistic skills, which were critical for creating the highly classified naval and aviation maps used by sailors and airmen in the Pacific. In a letter home, she noted that she could not share much about her work given its highly classified nature: "I'm not allowed to say much about what I'm doing because it's too vital and important and secretive," but she did confide that she had been assigned one of the most difficult art jobs in the unit, adding, "I confess I was terrified at all of the complications." Every member of the Hydro team, from Sears to Berkey, knew the work they were doing, no matter how technical or tedious, was essential to Allied progress in the Pacific.

Within six months of her arrival, Sears was promoted to director of the Oceanographic Unit, having been handpicked to oversee the ceaseless requests for oceanographic intelligence that swamped the office. Working with a combined section of Army and Navy personnel, she and her staff were charged with helping the Navy figure out where to land their ships. "In view of the probability of amphibious operations in many theaters," read a joint Army and Navy intelligence study, "it is of importance to compile and disseminate, as soon as possible, information on average sea and swell conditions, surf characteristics, tides, tidal and other currents, bottom material, probable underwater sound conditions and similar data." They secured that information from Sears.

On paper, their task seemed straightforward: translate academic oceanographic studies into useful insights for military commanders planning their operations in the Pacific and Indian Oceans. Sears and her team were asked for, and expected to provide, information on "ocean currents, wave and tide predictions, amphibious landing sites, and presence of propeller-fouling kelp or bioluminescent marine life." But the group lacked up-to-date information for many of the requests they received, forcing them to rely on whatever material they could obtain, pulled from all kinds of sources. Whether it be a fifty-year-old Dutch publication, a prewar Japanese survey published in an academic journal, information collected by a Navy survey vessel, or, in some cases, pure guesswork, Sears and her team were expected to use the limited information they had to provide accurate predictions.

Even in the face of these constraints, however, Sears and her team found ways to provide surprisingly precise assessments for naval commanders. Having spent her entire career developing the field of oceanography from scratch, Sears was accustomed to challenges like the one facing the Navy, and she thrived in the environment. Sears's first project, a study of the drift of debris and small rafts in the Atlantic and Pacific undertaken at the behest of Congress and completed entirely on her own, became the authoritative guide for rescuing pilots, crews, and ships that crashed or were sunk in naval combat and oversea flying. The intelligence provided by Sears and her team was not perfect, but it was far better than the paltry information that the Navy had relied on in the early days of the war, and the demand for her team's reports only grew.

As Sears's team and know-how expanded, her work became increasingly consequential. By 1944, Hydro was working on joint intelligence reports that broke down the key characteristics of military targets across the Pacific—including Sakhalin, the Kurils, Hokkaido, Palau, the Marianas, Java, Makassar Strait, Cam Ranh Bay, and the Singapore Strait—all areas the US Navy planned to land or transit in during the next two years. These comprehensive reports took up most of her team's time and focus, but Sears also recalled having to divert attention to urgent matters on the fly, often after a meeting of the combined British and American leadership. These quick-turn taskings were sometimes so secretive that only Sears was cleared to work on them, but she never failed to complete the expert analysis, even if it meant she worked overnight, alone, and exhausted.

The WAVES assigned to Sears's unit were inspired by her expertise and dedication, and eagerly followed her example. Sears's late nights and relentless pursuit of the answers to seemingly impossible requests told the WAVES at Hydro everything they needed to know about what would be expected of them. "It does feel good," wrote Berkey in a letter home, "to know my work is essential, that an error on my part would be drastic, and that my good work means victory is that much closer.

"That is absolutely all I can say about Hydro," she warned.

# 25

# "TO MAKE MEN FREE"

## VICTORY WON

IN THE SPRING OF 1945, THE AMERICAN MILITARY was reaping the dividends of investments it had made in the Pacific two years earlier. In 1943 and 1944, Navy planners, shifting their focus eastward, had begun funneling troops and equipment to the region. In 1943 alone, US troop totals arrayed against Japan already neared 1.7 million personnel, with nearly 8,000 aircraft and 700 combat ships, including 28 aircraft carriers, in the theater. By 1945, the Navy had committed almost two-thirds of its personnel, over 1.3 million sailors, to the Pacific. As the Navy sent more men to the Pacific, the WAVES, SPARS, and Women Marines who had been confined to serving stateside watched on, hoping to get closer to the action.

But up until 1944, the Navy had, quite intentionally, prevented their women's units from serving anywhere beyond the continental United States. McAfee attributed the resistance to sending WAVES abroad to the conservative attitudes of southern congressmen on the naval affairs committee, who, she determined, thought they were "protecting womanhood between them for various motives." McAfee also knew that the Navy felt it could better "control the situation" if the women were at home than if they were sent farther afield. The WAVES' authorizing legislation had, therefore, been clear that "members of the Women's reserve shall be restricted to the performance of short duty within the continental United States only."

The Navy had reason for their concerns. Harassment was rampant abroad, and Navy leaders also worried about exposing the women to the extreme physical hardships of serving in the Pacific region. But the war for which the WAVES had been authorized turned out to be quite a different conflict in its closing days. In 1945, the Navy was facing an expansive war in the Pacific, requiring the defense of existing holdings and amphibious assault operations that stretched supply lines and continued to strain manpower.

By late 1944, the manpower demands of the final push in the Pacific had caught up with the Navy. After three years of war, men were being pulled from anywhere they were not essential to meet the dual demands of the Pacific campaign and the final push in Europe. Adding to the operational pressure the Navy felt, precedents in other services bolstered the case for sending WAVES abroad. The WACs, as well as the Army and Navy Nurse Corps, had proved time and time again that women, when assigned to the right tasks, could successfully be deployed to the field. In the Pacific alone, the WAC had grown impressively, with women serving in New Caledonia, Australia, India, Burma, and China. The WAVES' inability to send women abroad was a considerable point of disappointment, especially as women from other programs boarded ships to theaters where Navy men were fighting. "The girls were simply infuriated about the fact that they were not being allowed to go overseas," remembered McAfee. The ongoing personnel shortage, combined with the compelling positive evidence of women serving abroad in other services, forced the Navy to amend its stance on sending women abroad.

Even so, the Navy wanted to impose clear geographic constraints on overseas service. McAfee, along with her staff, had studied the issue at length, including weighing the Army's success in using handpicked women for overseas service. They developed a comprehensive list of qualifications for women selected to go abroad, including proof of having completed six months of service with satisfactory reviews; "demonstrated maturity, a sense of responsibility, adaptability, and emotional stability"; and no dependents at home. In addition, the qualifications placed a strong emphasis on motivation, good health, and stable personality.

With these standards in place, the WAVES' authorizing legislation was amended, and, by the end of 1944, the inaugural group of WAVES found themselves on ships to Hawaii. Weeks later, the first WAVES to serve abroad marched down the gangplank in their gray-and-white seersucker summer uniforms to receive the traditional welcoming lei. They were soon joined by over four thousand more WAVES deployed to the island.

These women could be found working behind desks and under the engines at six naval air stations on the island. Within weeks, the Marines had also sent over one thousand women to join the WAVES, and the SPARS were not far behind. But even though the women posted in Hawaii found life there to be charming and beautiful, their jobs were taxing, and their schedules left little time for relaxation and sightseeing. As one WAVE aptly put it, "Be it Maryland or Maui, the Navy is the Navy."

The women's work was taxing because it was essential, and the demand for their skills was relentless on the strategically placed island, which served as a waypoint for the Navy troops and equipment en route to engagements deeper into the Pacific. The women posted there filled a variety of jobs, driving sailors around the base as they waited for their deployment, maintaining supply depots that furnished ships with essential provisions on their way out to sea, and repairing Navy equipment to be sent back to the front. Though miles away from the battles that raged in the Pacific, this work provided the vital support that the American forces relied on as the final stages of combat in the Pacific intensified.

\* \* \*

There is a famous photo of General MacArthur wading ashore at Leyte, the landing point in the Philippines that the United States selected for its initial invasion of the island nation in October 1944. Knee-deep in the ocean, he is flanked by several men, his uniformed stomach escaping over his belt and signature sunglasses sitting snuggly under his field-marshal cap. He is slightly ahead of the rest of the group, as though he is rushing to get to shore— which, it turns out, he was. MacArthur had been waiting to return to the Philippines since forced by the Japanese invasion to evacuate back in March 1942. He was eager to make good on his departing promise, "I shall return."

MacArthur was also very annoyed. His command headquarters, situated on the USS *Nashville,* had been listing with the tide on

General Douglas MacArthur wades ashore during initial landings at Leyte, Philippine Islands. **Courtesy National Archives, photo no. 531424.**

Red Beach for five hours after the US forces had made their initial assault. MacArthur decided he could no longer wait to get ashore, and he ordered his staff to take him to the beach. They summoned a small craft to get them there, bringing them within fifty yards of the landing site. The area had been secured by Allied forces hours earlier but was still under threat of Japanese mortar and artillery fire. The captain radioed the beachmaster to request a landing craft to ferry MacArthur and his entourage the final short distance to the beach.

The beachmaster, still intensely focused on securing the area and ensuring the organized flow of forces onto shore, had heard the request to send a smaller landing craft out to a command party's boat and allegedly replied, "Let 'em walk."

MacArthur, notoriously impatient and now mad, apparently heard the response and jumped out, landing knee-deep in seawater. His staff scrambled in to join him, and off they went. After delivering short remarks on the beach, MacArthur returned to the *Nashville*, just as the Japanese began their counterattack.

Back on board, he found a cable from President Roosevelt: "I know well what this means to you. I know what it cost you to obey my order that you leave Corregidor in February 1942, and proceed to Australia," wrote Roosevelt, continuing, "Ever since then you have planned and worked and fought with whole-souled devotion for the day when you would return." MacArthur, soaked to his knees in seawater, had done just that.

MacArthur's success at Leyte did not bode well for the Japanese. They were surrounded. As MacArthur swept north, the Navy forces had made their way through the Central Pacific and were now in position on Tokyo's doorstep.

This success paved the way for the first three months of 1945, which marked a dramatic escalation of the American effort to dislodge the Japanese from their island holdings and force a last stand on the Japanese mainland. The American strategy of taking parallel approaches to the home islands through the Southwest and

Central Pacific had proved highly effective, and it forced the Japanese to mount their final defense in three places: Luzon, against MacArthur and his Army forces, and Iwo Jima and Okinawa, against two punishing assaults conducted in swift succession by the Navy and Marine Corps.

Facing near-certain defeat, however, the Japanese calculus on losses had changed in the fall of 1944. The Japanese forces, benefiting from their knowledge of the rugged terrain and determined to go down fighting, wreaked havoc on the American landings. "Although the American public was only vaguely aware of the new tactics," writes one historian of the campaign, "the war in the western Pacific had entered a new phase that increased the cost of a continued American advance." The Japanese knew they were going to lose but intended to bleed the Allies as much as possible before they did.

In January 1945, MacArthur began his assault on the island of Luzon, the home of the Filipino capital. Equipped with an impressive force of the Sixth and Seventh Armies, supported by the Navy's 7th Fleet, MacArthur's troops drove into the heart of the island. The Americans held considerable advantages, especially when it came to conventional fighting in fields and plains in the lowlands. But the Japanese strategy of attrition proved far more effective—and bloody—in the mountains and cities that occupied most of the island.

The Japanese extracted a heavy toll on the Americans as they made their way through Luzon. It took MacArthur over a month to recapture the island, and the operation proved especially violent for civilians, with over one hundred thousand Filipinos dying in Manila as it was pounded by artillery. While the Japanese took far greater losses, the American forces suffered too. The Army alone sustained ten thousand casualties in taking back the island, and, in the Navy's first major confrontation with the kamikaze forces, twenty-seven ships were lost or damaged in just three particularly violent days of fighting. But while the Japanese defense at Luzon had been fierce and demoralizing, inflicting outsize casualties on the American forces, it did little to change the strategic balance in the region. By the end of the month, MacArthur had made good on his promise: he had returned to the Philippines, and he had liberated it.

Over the next four months, US forces faced the same ferocity in the final push to capture Iwo Jima and Okinawa, both deemed operationally critical for a final invasion of the Japanese mainland given their proximity to Tokyo. Iwo Jima, remembered by those who fought there as an otherworldly island of volcanoes and jagged rock, was the site of a particularly fierce engagement for the Navy and Marine forces. The Japanese used an extensive network of cave and bunker defenses, which proved nearly impossible to root out with air and naval attacks, and went down fighting. As one historian notes, "Japanese defenders would hold their positions and fire their weapons until they died." And, indeed, the desperate Japanese forces inflicted significant damage on the Marine infantry and ground forces fighting to take the island, with six thousand Marines killed and another twenty thousand wounded in the monthlong campaign. Victory at Iwo Jima was deemed operationally critical in order to secure a base for American airpower, but the tremendous costs of taking the island became and remain notorious.

Even at the end, there were no easy victories to be found in the Pacific campaign.

No one felt the desperation and devastation of combat in the Pacific, however, more than the prisoners of war who had been captured in the opening salvos of the conflict almost four years earlier. "One night as I lay in my bed," wrote Dorothy Still, one of the Navy nurses who remained in Japanese captivity in the Philippines for the duration of the war, "I drowsily became aware that I wasn't breathing, and thought I could no longer hear the pulsating sound of my heart. I must be dead, I felt," adding, "What a pleasant feeling."

For the Army and Navy nurses that had been interned in the

Philippines, the final days of the war were the most desperate. Hearing news of the American invasion, the Japanese captors became more brutal, taking what they could before they became prisoners themselves and exacting preemptive vengeance on the prisoners that remained.

But the American captives knew that an invasion was underway. They heard the distant gunfire and increasingly saw Allied planes flying overhead, scoping out the camps for an eventual rescue raid. Even with the prospect of being liberated, however, the prisoners had little left to give. With ever smaller rations and rescue still weeks away, they struggled to hold on.

The prisoners also feared, with good reason, that the Japanese would kill them if and when the liberators arrived. As months passed after the first glimpse of American bombers in the skies over Manila, the nurses in captivity wondered whether they would be among the last, tragic casualties of the war.

MacArthur had never stopped thinking of the thousands of men and women he had left behind in the spring of 1942 and, although it was taking longer than he hoped for, the liberation of the Japanese prison camps in Manila topped his list of objectives. The initial liberation effort focused first on the largest internment camp, Santo Tomas, where the Army nurses had spent most of their captivity. Ultimately, the dangerous raid was a success: on February 3, two columns of infantry with tank, howitzer, and air support overran the gates at Santo Tomas and liberated nearly four thousand prisoners, among them over sixty Army nurses.

Dorothy Still, however, needed to wait three more weeks to be freed. In 1943, the Japanese had transferred Still from Santo Tomas to Los Baños, the camp where she and over two thousand prisoners remained for the duration of the war. But Los Baños was located just outside Manila, and rescuing the prisoners there required a raiding force to get the prisoners out and needed to be carefully planned and executed.

Meanwhile, the conditions continued to deteriorate at Still's camp. The Japanese guards, spooked when the initial invasion force arrived, had left the prisoners for nearly a week—during which time the camp administrators had declared the prison "Camp Freedom"—only to return and attempt to reimpose order. The prisoners, anticipating liberation, became less compliant. It was a tense combination.

On the morning of February 23, Still was feeding one of the infants who had been born into captivity at Los Baños with a mix of powdered milk and water, since her mother was too ill to care for the baby. The bottle she used to feed the girl, "little princess," as she called her, had nearly disintegrated. "Careful there, little lady," whispered Still, as she tried to keep the baby warm and placed her over her shoulder to burp her.

Army nurses held captive in Santo Tomas are reunited with their colleagues. **Courtesy National Archives, photo no. 204951909.**

Moments later, with the sun just coming over the horizon, the American GIs arrived by air and by truck. Still, terrified by the noise, gripped the baby close to her chest and peered out the window to see what was going on. She had little time to take in the scene. The Americans had to move quickly. First, they picked off the Japanese forces on the base, then assembled the internees into a line, burned the barracks, and hurried to the nearest beach, where trucks awaited to take Still and her fellow escapees across a small bay to Allied territory, all before the nearby Japanese hold-outs took notice of the commotion.

Still, rail thin and bone-tired, also worked quickly. Seeing that the injured and disabled were being evacuated first, she changed the baby girl into a fresh diaper, wrapped her in an extra blanket, and tucked a bottle of powdered milk into her swaddle. She passed the infant off to her mother and began to collect her own things.

By the time Still and the rest of the captives had walked the mile and a half to the landing beach, three years of exhaustion and desperation had settled deeply into their bones. They could barely register what awaited them on the other side of the water—a clean change of clothes, new shoes, and real food. Still, assured that the little girl had made it onto one of the first evacuation ships, was now waiting her turn to make the final escape. She nestled herself under a nearby tree and, lulled by the sound of American C-47s overhead, fell asleep.

At that same moment, hundreds of miles away, Mary Sears and the women assigned to the Hydro office were working late. They, too, were exhausted, as they often were, working well past the end of the normal workday. But they knew there was no time to rest. Unlike for Still, the war was not over for them. They knew the Navy's most senior commanders would be relying on their analysis the following morning to make operational decisions about the next several weeks. Blinking hard to wake themselves up, the WAVES at Hydro—Sears first among them—straightened their uniforms and got back to work.

The question that consumed Sears and her colleagues in the waning days of the war was predicting the surf conditions on Hagushi Beach, the preferred location for the landing of sixty thousand American soldiers and Marines that was planned for early April— the first day of the Battle of Okinawa. The Navy would only proceed if Sears and her team assessed that the surf would be calm enough to support the landing. Just before the scheduled assault, Sears's team delivered their verdict: the ocean would be calm, and the landing could proceed. On the appointed morning, the sea bore out their prediction near perfectly, and the waves lapped calmly against the sides of American ships as they approached the island.

The Japanese defense of Okinawa extracted a high toll on the American forces sent there to take it. In nearly three months of fighting on the island, the losses were staggering. The 5th Fleet suffered 10,000 casualties and massive damage, while the Tenth Army alone suffered over 7,000 dead and 32,000 wounded. It was a violent and tragic battle, but Sears and her team helped ensure it ended in an Allied victory.

Only months before the Battle of Okinawa, Ann Baumgartner, having settled into her assignment as a test pilot for the Army Air Forces, sat on a busy runway at Wright Field going through her preflight checklist. She and her copilot were preparing for a long flight. Seated in the cockpit of the B-29 Superfortress, they had been given the unenviable task of taking the plane for a long-range test. This meant hours of aimless flying at thirty thousand feet, monitoring the instruments for anything unusual.

The B-29 was an enormous plane. Modeled after the B-17 Flying Fortress, it was capable of longer ranges and heavier payloads to meet the combat demands of the Pacific theater and was already being deployed with great success abroad. But Baumgartner's test flight of the B-29 had a very specific purpose: the Army Air Forces wanted to know if the plane could handle a nine-ton bomb load, packaged into an area of about ten feet by two feet for long-duration flights. In their tests of the plane, Baumgartner and her crew encountered few problems carrying dummy payload, aside from the occasional overheated engine. If anything, she found the whole ordeal a bit boring. But, as always, Baumgartner reveled in the flying, in watching "the light over the land turn pink and then fade into darkness."

Months later, on August 6, 1945, another pilot, Lieutenant Colonel Paul Tibbets, sat in the cockpit of a silver B-29 carrying a payload with nearly identical dimensions to the one that Baumgartner tested months earlier. Tibbets had worked over the preceding weeks with Baumgartner and the other test pilots at Wright Field to manage some of the quirks of the plane, and made a few modifications to address its hot engine. Given the nature of his upcoming mission, Tibbets needed to feel completely confident the plane would perform to the necessary specifications, and the team at Wright Field ensured he had the information he required.

The morning of his mission, however, Tibbets made one last small change to the bomber: he had the plane's name—shared by his mother, Enola Gay—painted below the cockpit window. Then Tibbets took off from a runway on the small island of Tinian and flew the B-29 over the Japanese port city of Hiroshima, where he dropped his payload, "Little Boy," the first atomic bomb used in human history. Days later, the Japanese communicated their intention to surrender.

Like most Americans, Baumgartner was probably at home when she heard the news of the atomic bomb being dropped. The WASP had been deactivated, she was no longer flying Army Air Force planes, and her life had transformed considerably since leaving Wright Field. She was now married and focused on building a home. But when she heard about the Allies' final victory in the Pacific, Baumgartner would have known, more than most, exactly what it took to get there.

Over the next several months, the remaining women of the

WAC, WAVES, SPARS, and MCWR were released from duty. With their discharge papers in hand, they arrived at processing centers around the country, and were unceremoniously returned to the lives they had left behind. Some women were thrilled to be going home, others had mixed emotions, and still others never looked back.

Waiting in line for the official discharge papers, many of the women were given an informational pamphlet that provided instructions for their formal separation from the military. Inside the front cover was a short commendation:

"A job accomplished, a victory won."

Servicewomen stand at attention in front of the Capitol. **Courtesy National Archives, photo no. 74243676.**

# EPILOGUE

# "GOOD SOLDIER"

ON MAY 19, 1995, DOROTHY STRATTON SAT AT HER typewriter. Retired and living in West Lafayette during her twilight years, she took an exasperated breath and tapped out a note to Richard Holtz, the editor of her local paper, the *Lafayette Journal Courier*.

Stratton complimented Holtz for his comprehensive coverage of World War II in a recent issue marking the fiftieth anniversary of the war's conclusion. But, she added, he had missed one thing. "If there was mention . . . of the American women who served in uniform during the war," she wrote, "I missed it." Stratton reminded him that the women who served had all been volunteers and that they performed so well that the military services had requested permission to retain them after the war. "I do not mean to imply that your lack of coverage was intentional," she concluded, adding, "I feel sure that it was not."

Stratton's frustration was well founded. In the fifty years after she was selected to lead the Coast Guard's first women's program, and since, much of the story of women in World War II has been forgotten. The fault lies with the rest of us. It should not fall to the veterans of any war—least of all this one—to remind us of their service.

Beyond having this basic obligation, however, every American also stands to gain from fully grasping the contributions of women during this watershed moment in American history. Providing this more nuanced portrayal of the war has been the singular goal of this book, and if reading about these women deepened your understanding of World War II, then it has succeeded.

But the story of women in World War II does not end with the cessation of hostilities. The postwar lives and careers of many of the women veterans of World War II are a testament to what happens when women are given new skills and new tools, and the opportunity to unleash their talents and ambitions on the world. Often, what happens next is extraordinary.

The female directors who led the women's program, for instance, reached exceptional professional heights for the time. Oveta Culp Hobby, director of the WAC and arguably the highest-profile woman in the US armed forces, became a close friend and confidante to Eisenhower after the war. When he was elected to the presidency in 1952, he appointed Hobby to lead the Department of Health, Education, and Welfare, where she oversaw the distribution of the polio vaccine. Her exemplary tenure was marred by the controversy caused after process errors led to the deaths of several children, but she remained a fixture of the national political and social establishment until her death in 1995.

Mildred McAfee, director of the WAVES, returned to Wellesley College at the end of the war, where she continued as its president until 1948. She oversaw a critical period in the history of women's higher education, even as she became more involved in the ecumenical movement in the United States. After leaving Wellesley, she became one of the foremost advocates for the ordination of women in the Presbyterian church.

Similarly, Dorothy Stratton, director of the SPARS, returned to Purdue University and joined forces with her longtime friend and companion, Helen Schleman, the dean of women at the university, to expand and manage women's enrollment. Stratton later became the executive director of the Girl Scouts of America, where she remained an outspoken advocate of expanding opportunities for young women and girls in the United States.

Ruth Cheney Streeter, director of the MCWR, returned to a quiet life in New Jersey but remained a fixture of her community, participating in the 1947 New Jersey constitutional convention and serving on the state's Veterans' Service Committee.

Jackie Cochran, director of the WASP, who had been forced to demobilize her unit in 1944, never gave up on integrating women fliers into the Air Force and she became an Air Force reservist after the war, retiring as a colonel. Cochran also continued to be a trailblazer in the era of the jet plane, and by 1953 she had set new speed records in a Sabre jet over the deserts of California and became the first woman to break the sound barrier. "I was opposed to women's records as such," she would remember of her jet flights, adding, "I wanted to break men's records only." Later, she personally helped finance the Mercury 13 program, an initiative to prove that women could successfully meet the NASA standards for space travel.

While the directors of the women's programs went on to have some of the more prominent postwar careers, other women veterans achieved less public but still noteworthy professional successes. Mary Sears's oversight of the Navy's Oceanographic Unit laid the foundation for its transformation into the Naval Oceanographic Office (NAVOCEANO), currently headed by a rear admiral and responsible for providing the Navy with the same type of vital intelligence Sears's unit provided in World War II. After the war, Sears continued her work as a senior scientist at the Woods Hole Oceanographic Institution and was widely regarded as one of the most influential forces in the development of the field of oceanographic studies. For her groundbreaking work, she received honorary degrees from Mount Holyoke College and the University of Massachusetts, Dartmouth.

Charity Adams, the commander of the 6888th Central Postal

Directory Battalion, received a master's degree from Ohio State University and became an institution in her community of Dayton, Ohio. She frequently spoke about her work with the Six Triple Eight and was a beacon of hope for generations of Black military women. In 2022, Congress awarded her unit a long-overdue Congressional Gold Medal, and, in the same year, the United States Naming Commission, tasked with providing the Department of Defense with name recommendations for military bases that commemorate the nation's values, advised that Fort Lee, Virginia, be renamed in Adams's honor.

Susan Ahn, after spending the war training naval aviators in flying and gunnery as a WAVES officer, was transferred to naval intelligence at the end of the war. She would spend the next ten years working for the National Security Agency on top-secret defense projects, along with many women veterans who successfully made the transition into the civil service.

Other women's veterans of World War II returned home and became pillars of their communities in the postwar years. Millie Corbett, for instance, worked for the rest of her career as a civil servant and became a community leader in Howard County, Maryland. In the last year of her life, Corbett, who married and became Millie Bailey, continued her tradition of sending hundreds of care packages to soldiers serving overseas, distributing almost 250 of the renowned "Bailey's Bundles" in 2021. At her funeral several months later, every pew of the church was filled with friends, colleagues, and admirers paying their final respects to the beloved, 104-year-old "Ms. B."

Ann Baumgartner's first flight in a jet plane was one of her last as a military test pilot, and she spent the rest of the war starting a family with her husband, the designer of the F-82 Mustang. She traveled extensively after the war, sailing the world and writing about her adventures, and continued to fly for United Airlines. Later in life she became a passionate advocate for environmental causes, documenting the impact of climate change as a journalist for many years.

Joy Lemmon, who had come a long way since bemusedly staring up at the escalator in Penn Station, remained an institution in her southern Illinois community, where she dedicated years of her life to sewing and donating dresses for girls living in poverty. What started as a hobby soon ballooned into a calling, and by her ninety-seventh birthday, Joy had sewn and donated ten thousand dresses globally.

From all of these stories, a clear theme emerges: almost without exception, the women veterans of World War II continued their service in some form, whether in the highest levels of government, in their communities, or in their families, for the rest of their lives.

While the individual achievements of these women were undeniably trailblazing, the most lasting impact of the women who served in World War II belongs to their collective legacy. With some notable exceptions, including Tanya Roth's recently published study, *Her Cold War*, few histories have fully captured the extent of their contribution in the postwar era. This is unfortunate, since the legacy left by these women is as interesting and as important as the experiences that created it.

The seeds of this legacy began in the immediate aftermath of Allied victory. As leaders of a superpower now in competition with the Soviet Union, and with occupation forces in Germany and Japan, American policymakers decided soon after the war that they needed to maintain a substantial peacetime military to support American commitments abroad. But the end of the wartime draft left military commanders facing an almost identical puzzle to the one that had confronted them at the start of World War II: how to supply the manpower for their sustained, expanded commitments around the globe.

Eisenhower, who succeed Marshall as Army chief of staff, again saw the writing on the wall. This time, he knew immediately where to look to meet the manpower requirements of the postwar era: women had been indispensable in supporting the combat operations he led during the war, and he was certain they could again serve their country in critical ways.

The bureaucratic challenge facing Eisenhower after the war, however, was that women had only been authorized to serve in the military "for the duration of the war and six months." Staring down this deadline, he directed his staff to draft legislation authorizing women to serve permanently in peacetime programs. By 1947, the Army general staff had pushed its proposed legislation through the Senate and House Armed Services Committees with the enthusiastic backing of the secretary of defense, James Forrestal, and the senior-ranking commanders of every military service.

By the time congressional hearings on the legislation began, Eisenhower had left the military for the presidency of Columbia University. As the most vocal advocate of the proposal, however, he felt obliged to return to Washington to provide testimony emphatically supporting the permanent integration of women into the armed forces. He testified that his experience in World War II had convinced him that women could be used productively and efficiently in the military establishment. "When this project was proposed in the beginning of the war, like most old soldiers, I was violently against it," he stated. "I thought a tremendous number of difficulties would occur," he continued, but noted that "none of that occurred." Facing down an equally perplexing manpower shortage, he argued, Congress should approve the legislation. The military service chiefs agreed and forcefully supported the legislation in their own testimonies.

Congress, however, was not easily convinced, and a contentious debate ensued for almost two years. As it had during World War II, the argument centered on the official classification of the women. Many congressmen balked at the prospect of making women a permanent part of the regular forces and, instead, pushed for the inclusion of women in the reserves. Military leaders, on the other hand, knew that such an arrangement would backfire, as it had in the early days of the WAC. They leveraged their prior experience in litigating this debate with Congress and were prepared to forcefully hit back against the lawmakers' arguments that a reserve force would be sufficient. Their vigorous and tenacious support of the bill won the day.

In June 1948, the Women's Armed Services Integration Act was signed into law by President Harry Truman. The act formally authorized women to serve in both the regular and reserve armed forces of the United States during peacetime. It was an extraordinary turning point for the women in the military, recognizing women as equal contributors to national defense, and it rested on the shoulders of the women who served in World War II.

But, as was the case in World War II, the legislation imposed considerable limits on the degree of this integration. Women were explicitly barred from serving in combat roles, barred from attaining full command authority over men, and barred from receiving any rank above colonel or captain. Women under twenty-one were required to have parental permission before signing up for the military, while men needed permission only if they were under eighteen. Women were also employed by the military at will, meaning they could be dismissed for any reason, including if they became pregnant. Finally, the legislation stipulated that military women could not claim men or children as their dependents without extensive paperwork demonstrating their spouses' incapacitation. Though the act marked a moment of extraordinary progress, it would take decades for these limitations to be lifted.

In 1973, however, the moment for challenging these restrictions had arrived, and the dependency policy in particular came under criticism. The policy was so egregious, critics argued, that it could make the perfect test case for legal action against discrimination on the basis of sex. The critics were right. The regulation was challenged in one of the most pivotal sex-discrimination cases in American legal history, *Frontiero v. Richardson*.

In the case, Sharron Frontiero, a lieutenant in the Air Force, filed suit against the federal government. Her legal team, led by Joseph J. Levin Jr. of the Southern Poverty Law Center—who was joined by an up-and-coming lawyer from the American Civil Liberties Union, Ruth Bader Ginsburg—argued before the Supreme Court that Frontiero was entitled to the same benefits for her husband that were provided to the spouses of male personnel, including housing allowances, medical benefits, and dental benefits. The court decided in favor of Frontiero by an 8 to 1 majority, and the precedent paved the way for significantly greater workplace protections for women.

Like so many pieces of twentieth-century history, the case is a testament to the ripple effects of women's service in World War II. Though frequently overlooked, the women of the greatest generation, and especially the women veterans of World War II, are often the ultimate source of some of the most important victories of the contemporary women's movement. It is time they get their deserved credit for this contribution too.

The conventional view of women's history, however, often excludes the women of the greatest generation from its narrative, implying that they had little part to play in the march toward women's equality. The contributions of the women of World War II, and especially military women, have often been overlooked or ignored by generations of feminists that came after them.

This is especially disappointing given that, time and time again, women in uniform fought the first battles of the women's liberation movement. Before Betty Friedan wrote *The Feminine Mystique*, the

US military published *Sex Hygiene*. Before Gloria Steinem started *Ms.* magazine, the Navy started the *WAVES News Letter*. And before Mary Tyler Moore donned capris, the Army Air Forces allowed its women pilots to wear pants. Long before the women's liberation movement existed, the women of World War II changed the way Americans thought about the role of women in the workplace, the nature and content of femininity, homosexuality, and intersectionality.

To be sure, it took the work of future generations to advance the gains of the women who served in World War II, but, wittingly or not, the women of World War II forever changed the place of women in American society. Quietly, diligently, and persistently, the military women of World War II brought the women's movement into the modern era.

Too often, this essential contribution has been forgotten or, worse, willfully ignored. For decades, it has fallen to women like Dorothy Stratton to write her local editor asking him, gently but firmly, to remember those women who served and the paths they paved for all of us.

On a dreary gray day in March 2012, a motorcade made its way to Coast Guard Island in Alameda, California. A fierce spring storm had descended on the artificial island, and rain whipped across the hundreds of bystanders lining the motorcade's route. The weather was brutal, especially for California, with gusting winds forcing many of the typical celebrations indoors.

The unusual downpours, however, did not diminish the occasion for the rain-soaked observers. A new Coast Guard ship was being commissioned for service, and First Lady Michelle Obama had made the trip from Washington to launch the newest, most versatile, and largest cutter into service. A First Lady had never sponsored such a ship, and the Coast Guard had pulled out all the stops for the event. Two years earlier, Obama had broken a bottle of champagne across the bow of the cutter and, given her unprecedented sponsorship of the vessel, she was now on hand to send it out to sea.

By the time the ceremony began, the rain had ebbed slightly, and hundreds of spectators perked up as Obama made her way onto the stage. Most of the ceremony went as planned, with the pomp and circumstance on display in full force. The commandant of the Coast Guard, Admiral Robert Papp Jr., made introductory remarks; the Coast Guard band played; and the ship's crew stood at attention, seemingly unbothered as the pouring rain soaked through their uniforms. When the time came for Obama to deliver her remarks, she effusively praised the Coast Guard. She noted what an honor it was to be the first First Lady to sponsor a Coast Guard vessel, and added that she brought her daughters, Sasha and Malia, to witness the occasion.

At the end of the ceremony, Papp put on his white gloves, called the crew to attention, and placed the ship in commission with the invocation, "May God bless and guide this cutter and all who sail her." With that, he turned to Obama and asked her to bring the ship to life, the final formality in getting it underway. Obama stepped up to the podium and gave the traditional command: "Officers and crew of the US Coast Guard Cutter *Stratton*," she said into the microphone, "lay aboard and bring our cutter to life."

And so, almost twenty years after Stratton had penned her frustrated letter to the editor of the *Lafayette Journal Courier*, one hundred guardsmen shouted "Aye, aye" and marched aboard the US Coast Guard Cutter *Dorothy Stratton*.

Obama, reflecting on the significance of Stratton's contribution and legacy, noted how much she regretted never having the privilege of meeting her: "Like most of you, I wasn't fortunate enough to know Captain Stratton personally," she remarked. "But I have come to know her story."

First Lady Michelle Obama at the commissioning of USCG Cutter *Stratton*.
**Courtesy US Department of Defense.**

# ACKNOWLEDGMENTS

My first and greatest thanks are reserved for the women that served in World War II, and especially the women whom I met and interviewed while researching this book: Vivian "Millie" Bailey, Merle Caples, Joy Casino, Jessie Dunbar, Helen Garth, and Beth Leeper. I was assisted in arranging and conducting these interviews by a cast of their friends and family, who are caring for these incredible women as they age and safeguarding their stories along the way, including Amy Caples; Gloriane Garth; Vikki Garth; Carol Montgomery; Captain Wanda Riddle, US Navy (retired); Patti Ryan; and Jean Schreiber. I am also grateful to Laurie and Fred Iskowitz, family of Ethel Small; and Colonel Edna W. Cummings, US Army (retired), and Master Sergeant Elizabeth Helm-Frazier, US Army (retired), friends of Deloris Ruddock, for offering their insights into the lives and experiences of both women. Although Ms. Small and Ms. Ruddock passed away before I could meet with them, their stories still greatly informed my understanding of women's experiences in World War II.

In the absence of firsthand accounts, the close friends and family of women veterans have also provided some of the richest material for this book. Children, nieces, nephews, and grandchildren have been among the most enthusiastic stewards of their relatives' stories and generously allowed me into their homes and family histories. Phil Burnham, Nan Denton, Debra Frankel, Kathy Gonzales, Elissa Weidaw, Liz Hansen, Mary Lardinois, Liz Rosenberg, and Robert Trisciuzzi all provided answers to seemingly endless questions about their loved ones. They brought to life the stories of veterans Ruth Burnham, Mabel Johnson, Ruth Potier, Freda Rosenberg, Adele Mary Sabbagh, Mary Sears, and Evelyn Weidaw. The experiences of women veterans are the heartbeat of this book, and I am both grateful and deeply honored that so many people were willing to share their stories with me. Talking and, often, laughing with these exceptional women and their families has been the greatest joy of this project.

In addition to the interviews I conducted with veterans and their families, I also benefited from memoirs and oral histories of women veterans who served in World War II. These books and recordings are utterly transporting and include many extraordinary anecdotes. Military and archival institutions, including the Betty H. Carter Women Veterans Historical Project at the University of North Carolina, Greensboro, and the Veterans History Project maintained by the American Folklife Center at the Library of Congress, have also done the painstaking work of recording and digitizing many of these stories in online oral history repositories, which proved extremely valuable during my research.

The narrative of this book is also a product of several months of research at archives around the country. This would have been impossible but for the patience and expertise of the archivists at these institutions. Lauren Theodore at the National Archives and Research Administration, College Park, went above and beyond the call of duty to assist me in locating documents during COVID-related archival closures and found several hidden treasures that are featured in these pages. Several university archivists were also essential in helping me access the individual papers of women veterans, including Traci Patterson at the Woodson Research Center at the Fondren Library at Rice University; Katey Watson and Tiffany Eakin at the Purdue University Archives and Special Collections; Rebecca Goldman and Sara Ludovissy at the Wellesley College Archives; Sarah Hutcheon and Jennifer Fauxsmith at the Schlesinger Library, Harvard Radcliffe Institute; Kate Long at the Smith College Special Collections; Leslie Fields and Debbie Richards of the Mount Holyoke College Archives and Special Collections; Shelia Bickle and Kimberly Johnson at the Woman's Collection, Texas Woman's University; and Myles Crowley at the Department of Distinctive Collections, MIT Libraries. Many of these archivists went out of their way to supply me with documents during the pandemic, and I am extremely grateful for their efforts and assistance during a difficult time. Sandi Fox, Megan Casey, and Christian Higgins at the Histories and Archives Division, Naval History and Heritage Command, were also essential in granting access to the Navy's official histories of its women's programs, and the Atwood House Museum Archives at the Chatham Historical Society also provided helpful information on Unit 21 of the SPARS posted there.

Since the bulk of this research was conducted in the midst of a global pandemic, I am especially grateful for the efforts of these and other archivists who came into the office to digitize folders for me and many others. While that work was surely tedious, it provided a critical foundation on which I could build when we were able to return to the archives in person. These archivists are the shepherds of our national memory, and it has been a pleasure to work with them.

Often, American women veterans have themselves taken up the mantle of keeping this history alive. I have found some of my richest source material in the histories of women's service written by other veterans, and these extraordinary women have done the equally important work of encouraging women who served in World War II to share their stories at churches, schools, libraries, and any other community organizations that show an interest. I am deeply indebted to the work of this community, both formal and informal, which ensures that the stories of their forebearers are honored.

The individual services of the US military have also done considerable work to record official histories of their servicewomen during World War II. The US Army Center for Military History has sponsored several excellent studies of women's service, including an incredibly comprehensive history of the WAC by Mattie Treadwell, as well as monographs on the Army Nurse Corps. The Naval History and Heritage Command also holds several comprehensive histories of WAVES and MCWR, written in the immediate aftermath of the war, which are very useful to those looking for a first draft of their history.

The stark reality for anyone interested in this slice of American history is that we are losing veterans of World War II every day. According to the US Department of Veterans Affairs, fewer than two hundred thousand veterans of this war are still alive today—and that number will be cut in half in less than two years. The youngest of this small, and shrinking, group are in their late nineties and the oldest are well over one hundred. This reality is even more pronounced when it comes to women veterans of World War II, where the numbers are dwindling. Just in the course of my research, three of the women whom I contacted—Millie Bailey, Ethel Small, and Deloris Ruddock—passed away.

Even more commonly, many of the requests I sent to women veterans were met with apologetic emails from loved ones, noting that their mother or grandmother or aunt was struggling with memory issues and would not be able to discuss her experiences. This should serve as an important reminder to all of us: if you have the privilege of knowing a woman veteran of this war—or any war—take a moment to ask her about her service, and then listen carefully to what she tells you.

My final thanks are reserved for friends and colleagues who supported my efforts and considerably improved this book. My agent, Peter McGuigan, has shown unrivaled enthusiasm for this project—and my ability to complete it—at every turn, and patiently guided me through each step of the process. Peter Hubbard, my editor at Mariner Books, has been a wonderful collaborator and sounding board, and working with him made this book sharper, more readable, and also much more fun to write.

Janis Rothbard carefully and doggedly read every page of this book, correcting some of its more egregious errors and softening many of its hard edges. Lieutenant Commander Erik Sand, US Navy Reserve; Barry Posen; Jim Steinberg; Veronica Voll; and Colonel Stephane Wolfgeher, US Air Force (retired), also read the manuscript with great care and offered helpful feedback and corrections that greatly improved the story.

My parents, Jane Etish-Andrews and Kevin Andrews, encouraged me to pursue this book project with their trademark enthusiasm and confidence, for which I am—and have always been—extremely grateful. I am also indebted to many friends for their steadfast support as I wrote, and I am especially thankful for the levity and encouragement of Alice Graff, Amanda Harwood, and Rebecca Lissner. Finally, Jacquie Tuyishme helped me find the time necessary to finish this book, and brings joy and order to our home daily.

My husband and partner, David, supported me throughout this entire process and provided exactly the right encouragement at exactly the right moments. This book would not exist without his patient, persistent belief in me. For that, and so much more, I am exceptionally lucky to have him in my life.

Lastly, my deepest thanks are reserved for my son, Charles, since his arrival ensured that I completed the manuscript on time. I hope that one day he will read this book and be inspired by the women found in its pages, and proud of the woman who wrote them.

# SOURCES

## VETERAN AND FAMILY INTERVIEWS

Vivian "Millie" [Corbett] Bailey*
Phil Burnham
Merle Jean [Selma] Caples*
Joy [Lemmon] Casino*
Nan Denton
Jessie [Kontrabecki] Dunbar*
Debra Frankel
Helen [Hayden] Garth*
Kathy Gonzales
Liz Hansen
Laurie Iskowitz
Fred Iskowitz
Mary Lardinois
Beth [Montgomery] Leeper*
Wanda Riddle
Liz Rosenberg
Robert Trisciuzzi
Elissa Weidaw

## ARCHIVAL INSTITUTIONS AND PERSONAL PAPERS

National Archives and Research Administration, College Park
Woodson Research Center, Fondren Library, Rice University
    Papers of Oveta Culp Hobby

---

* Served in World War II. Maiden names referenced in text are included here in brackets.

Purdue University Archives and Special Collections
    Papers of Helen Schleman
    Papers of Beverly Stone
    Papers of Dorothy Stratton
Wellesley College Archives
    Papers of Mildred McAfee
Schlesinger Library, Harvard Radcliffe Institute
    Papers of Bertha Clark
    Papers of Winifred Quick Collins
    Papers of Ernestine R. Etienne
    Papers of Katherine M. Keene
    Papers of Elizabeth Reynard
    Papers of Ruth Streeter
Mount Holyoke College Archives and Special Collections
    War Collection
History and Archives Division, Naval History and Heritage Command
    History of Hydrographic Office
    History of MCWR
    History of WAVES
Atwood House Museum and Archives
Department of Distinctive Collections, MIT Libraries
Dwight D. Eisenhower Presidential Library
    WASP Collection
Texas Woman's University
    Women's Collection
Franklin D. Roosevelt Presidential Library
Betty H. Carter Women Veterans Historical Project, University of North
    Carolina, Greensboro
Veterans History Project, American Folklife Center, the Library of
    Congress

# NOTES

## EPIGRAPH

vii  *"Our debt"*: Harry S. Truman, Transcript of First Address to
Congress, April 16, 1945, https://millercenter.org/the-presidency
/presidentiasl-speeches/april-16-1945-first-speech-congress.


## CONTENTS

viii  *Chapter titles are drawn:* For more, see "World War II Posters, 1942–
1945" Record Group 44: Records of the Office of Government
Reports, March 9, 1943–September 15, 1945, National Archives and
Records Administration, College Park.


## PROLOGUE: "THANK YOU FOR EVEN THINKING OF ME"

1  *"Thank You for Even Thinking of Me"*: "World War II Posters, 1942–
1945" Record Group 44: Records of the Office of Government
Reports, March 9, 1943–September 15, 1945, National Archives and
Records Administration, College Park.

1  *"The future of women"*: Charity Adams Earley, *One Woman's Army:
A Black Officer Remembers the WAC* (College Station: Texas A&M
University Press, 1995), ix.

1  *"Oh my god"*: Unless otherwise noted, the sections on Merle Caples's
experience in the Marine Corps are drawn primarily from Merle
[Selma] Caples, Interview with Author, Virtual, March 16, 2021.

2  *"My memory's"*: Beth [Leeper] Montgomery, Interview with Author,
Virtual, August 24, 2021.

2  *"Thank you":* Jessie [Kontrabecki] Dunbar, Interview with Author, Virtual, August 2, 2021.

### INTRODUCTION:
### "AMERICA WILL BE AS STRONG AS HER WOMEN"

7  *"Would I always":* The recollections that follow about Ann Baumgartner's life are drawn primarily from her memoir, Ann B. Carl, *A WASP Among Eagles: A Woman Military Test Pilot in World War II,* ill. ed. (Washington, D.C.: Smithsonian Books, 2010), 12.

8  *"something with adventure":* Ibid., 19.

8  *"Would I really want":* Ibid., 19.

8  *"a colorful":* Ibid., 5.

10  GERMAN ARMY: "German Army Attacks Poland," *New York Times,* September 1, 1939, https://timesmachine.nytimes.com/times machine/1939/09/01/issue.html.

10  *"the finest soldier":* Robert E. Sherwood, Wilson Miscamble, and Irwin F. Gellman, *Roosevelt and Hopkins: An Intimate History,* 60th anniversary ed. (New York: Enigma Books, 2008), 130.

11  *The war:* George Catlett Marshall, *The Papers of George Catlett Marshall,* vol. 2, *"We Cannot Delay," July 1, 1939–December 6, 1941,* ed. Larry I. Bland, Clarence N. Wunderlin Jr., and Sharon Ritenour Stevens (Baltimore: Johns Hopkins University Press, 1986), 47.

12  *"ranked approximately seventeenth":* Christopher Gabel, *The US Army GHQ Maneuvers of 1941,* CMH Pub 70–41–1 (Washington, D.C.: US Army Center of Military History, 1991), 8.

13  *"The women walked":* Carl, *WASP Among Eagles,* 20.

13  *"This was a time":* Ibid., 22.

13  *"Get all of this":* Marshall, *Papers of George Catlett Marshall,* 2:210.

14  *Given the deteriorating circumstances:* Forrest C. Pogue, *George C. Marshall: Interviews and Reminiscences,* ed. Larry I. Bland, rev. ed. (Lexington, Va.: George C. Marshall Research Foundation, 1991), 329.

14  *"Recalling that a man":* Ibid., 330.

14  *"I don't know":* Ibid.

15  *The United States also produced:* Allan R. Millett, Peter Maslowski, and William B. Feis, *For the Common Defense: A Military History of the United States from 1607 to 2012,* 3rd ed. (New York: Free Press, 2012), 388; "War Production," *The War,* PBS, accessed April 15, 2022, https://www.pbs.org/kenburns/the-war/war-production.

16  *"everything begged"*: Marshall, *Papers of George Catlett Marshall*, 2:87.

16  *"If you want to determine"*: James F. Dunnigan, *How to Make War: A Comprehensive Guide to Modern Warfare in the Twenty-First Century*, 4th ed. (New York: William Morrow Paperbacks, 2003), 501.

17  *"We have spent"*: Franklin Delano Roosevelt, "Fireside Chat, May 26, 1940," Washington, D.C., May 26, 1940, https://www.presidency .ucsb.edu/documents/fireside-chat-10.

18  *"We are constantly improving"*: Ibid.

18  *"Personnel is our most"*: Marshall, *Papers of George Catlett Marshall*, 2:231.

19  *"he did wear"*: Carl, *WASP Among Eagles*, 22.

19  *"I shall learn"*: Ibid., 23.

## 1: "THE FIGHTING FILIPINOS"

23  *Dorothy Still:* Unless otherwise noted, the stories that follow in this chapter on Dorothy Still's experience in the Pacific are drawn primarily from her memoir, Dorothy Still Danner, *What a Way to Spend a War: Navy Nurse POWs in the Philippines* (Thorndike, Maine: G. K. Hall, 1997).

23  *"I loved to stand"*: Ibid., 30.

24  *"Formals and party dresses"*: Ibid.

24  *"A delightful setting"*: Ibid.

24  *"6 December 1941"*: Ibid., 41.

26  *"it would take"*: Douglas MacArthur, *Reminiscences* (Annapolis, Md.: Naval Institute Press, 2012), 102.

26  *"Washington had not"*: Ibid., 108.

26  *"offensive naval war"*: Marshall, *Papers of George Catlett Marshall*, 2:100.

27  *By late 1940:* Millett, Maslowski, and Feis, *For the Common Defense*, 371–72.

27  *"We stand to lose"*: Marshall, *Papers of George Catlett Marshall*, 2:360.

27  *"began an eleventh-hour"*: MacArthur, *Reminiscences*, 109.

27  *By December, over thirty thousand:* Louis Morton, *The Fall of the Philippines* (Washington, D.C.: US Army Center of Military History, 1953), 48, https://history.army.mil/html/books/005/5-2-1/CMH_Pub_5-2-1 .pdf.

27  *Along with this growth:* Morton, *The Fall of the Philippines*, 48.

28  *"meet to the fullest"*: Ibid.

28  *In fact, on December 7, 1941:* Ibid.

**28**   *"You girls ready":* Danner, *What a Way to Spend a War,* 54.

**29**   *"there was almost":* Barbara Brooks Tomblin, *G.I. Nightingales: The Army Nurse Corps in World War II* (Lexington: University Press of Kentucky, 2003), 22.

**29**   *The aircraft warning service:* Morton, *Fall of the Philippines,* 84.

**30**   *By the conclusion:* Ibid., 86.

**30**   *"The fact is":* Franklin D. Roosevelt, "Remarks to Cabinet Members and Legislative Leaders," December 7, 1941, Master Speech File, 1898–1945, Box 63, Franklin D. Roosevelt Presidential Library and Museum, http://www.fdrlibrary.marist.edu/_resources/images/msf /msfb0001.

**31**   *"Unmarried women":* Evelyn Monahan and Rosemary Neidel-Greenlee, *And If I Perish: Frontline U.S. Army Nurses in World War II* (New York: Anchor, 2004), 10.

**31**   *"suppress prostitution":* "Semi-Annual Report of Conditions in Leesville and Vernon Parish, Louisiana," n.d., RG 160, Entry NM-25 21, Army Service Forces, Director of Administration, Decimal Correspondence File, 1942–43, 333–383.6, Box 3, "Leesville, Louisiana," National Archives and Records Administration, College Park.

**32**   *"In the face of":* Monahan and Neidel-Greenlee, *And If I Perish,* 11.

**32**   *"I needed a job":* Edith A. Aynes, *From Nightingale to Eagle: An Army Nurse's History* (Englewood Cliffs, N.J.: Prentice-Hall, 1973), 37, 38.

**32**   *"Hold on":* MacArthur, *Reminiscences,* 142.

**33**   *St. Stephen's College massacre:* Charles G. Roland, "Massacre and Rape in Hong Kong: Two Case Studies Involving Medical Personnel and Patients," *Journal of Contemporary History* 32, No. 1 (1997): 53.

**34**   *Despite the risks:* Judith Bellafaire, *The Army Nurse Corps: A Commemoration of World War II Service,* Campaigns of World War II, CMH Pub 72–14 (Washington, D.C.: US Army Center of Military History, n.d.), 5.

**34**   *"Even all the rumors":* Walter Macdougall, *Angel of Bataan: The Life of a World War II Army Nurse in the War Zone and at Home,* 1st ed. (Camden, Maine: Down East Books, 2015), 41.

**35**   *Even after receiving:* Aynes, *From Nightingale to Eagle,* 178.

**35**   *"She knew":* Jonathan M. Wainwright, *General Wainwright's Story: The Account of Four Years of Humiliating Defeat, Surrender, and Captivity by General Jonathan M. Wainwright, Who Paid the Price of His Country's Unpreparedness,* ed. Robert Considine, 1st ed. (Garden City, N.J.: Doubleday, 1946), 109.

35 *"waiting for the American forces":* Danner, *What a Way to Spend a War*, 147.

## 2: "THEY CAN'T DO ANY MORE, BUT YOU CAN"

36 *BOMBS DEMOLISH:* Danner, *What a Way to Spend a War*, 142.

36 *CORREGIDOR FALLS:* Ibid., 144.

36 *JAPAN SET:* Ibid., 175.

37 *In the earliest days:* Gabel, *US Army GHQ Maneuvers of 1941*, 13–15.

37 *in 1941, the United States had produced:* Wesley Frank Craven and James Lea Cate, eds., *The Army Air Forces in World War II*, vol. 6 (Washington, D.C.: Office of Air Force History, 1983), 350.

37 *In almost the same period:* Allan R. Millett and Williamson Murray, eds., *Military Effectiveness, volume 3, The Second World War*, 2nd ed. (Cambridge: Cambridge University Press, 2010), 47.

38 *"Time is the dominant":* Marshall, *Papers of George Catlett Marshall*, 2:267.

38 *"American shipyards":* Mark R. Wilson, *Destructive Creation: American Business and the Winning of World War II* (Philadelphia: University of Pennsylvania Press, 2018), 55.

39 *By one account:* Alan Gropman, *The Big "L": American Logistics in World War II*, 1st ed. (Washington, D.C.: National Defense University Press, 1997), 78.

39 *In 1942:* Ibid., 79.

39 *Ultimately, women made up:* Ibid., 78.

40 *Combat support forces, such as:* John McGrath, "The Other End of the Spear: The Tooth to Tail Ratio (T3R) in Modern Military Operations," in *The Long War Series Occasional Paper 23* (Fort Leavenworth, Kans.: Combat Studies Institute Press, 2007).

41 *According to the 1940 census:* US Census Bureau. Decennial Census Official Publications, 1940. https://www.census.gov/programs-surveys/decennial-census/decade/decennial-publications.1940.html.

42 *Indeed, by the Army's:* Maurice Matloff, *Strategic Planning for Coalition Warfare, 1943–1944*, CMH Pub 1–4 (Washington, D.C.: US Army Center of Military History, 1959), 112.

42 *"There are a great":* George Catlett Marshall, *The Papers of George Catlett Marshall, vol. 3, "The Right Man for the Job," December 7, 1941–May 31, 1943*, ed. Larry I. Bland and Sharon Ritenour Stevens, 1st ed. (Baltimore: Johns Hopkins University Press, 1991), 484–85.

### 3: "I'M IN THIS WAR TOO!"

**43**  *"Women," wrote Eleanor Roosevelt:* Eleanor Roosevelt, "My Day," September 1, 1942, https://www2.gwu.edu/~erpapers/myday /displaydoc.cfm?_y=1942&_f=md056279.

**43**  *"I was eager":* Carl, *A WASP Among Eagles*, 29.

**43**  *"This is what":* Ibid., 25.

**44**  *"Nothing but fruitless":* Mattie E. Treadwell, *The Women's Army Corps, United States Army in World War II*: Special Studies (Washington, D.C.: US Army Center of Military History, 1991), 13.

**44**  *"no one seems":* Ibid., 15.

**45**  The Chicago Women's Defense League: Ibid., 16.

**45**  *"Women must play":* "Form Women's Ambulance Corps," *California Eagle*, March 13, 1941.

**45**  *"Knitting would drive":* Mary Hale, "Committing Crimes in Movies Takes Toll of Feminine Stars," *Lancaster New Era*, July 12, 1941.

**45**  *"provide some outlet":* Treadwell, *Women's Army Corps*, 16.

**46**  *"Take the women":* Ibid., 45.

**46**  *"I hope":* "Rogers, Edith Nourse, US House of Representatives: History, Art & Archives," accessed May 10, 2022, https://history. house.gov/People/Listing/R/ROGERS,-Edith-Nourse-(R000392)/.

**46**  *"I saw the women":* Treadwell, *Women's Army Corps*, 17.

**47**  *"The desire is":* Hearings on H.R. 6293: A Bill to Establish a Women's Army Auxiliary Corps for Service with the Army of the United States, Before the Committee on Military Affairs, 77th Cong., 2nd Sess. (1942) (Major General John Hilldring, Assistant Chief of Staff, US Army).

**48**  *"Representative Somers":* Nona Baldwin, "Bill for Women's Auxiliary Corps of 150,000 Passed by the House," *New York Times*, March 18, 1942.

**48**  *"for noncombatant service":* H.R. 6293: A Bill to Establish a Women's Army Auxiliary Corps for Service.

**48**  *"For the first":* "Mrs. Oveta Culp Hobby Takes Oath as Women's Army Auxiliary Corps Director," *Fort Worth Star-Telegram*, May 17, 1942.

## 4: "RELEASE A MAN TO FIGHT!"

50 *"Her enemies"*: "She's in the Army Now," *Vogue*, July 1, 1942, 59.

51 *"Slim and gracious"*: Emily Newell Blair, "Woman Soldier Number One," *Liberty Magazine*, n.d., Oveta Culp Hobby Papers, Box 58, Folder 2, Woodson Research Center, Rice University.

52 *"Almost every phase"*: Oveta Culp Hobby, "Information Prepared for Furman Features," n.d., Oveta Culp Hobby Papers, Box 57, Folder 1, Woodson Research Center, Rice University.

52 *"How many of us"*: Oveta Culp Hobby, "Women's City Club of Cleveland, Ohio, 'Women's Role in Government,'" October 29, 1964, Oveta Culp Hobby Papers, Box 53, Folder 7, Woodson Research Center, Rice University.

52 *"is a citizen"*: Oveta Culp Hobby, "Women in Elective Office," n.d., Oveta Culp Hobby Papers, Box 4, Folder 4, Woodson Research Center, Rice University.

53 *"The Army has"*: "Cleveland Newspaper, Saturday Morning," August 2, 1941, Oveta Culp Hobby Papers, Box 56, Folder 1, Woodson Research Center, Rice University.

53 *"how the men"*: Hobby, "Information Prepared for Furman Features."

54 *"The war department"*: "Mrs. Hobby Sworn In as WAAC Head," *The State: South Carolina's Progressive Newspaper*, May 17, 1942.

54 *"the actual"*: Oveta Culp Hobby, "Responses to Questions for *Ladies' Home Journal* Article," March 6, 1952, Oveta Culp Hobby Papers, Box 57, Folder 1, Woodson Research Center, Rice University.

55 *"it must have"*: Eleanor Roosevelt, "Letter from Eleanor Roosevelt to Oveta Culp Hobby," June 13, 1936, Oveta Culp Hobby Papers, Box 21, Folder 11, Woodson Research Center, Rice University.

55 *"How about girdles?"*: Treadwell, *Women's Army Corps*, 48.

56 *"Here at this first conference"*: Ibid.

56 *Years earlier, Hobby had assisted Roosevelt*: Eleanor Roosevelt, "Letter from Eleanor Roosevelt to Oveta Culp Hobby," July 14, 1936, Oveta Culp Hobby Papers, Box 21, Folder 11, Woodson Research Center, Rice University; Eleanor Roosevelt, "Letter from Eleanor Roosevelt to Oveta Culp Hobby," May 12, 1943, Oveta Culp Hobby Papers, Box 21, Folder 11, Woodson Research Center, Rice University.

56 *"charming, intense"*: Sylvia J. Bugbee, ed., *An Officer and a Lady: The World War II Letters of Lt. Col. Betty Bandel, Women's Army Corps* (Hanover, N.H.: UPNE, 2004), 38.

57 *"on the lovely spreads":* Ibid.

58 *"Our uniform":* Bertha Marie Strittmatter Clark, "When WAC Was a Dirty Word," 1977, 10, Papers of Bertha Marie Strittmatter Clark, MC249, Box 1, Schlesinger Library, Harvard Radcliffe Institute, Harvard University.

58 *"more than 1000":* Hobby, "Responses to Questions for *Ladies' Home Journal* Article."

59 *As Martha Putney:* For a comprehensive history of Black WACs, see Martha S. Putney, *When the Nation Was in Need: Blacks in the Women's Army Corps During World War II* (Lanham, Md.: Scarecrow Press, 1992), 29–47.

59 *"There is a definite":* Ibid., 30.

## 5: "BRING HIM HOME SOONER, JOIN THE WAVES"

61 *"Is there any law":* Joy Bright Hancock, *Lady in the Navy: A Personal Reminiscence* (Annapolis: Naval Institute Press, 1972), 22.

61 *"Then enroll":* Ibid.

61 *By 1925, updated appropriations:* Ibid., 48.

62 *Between 1941 and 1945:* Kathleen Broome Williams, *Improbable Warriors: Women Scientists and the U.S. Navy in World War II* (Annapolis: Naval Institute Press, 2001), 2.

62 *Office of the judge advocate general:* Ibid., 4.

63 *According to Judy Tzu-Chun Wu:* The information that follows relies primarily on Wu's authoritative biography of Dr. Margaret Chung. For more, see Judy Tzu-Chun Wu, *Doctor Mom Chung of the Fair-Haired Bastards: The Life of a Wartime Celebrity* (Berkeley: University of California Press, 2005).

63 *"During her":* Ibid., 44.

63 *In the known:* Ibid., 103–15.

64 *"dedicate themselves":* Ibid., 121.

64 *"a good guy":* Ibid.

65 *"The evidence indicates":* "History of the Women's Reserve" (Washington, D.C.: Historical Section, Bureau of Naval Personnel, January 18, 1946), US Naval Administrative Histories of World War II, Navy Department Library, Naval History and Heritage Command.

66 *But what Knox:* Wu, *Doctor Mom Chung*, 161.

## 6: "WISH I COULD JOIN TOO!"

**68**  *MAY CHOOSE:* Nancy Wilson Ross, *The WAVES: The Story of the Girls in Blue* (New York: H. Holt, 1943), 133.

**68**  *"Soft, crowned":* Ibid.

**69**  *"The theory":* Mildred McAfee, Transcript of Oral History Interview of Mrs. Horton by John T. Mason Jr., August 25, 1969, 1, Mildred McAfee Horton Papers, 1DD7-McAfee, Box 9, Wellesley College Archives.

**70**  *"The Navy knew":* Ibid.

**70**  *Under the leadership:* Hancock, *Lady in the Navy*, 60.

**70**  *"Women Leaders":* Mildred McAfee, "Women Leaders and the Family" (University of Chicago, March 17, 1927), Mildred McAfee Horton Papers, 1DD7 University of Chicago Papers, 1927–1931, Wellesley College Archives, Digital Collections, https://repository.wellesley .edu/object/wellesley29583?search=mcafee.

**71**  *"intellectual honesty":* "Mildred McAfee 1920," Vassar College Encyclopedia, Vassar College, accessed August 20, 2021, https:// vcencyclopedia.vassar.edu/distinguished-alumni/mildred-mcafee/.

**71**  *"Wellesley College":* Claire Richter, "Committee on War Activities Pamphlet," n.d., World War II Collection, 1VW-World War II, Box 3, Wellesley College Archives.

**71**  *All the students:* "Wellesley College Receives 124 British Children," *Wellesley Ledger*, June 26, 1941, World War II Collection, 1VW-World War II, Box 2, Wellesley College Archives.

**71**  *"We were all eager":* McAfee, Transcript of Oral History Interview of Mrs. Horton by John T. Mason Jr.

**73**  *Some of the male:* Ibid.

**73**  *"Why, think nothing of that":* Ibid.

**73**  *"The theory":* Ibid.

**74**  *"assigns responsibility":* Mildred McAfee, "Draft Memoranda," Mildred McAfee Horton Papers, 1DD7 Official Correspondence and Reports: Drafts, 1943–1944, Wellesley College Archives, Digital Collections, accessed August 20, 2021, https://repository.wellesley.edu/object /wellesley29583?search=mcafee.

**75**  *"Where have you been":* McAfee, Transcript of Oral History Interview of Mrs. Horton by John T. Mason Jr.

**75**  *"As far as general policy":* Ibid.

**75**  *"I really":* Ibid.

75  *"We could go"*: Ibid.

76  *"You didn't even"*: Ibid.


## 7: "YOUR DUTY ASHORE, HIS AFLOAT"

77  *"inherent kindness"*: "Comments Made by Lt. Helen B. Schleman
(SPARS)–Fall 1941 (While Lt. Schleman Was Director of Residence
Halls for Women, Purdue University)," 1941, MSF 366 Dorothy
Stratton Papers, Box 1, Folder 1, Purdue University Archives and
Special Collections, Purdue University Libraries.

78  *"ever a bad"*: Margaret Kernodle, "Organization Work Old Story
to Head of SPARS, Former Purdue U. Dean," Associated Press,
November 29, 1942, MSF 366 Dorothy Stratton Papers, Box 1,
Folder 1, Purdue University Archives and Special Collections, Purdue
University Libraries.

78  *"I found that"*: Angie Klink, *The Deans' Bible: Five Purdue Women and
Their Quest for Equality* (West Lafayette, Ind.: Purdue University Press,
2017), 34.

79  *"If there was"*: Ibid., 113.

79  *"a sort of enlarged closet"*: Ibid., 117.

79  *"one of those"*: Kernodle, "Organization Work Old Story to Head of
SPARS, Former Purdue U. Dean."

80  *When it came:* Morris J. MacGregor, *Integration of the Armed Forces,
1940–1965,* Defense Studies Series, CMH Pub 50–1–1 (Washington,
D.C.: US Army Center of Military History, 1981), 100.

80  *"I didn't believe"*: Pat Meid, *Marine Corps Women's Reserve in World War II*,
Marine Corps Historical Reference Series No. 37 (Washington, D.C.:
Historical Branch, G-3 Division Headquarters, US Marine Corps,
1964), 2.

80  *"From Holcomb"*: Allan R. Millett, *Semper Fidelis*, rev., exp. ed. (New
York: Free Press, 1991), 374.

82  *By the end:* Denis A. Clift, "Lest We Forget: March of the Women
Marines: Colonel Ruth Cheney Streeter," *Proceedings* 43, No.
11 (November 2017), https://www.usni.org/magazines/
proceedings/2017/november/lest-we-forget-march-women-marines
-colonel-ruth-cheney-streeter.

82  *"Femarines"*: Peter A. Soderbergh, *Women Marines: The World War II Era*
(Westport, Conn.: Praeger, 1992), 21.

83  *"They are Marines"*: Ibid.

## 8: "THE ARMY AIR FORCES WANT YOU!"

85 *"good fellowship"*: "Charter Members," Ninety-Nines, accessed April 17, 2022, https://www.ninety-nines.org/charter-members.htm.

86 *"Until I was eight"*: Jacqueline Cochran, *The Stars at Noon* (Boston: Little, Brown and Company, 1954), 3.

87 *"kept them waving"*: Sally van Wagenen Keil, *Those Wonderful Women in Their Flying Machines: The Unknown Heroines of World War Two* (New York: Four Directions Press, 1994), 44.

87 *"Where's my husband?"*: Ibid., 45.

87 *"Do it well"*: Sarah Byrn Rickman, *Nancy Love: WASP Pilot* (Palmer Lake, Colo.: Filter Press, 2019), 1.

88 *"With all those"*: Henry Harley Arnold, *Global Mission*, 1st ed. (Blue Ridge Summit, Pa.: Tab Books, 1989), 156.

90 *By 1941, ATC was dealing*: Molly Merryman, *Clipped Wings: The Rise and Fall of the Women Airforce Service Pilots WASPs of World War II* (New York: NYU Press, 2008), 9.

91 *"I have been"*: "Air Force Historical Studies No. 55, Women Pilots with the AAF, 1941–1944" (AAF Historical Office, Headquarters, Army Air Forces, March 1945), 3.

91 *"We have about"*: Ibid., 2.

92 WOMEN WILL FORM: "Women Will Form a Ferry Command," *New York Times*, September 11, 1942.

92 *"Mrs. Love"*: Ibid.

92 *"He called General George"*: Sarah Byrn Rickman and Deborah G. Douglas, *WASP of the Ferry Command: Women Pilots, Uncommon Deeds* (Denton: University of North Texas Press, 2017), 26.

93 *"The formation of"*: "Press Release Regarding Jacqueline Cochran's Appointment as Director of Women's Flying Training," September 14, 1942, Jacqueline Cochran and the Women's Airforce Service Pilots (WASPs), Dwight D. Eisenhower Presidential Library, Digital Collection.

95 *In his 1942*: Franklin Delano Roosevelt, "State of the Union Address" (American Presidency Project, January 6, 1942), https://www.presidency.ucsb.edu/documents/state-the-union-address-1.

95 *He went on*: Ibid.

95 *By one estimate*: Craven and Cate, *Army Air Forces*, 304.

95 *In the same*: Ibid., 423–24.

95 *By the end of the year*: Wilson, *Destructive Creation*, 49.

95  *Rubber production:* Ibid., 80.
95  *Artillery production:* Millett, Maslowski, and Feis, *For the Common Defense,* 388.
95  *"convulsive, expensive":* Marshall, *Papers of George Catlett Marshall,* 2:248.
96  *By the end of 1942:* "Research Starters: US Military by the Numbers," National WWII Museum, New Orleans, n.d., accessed April 9, 2020.
96  *The Army alone:* Ibid.
96  *The first American:* Maury Klein, *A Call to Arms: Mobilizing America for World War II* (New York: Bloomsbury Press, 2013), 340.
96  *"One hundred thousand":* Matloff, *Strategic Planning,* 59.


9: "ARE YOU A GIRL WITH A STAR-SPANGLED HEART?"

98  *"The men lie":* Katherine Keene, "Memoir of Service in WAAC or WAC," n.d., Papers of Katherine Mildred Keene, MC817, Box 2, Schlesinger Library, Harvard Radcliffe Institute, Harvard University.
99  *"The freedom":* Oveta Culp Hobby, "Texas Society in Washington," May 16, 1943, Oveta Culp Hobby Papers, Box 43, Folder 16, Woodson Research Center, Rice University.
100  *On the first day:* Treadwell, *Women's Army Corps,* 55.
100  *According to the official:* Ibid.
100  *"a dean of women":* Ibid., 58.
101  *"hairpins, comb":* Doris E. Samford, *Ruffles and Drums* (Boulder: Pruett Press, 1966), 5.
101  *"I don't know":* Rebecca Fisk, "To Relieve Enlisted Men for Active Duty," *Mount Holyoke Alumnae Quarterly,* May 1943, War Series, World War II 1939–1945, Box 10, Folder 1, Mount Holyoke College Archives and Special Collections.
102  *"There is no sloppy guesswork":* Ibid.
102  *"It wasn't so bad":* Ruth G. Haskell, *Helmets and Lipstick: An Army Nurse in World War Two* (independently published, 2017), 43.
103  *"I feel as if":* Elizabeth R. Pollock, *Yes, Ma'am! The Personal Papers of a WAAC Private,* 2nd printing (Philadelphia: J. B. Lippincott, 1943), 15.
104  *"liked to make beds":* Doris Weatherford, *American Women and World War II* (Edison, N.J.: Castle Books, 2009), 97.
104  *"We have found":* "Mt. Holyoke's Marines Excel at Drilling," May 4, 1943, War Series, World War II 1939–1945, Box 10, Folder 1, Mount Holyoke College Archives and Special Collections.
104  *"You couldn't make":* Weatherford, *American Women,* 97.

104  *"had never seen"*: Bugbee, *Officer and a Lady*, 12.

104  *"From the first"*: Hobby, "Texas Society in Washington."

105  *"When a woman"*: Beverly Stone, "Essays by Stone About Women in the Military," 1944, MSF 466 Beverly Stone Papers, Box 4, Folder 6, Purdue University Archives and Special Collections, Purdue University Libraries.

105  *"I have been"*: Marcelle Fisher, "Letter from Marcelle Fisher to Her Mother, 1943," June 23, 1943, Betty Carter Women Veterans Historical Project, University of North Carolina, Greensboro, https://gateway.uncg.edu/islandora/object/wvhp%3A9208.

105  *"If at the end"*: Adeline LaPlante, "Letter from Adeline LaPlante to Parents, 1942," September 25, 1943, Betty Carter Women Veterans Historical Project, University of North Carolina, Greensboro, http://libcdm1.uncg.edu/cdm/ref/collection/WVHP/id/6268/rec/25.

105  *"I've never felt"*: Roberta Wooddell House, "Post Card from Roberta Wooddell House to Mr. and Mrs. Frank Anderson, 1942," August 13, 1942, Betty Carter Women Veterans Historical Project, University of North Carolina, Greensboro, http://libcdm1.uncg.edu/cdm/ref/collection/WVHP/id/10331/rec/304.

105  *"on account of nerves"*: Janet Mead, "Letter from Janet Muriel Mead to Her Mother, 20 August 1944," August 20, 1944, Betty Carter Women Veterans Historical Project, University of North Carolina, Greensboro, http://libcdm1.uncg.edu/cdm/ref/collection/WVHP/id/6222/rec/289.

106  *"Getting those gold"*: Jenny Lea, "Letter from Lt. Jenny Lea to Mary Kate Bonds, 1942," September 14, 1942, Betty Carter Women Veterans Historical Project, University of North Carolina, Greensboro, https://gateway.uncg.edu/islandora/object/wvhp%3A18005.

## 10: "LEARN A SKILL YOU'LL VALUE ALL YOUR LIFE"

107  *"Negroes on one side"*: Putney, *When the Nation Was in Need*, 4.

107  *Vivian "Millie" Corbett:* The recollections and information that follow about Millie Bailey's experience in the Army are drawn primarily from author interviews conducted with her in winter/spring 2021. Vivian "Millie" [Corbett] Bailey, Interview with Author, In Person, March 2021.

109  *"the corps offered"*: Sandra M. Bolzenius, *Glory in Their Spirit: How Four*

*Black Women Took On the Army During World War II*, ill. ed. (Urbana: University of Illinois Press, 2018), 22.

110 *Charity Adams, a tall, striking woman:* Unless otherwise noted, the following sections on Charity Adams's experience in the war are based on several publicly available interviews and the recollections in her memoir. For more, see Charity Adams Earley, *One Woman's Army: A Black Officer Remembers the WAC* (College Station: Texas A&M University Press, 1995).

110 *"The uncertainty":* Ibid., 11.

111 *"Let's take her":* Ibid., 12.

111 *"had some feeling":* Ibid., 19.

111 *"Here at":* Putney, *When the Nation Was in Need*, 51.

## 11: "THAT WAS THE DAY I JOINED THE WAVES"

113 *"Can I help":* The following sections on Joy Lemmon's experience in the Navy are drawn primarily from author interviews. Joy [Lemmon] Casino, Interview with Author, Phone, March 17, 2021.

115 *"The Navy, at no point":* McAfee, Transcript of Oral History Interview of Mrs. Horton by John T. Mason Jr.

116 *In its first:* "It's Your War, Too: Women in World War II," n.d., National WWII Museum, New Orleans.

116 *Like the WAAC:* "US Naval Training School (W.R.) Daily Worksheet," n.d., Papers of Elizabeth Reynard, A-128, Box 3, Folder 71, Schlesinger Library, Harvard Radcliffe Institute, Harvard University.

116 *"It has been brought":* "Commanding Officer's Orders," n.d., Papers of Elizabeth Reynard, A-128, Box 4, Folder 81, Schlesinger Library, Harvard Radcliffe Institute, Harvard University.

116 *"Telephones are":* Ibid.

117 *"President Davis":* McAfee, Transcript of Oral History Interview of Mrs. Horton by John T. Mason Jr.

117 *"It sounds":* Dorothy Kenyon, "Letter from Dorothy Kenyon to Miss Florence Snow," June 17, 1942, WAVES Files, College Archives, CA-MS-00007, Board of Directors 1942–1943, Smith College Special Collections.

117 *"With all possible":* Eleanor Edson, "Letter from Eleanor Edson to Miss Florence Snow," June 17, 1942, WAVES Files, College Archives, CA-MS-00007, Board of Directors 1942–1943, Smith College Special Collections.

## 12: "THE GIRL OF THE YEAR IS A SPAR"

120 *Among the many:* The recollections and information that follow about Merle Selma's experience in the Marine Corps are drawn primarily from author interviews. Caples, Interview with Author.

122 *"It is probable":* "The Women's Reserve of the United States Coast Guard Reserve, Progress Report, December 1942 through May 1943," n.d., MSF 334 Helen Schleman Papers, Biographical Information, Box 1, Folder 3, Purdue University Archives and Special Collections, Purdue University Libraries.

122 *"considerably more":* "History of the Marine Corps Women's Reserve: A Critical Analysis of Its Development and Operation" (Washington, D.C.: Historical Section, Bureau of Naval Personnel, December 6, 1945), US Naval Administrative Histories of World War II, Navy Department Library, Naval History and Heritage Command.

122 *"In stiff competition":* Mary C. Lyne and Kay Arthur, *Three Years Behind the Mast: The Story of the United States Coast Guard SPARS* (Historical Section, Public Information Division, U.S. Coast Guard 1946), 18.

123 *With the benefit:* "The Women's Reserve of the United States Coast Guard Reserve, Progress Report, December 1942 through May 1943."

123 *The MCWR also did well:* Meid, *Marine Corps Women's Reserve,* 11.

124 *"with walls knocked":* Lyne and Arthur, *Three Years Behind the Mast,* 26.

125 *The SPARS officer corps:* "The Coast Guard at War, Women's Reserve: A Preliminary Survey of the Development of the Women's Reserve of the United States Coast Guard" (Washington, D.C.: Historical Section, Public Information Division for the Women's Reserve Division, US Coast Guard Headquarters, April 1945), 43.

125 *"mortars, bazookas":* Meid, *Marine Corps Women's Reserve,* 17.

126 *"BAMs":* Soderbergh, *Women Marines,* 58.

126 *"dogs and n[****]rs":* Ibid.

126 *"They would not leave her alone":* Ibid., 57.

126 *"Information reaching":* Treadwell, *Women's Army Corps,* 275n.

127 *"practically unheard of":* Caples, Interview with Author.


## 13: "IF YOU WANT TO FLY"

128 *newly minted:* The recollections and information that follow about Florene Miller's experience in the WASP are drawn primarily from

Olga Gruhzit-Hoyt, *They Also Served: American Women in World War II* (Secaucus, N.J.: Birch Lane Press, 1995), 153–69; Florene Miller Watson, *Florene Miller Watson, Edited Oral History Transcript* (Tucson, Ariz.: NASA Headquarters Oral History Project, March 24, 2000); https://historycollection.jsc.nasa.gov/JSCHistoryPortal /history/oral_histories/NASA_HQ/Aviatrix/WatsonFM /Watson_3-24-00.htm; and Florene Miller, "Early Women Pilots in World War II in the Ferrying Division," Recorded Lecture, National Museum of the United States Air Force, n.d., https://www .nationalmuseum.af.mil/Portals/7/av/early_women_pilots_in_wwii .mp3?ver=2015-08-28-094738-200.

128  *The plane was so advanced:* "U.S. War Planes," *Life*, February 12, 1942, 47.

131  *"cross-country experience":* Merryman, *Clipped Wings*, 12.

132  *"an iron cot":* Rickman and Douglas, *WASP of the Ferry Command*, 34.

133  *"I didn't want":* Miller, "Early Women Pilots in World War II in the Ferrying Division."

133  *"If you weren't worried":* Ibid.

134  *"I got the right kind of screwdriver":* Ibid.

134  *two hundred hours:* Keil, *Those Wonderful Women*, 364.

135  *By one estimate:* Merryman, *Clipped Wings*, 14.

136  *Nearly thirty percent:* Keil, *Those Wonderful Women*, 380.

136  *"The engineer would":* Jean Hascall Cole and Dora Dougherty Strother, *Women Pilots of World War II* (Salt Lake City: University of Utah Press, 1992), 85.

136  *"You'd see these puffs":* Ibid., 87.

136  *"There was always":* Ibid., 85.

137  *"They began":* Carl, *WASP Among Eagles*, 51.

137  *"Our first test":* Ibid., 52.

137  *Over three dozen:* Keil, *Those Wonderful Women*, 382–84.

138  *"a sorry lot":* Doris L. Rich, *Jackie Cochran: Pilot in the Fastest Lane* (Gainesville: University Press of Florida, 2010), 120.

138  *by some accounts:* Merryman, *Clipped Wings*, 30.

138  *"I don't know":* Rich, *Jackie Cochran*, 120.

138  *"Look Mrs. Hobby":* Ibid.

138  *"would result in confusion":* Henry Harley Arnold, "Memorandum for General Marshall, 'Incorporation of Women Civilian Pilots and Trainees into Army Air Forces,'" June 14, 1943, Jacqueline Cochran and the Women's Airforce Service Pilots (WASPs), Dwight D. Eisenhower Presidential Library, Digital Collection.

139   *director of Women's Flying Training:* Henry Harley Arnold, "Memorandum for Assistant Chief of Air Staff, Operations, Commitments and Requirements, 'Establishment of Office of Special Assistant for Women Pilots,'" June 21, 1943, Jacqueline Cochran and the Women's Airforce Service Pilots (WASPs), Dwight D. Eisenhower Presidential Library, Digital Collection.

### 14: "SOMEONE TALKED!"

140   *"Contraceptives and prophylactic":* John O'Donnell, Capitol Stuff, June 8, 1943.

142   *"Hanlon, Anna":* "Chart—Replacement of Enlisted Men by WAAC Personnel," n.d., RG 18, Entry NM-53 292-A, General Correspondence, 1941–5/1944, 220.31, Box 426, National Archives and Records Administration, College Park.

143   *"Get that damn":* Treadwell, *Women's Army Corps,* 212–13.

143   *"You join":* Ibid., 212.

143   *"I have been in gatherings":* "Letter to Colonel Hobby on Reputation of WACs," April 21, 1944, RG 165, Entry NM-84 54-C, Records of the War Department General and Special Staffs, Women's Army Corps Numerical Files 1942–1949, Box 91, National Archives and Records Administration, College Park.

145   *"a shameful thing":* "Press Conference #902," June 11, 1943, Press Conferences of President Franklin D. Roosevelt, 1933–1945, Franklin D. Roosevelt Presidential Library and Museum, http://www.fdrlibrary.marist.edu/_resources/images/pc/pc0150.pdf.

145   *"The Secretary of War":* George Catlett Marshall, *The Papers of George Catlett Marshall, vol. 4, "Aggressive and Determined Leadership," June 1, 1943–December 31, 1944,* ed. Larry I. Bland and Sharon Ritenour Stevens (Baltimore: Johns Hopkins University Press, 1996), 15–16.

145   *"if this report":* JW Mathews, "Letter from JW Mathews to Oveta Culp Hobby," October 18, 1944, RG 165, Entry NM-84 54-C, Records of the War Department General and Special Staffs, Women's Army Corps Numerical Files 1942–1949, Box 91, National Archives and Records Administration, College Park.

145   *"Yes, we've heard":* Vida Williamson, "What About Our Girls in Uniform? What Kind of People Are They?," *Bureau of Naval Personnel Information Bulletin,* July 1943, MSF 366 Dorothy Stratton

Papers, Purdue University Archives and Special Collections, Purdue University Libraries.

**145** *"a line of"*: Treadwell, *Women's Army Corps*, 206.

**146** *"When I went"*: Ibid., 204.

## 15: "GOING WHERE WE'RE NEEDED MOST!"

**149** *"NONE OF US"*: The recollections and information that follow about Miriam Stehlik's experience in North Africa are drawn from her letters, found in Alma Lutz and Marta C. Gorick, *With Love, Jane: Letters from American Women on the War Fronts* (New York: John Day, 1945), 81–84.

**150** *"We know"*: Ibid., 84.

**150** *"What work"*: Ibid., 80.

**150** *"We have gone"*: Ibid., 83–84.

**151** *"was probably"*: Omar N. Bradley and Clay Blair, *A General's Life* (New York: Simon and Schuster, 1983), 128.

**154** *Ruth Haskell:* The following sections about Ruth Haskell's experience in North Africa are drawn primarily from her memoir, Haskell, *Helmets and Lipstick.*

**155** *"Remember that you live"*: Ibid., 18–19.

**155** *"Sea sickness, like love"*: Ibid., 63.

**155** *"We passed slowly"*: Ibid., 21.

**156** *"mosquito cream"*: Ibid., 64.

**156** *"leggings, cartridge belts, canteens"*: Ibid., 68.

**157** *On the day of the Pearl Harbor bombing:* Carolyn Feller and Constance Moore, *Highlights in the History of the Army Nurse Corps*, CMH Pub 85–1 (Washington, D.C.: US Army Center of Military History, 1995).

**157** *The Navy Nurse Corps:* Jeanne M. Holm, ed., *In Defense of a Nation: Servicewomen in World War II* (Washington, D.C.: Vandamere Press, 1998), 32.

**157** *For example, Army nurses were not:* Monahan and Neidel-Greenlee, *And If I Perish*, 14.

**158** *"Hi, Ho, Silver!"*: Haskell, *Helmets and Lipstick*, 82.

**159** *"the unmistakable odor"*: Ibid., 82.

## 16: "DON'T MISS YOUR GREAT OPPORTUNITY"

161   *Helen Hayden:* The details included in this chapter regarding Helen
Hayden's experience in Italy are drawn primarily from author
interviews. Helen [Hayden] Garth, Interview with Author, Virtual,
February 26, 2021.

162   *"information programs":* Meg Metcalf, "Research Guides: Rosie
the Riveter: Working Women and World War II: Office of
War Information," n.d.

165   *"We came":* Antony Beevor, *The Second World War* (New York: Back Bay
Books, 2013), 403.

169   *Among the most experienced:* Unless otherwise noted, the recollections and
information that follow about Agnes Jensen's experience in Albania
are drawn from her memoir, Agnes Jensen Mangerich, *Albanian
Escape: The True Story of U.S. Army Nurses Behind Enemy Lines* (Lexington:
University Press of Kentucky, 2006), 11.

171   *"smoothed out":* Judith Barger, *Beyond the Call of Duty: Army Flight Nursing
in World War II* (Kent, Ohio: Kent State University Press, 2013), 98.

172   *"Dead bodies piled up":* Diane Burke Fessler, *No Time for Fear: Voices of
American Military Nurses in World War II* (East Lansing: Michigan State
University Press, 1997), 92.

172   *"It was wall-to-wall":* Danner, *What a Way to Spend a War*, 130.

173   *by 1943, the rate:* For more on the changes of battlefield nursing in
World War II, see Barger, *Beyond the Call of Duty*, xi.

177   *"For a long time":* Marshall, *Papers of George Catlett Marshall*, 4:68–69.

178   *"The ship was torpedoed":* "Press Conference #875," January 24, 1943,
Press Conferences of President Franklin D. Roosevelt, 1933–1945,
Franklin D. Roosevelt Presidential Library and Museum, http://
www.fdrlibrary.marist.edu/_resources/images/pc/pc0144.pdf.

178   *"an unnamed":* Lutz and Gorick, *With Love, Jane*, 79.

178   *If the women died:* Treadwell, *Women's Army Corps*, 113–15.

## 17: "WHICH ONE OF THESE JOBS WOULD YOU LIKE?"

181   *in 1943, it took divisions:* Matloff, *Strategic Planning*, 114.

181   *Susan Ahn grew:* The details that follow about Susan Ahn's experience
in the WAVES are drawn primarily from John Cha, *Willow Tree Shade:
The Susan Ahn Cuddy Story* (Washington, D.C.: Korean American
Heritage Foundation, 2002).

181  *"I was the oldest":* Ibid., 55.

182  *"This is the life":* Ibid., 88.

183  *"I still seem":* Ibid., 91.

183  *"landmarks he would":* Fisk, "To Relieve Enlisted Men for Active Duty."

187  *It took over six months:* Millett, Maslowski, and Feis, *For the Common Defense*, 397.

187  *"The myth":* Ibid., 399.

188  *"During the war's":* Holm, *In Defense of a Nation*, 66, 74.

188  *There is a story:* Stone, "Essays by Stone About Women in the Military."

189  *According to one estimate:* Millett and Murray, *Military Effectiveness*, 63.

189  *between 1942:* Millett, Maslowski, and Feis, *For the Common Defense*, 388.

189  *The solution:* The recollections and details that follow about Jessie Kontrabecki's experience in the WAVES are primarily drawn from author interviews. Dunbar, Interview with Author.

192  *The Marine aviation:* Holm, *In Defense of a Nation*, 86.

192  *Serving as motor:* Ibid., 91.

193  *"women couldn't do":* Ibid., 69.

193  *McAfee often told:* McAfee, Transcript of Oral History Interview of Mrs. Horton by John T. Mason Jr., 73.

## 18: "HAVE YOU GOT WHAT IT TAKES TO FILL AN IMPORTANT JOB LIKE THIS?"

195  *For instance, in one request:* "Request for WAAC Personnel," June 19, 1943, RG 18, Entry NM-53 292-A, General Correspondence, 1941–5/1944, 220.31, Box 426, National Archives and Records Administration, College Park.

195  *Similarly, at the peak:* Treadwell, *Women's Army Corps*, 289.

196  *"Typist":* Gardner Brown, "Memorandum to the Commanding General, Army Air Forces, Washington, DC 'List of WAC Personnel by MOS,'" March 28, 1944, RG 18, Entry NM-53 292-A, General Correspondence, 1941–5/1944, Box 426, National Archives and Records Administration, College Park.

196  *In the Army Ground Forces:* Treadwell, *Women's Army Corps*, 299.

196  *"Ike's Little Carrier Pigeon":* Gruhzit-Hoyt, *They Also Served*, 86.

196  *"The boys":* McAfee, Transcript of Oral History Interview of Mrs. Horton by John T. Mason Jr., 18.

196  *"The simple headquarters":* Dwight D. Eisenhower, *Crusade in Europe*, rpt. ed. (Baltimore: Johns Hopkins University Press, 1997), 132–33.

197  *One worksheet: US Coast Guard Instruction Pamphlet*, 1943, Personal Collection of Mabel Johnson.

198  *Among the many:* Bailey, Interview with Author.

200  *In fact, the task:* Stephen E. Bower, "A Short History of the U.S. Army Adjutant General's Corps, 1775–2013" (US Army Soldier Support Institute, 2013), 36.

202  *"You can ask": WAC Recruiting Pamphlet*, n.d., Oveta Culp Hobby Papers, Box 4, Folder 5, Woodson Research Center, Rice University.

202  *"Morale stayed high":* Hobby, "Responses to Questions for *Ladies' Home Journal* Article."

202  *"I never worry":* Dorothy Stratton, "Notes on Mildred McAfee Obituary, 1993–4," September 6, 1994, MSF 366 Dorothy Stratton Papers, Box 2, Folder 3, Purdue University Archives and Special Collections, Purdue University Libraries.

202  *"an adventure":* McAfee, Transcript of Oral History Interview of Mrs. Horton by John T. Mason Jr., 25.

202  *"We cannot have":* Ibid.

203  *"Less than a year":* Brenda L. Moore, *To Serve My Country, to Serve My Race: The Story of the Only African-American WACS Stationed Overseas During World War II* (New York: NYU Press, 1997), 2.

203  *In one instance:* Meyer, *Creating G. I. Jane*, 93–94.

204  *"Kill 'em":* Ibid.

204  *According to the Navy's:* "African American Sailors in the U.S. Navy Chronology," accessed June 3, 2022, http://public2.nhhcaws.local /browse-by-topic/diversity/african-americans/chronology.html.

205  *"couldn't see any":* McAfee, Transcript of Oral History Interview of Mrs. Horton by John T. Mason Jr., 44.

205  *"With very little notice":* Ibid., 45.

205  *Pickens and Wills's initial entry:* Frances Wills Thorpe, *Navy Blue and Other Colors* (New York: Xlibris, 2007), 84.

206  *"two brown skinned":* Ibid.

206  *"We knew the score":* Ibid., 85.

206  *"troubled by":* Laura Rapaport Borsten and Orin Borsten, *Once a Wave: My Life in the Navy, 1942–1946* (Studio City, CA: Amber Publishing Company, 1998), 40.

206  *"she would get up":* Thorpe, *Navy Blue and Other Colors*, 91–92.

207   *"I became aware"*: Ibid., 89.

207   *"another brown one"*: Ibid.

207   *"When the Navy"*: Ibid., 83.

207   *"It was not"*: Ibid., 87.


### 19: "MAKE A DATE WITH UNCLE SAM"

209   *The leave pass:* Ethel [Becker] Small, Family Recording Provided to Author, n.d., Personal Collection of Fred and Laurie Iskowitz.

210   "Ethel Becker handles the passes": Ethel Becker [Small], Newspaper Clipping Provided to Author, n.d., Personal Collection of Fred and Laurie Iskowitz.

211   *"You are no longer"*: Oveta Culp Hobby, "Greetings to Officer Candidates," July 23, 1942, Oveta Culp Hobby Papers, Box 43, Folder 15, Woodson Research Center, Rice University.

212   *"The WACs themselves"*: Hobby, "Responses to Questions for *Ladies' Home Journal* Article."

212   *"Parties just happened"*: Helen Gilbert, *"Okay, Girls—Man Your Bunks!" Tales from the Life of a WWII Navy WAVE*, 2nd ed. (Toledo, Ohio: Pedestrian Press, 2006), 68.

212   *"There were so many"*: Ibid., 69.

213   *"one of my"*: Ibid., 91.

213   *"I looked at"*: McAfee, Transcript of Oral History Interview of Mrs. Horton by John T. Mason Jr.

214   *"One of the main"*: *Sex Hygiene for Women Officers and Women Officer Candidates of the Armed Forces,* Joint Army, Navy, Air Force Pamphlet, n.d., RG 165, Entry NM-84 54-C, Records of the War Department General and Special Staffs, Women's Army Corps Numerical Files 1942–1949, Box 165, National Archives and Records Administration, College Park.

214   *"adequate sex education"*: Ibid.

214   *"always been"*: Ibid.

215   *"You goddam WACs"*: Keene, "Memoir of Service in WAAC or WAC."

215   *Some pilots flew over:* Clark, "When WAC Was a Dirty Word."

215   *"Join the Navy"*: Gruhzit-Hoyt, *They Also Served*, xvi.

215   *"The phrase"*: Keene, "Memoir of Service in WAAC or WAC."

216   *"There was nothing"*: Jessie [Kontrabecki] Dunbar, Interview with Author.

216  *"fairly astounding"*: Leisa Meyer, *Creating G. I. Jane* (New York: Columbia University Press, 1997), 142.

216  *taking police reports*: Kathy Gonzales, Interview with Author, In Person, September 2021.

216  *"boy crazy"*: Meyer, *Creating G. I. Jane*, 143–44.

217  *"One commander"*: Hobby, "Responses to Questions for *Ladies' Home Journal* Article."

217  *"would be locked"*: Meyer, *Creating G. I. Jane*, 139.

## 20: "NOW IS THE TIME TO INVESTIGATE THE OPPORTUNITIES OFFERED"

218  *When military:* The insights that follow in this chapter rely primarily on the Army's official investigation of the alleged conduct. For more, see Major General Howard Snyder, "Investigation of Conditions in the 3d WAC Training Center, Fort Oglethorpe, Georgia" (Office of the Inspector General, War Department, US Army, July 29, 1944), RG 159, Entry NM-37 26-E, "General Correspondence {Formerly Confidential Correspondence}, 1939–1947," Records of the Office of the Inspector General, 3rd WAC Training Center, 333.9, Box 17A, National Archives and Records Administration, College Park.

220  *"argyle socks"*: Allan Bérubé, *Coming Out Under Fire: The History of Gay Men and Women in World War II* (Chapel Hill: University of North Carolina Press, 2010), 32.

220  *"of course not!"*: Ibid., 33.

221  *"Individuals guilty"*: "History of the Marine Corps Women's Reserve: A Critical Analysis of Its Development and Operation," 231.

221  *"All commanding officers"*: Ibid., 236.

222  *The Fort Oglethorpe investigation:* Snyder, "Investigation of Conditions in the 3d WAC Training Center, Fort Oglethorpe, Georgia."

223  *"I think these"*: Ibid.

223  *"the latest circular"*: Ibid.

224  *While estimates:* John D'Emilio, "The Other War," Queer America, accessed October 18, 2022, https://www.learningforjustice.org /podcasts/queer-america/the-other-war.

## 21: "GIVE US MORE P-47'S"

225   *Marjorie Kumler:* William M. Miller, *To Live and Die a WASP: 38 Women Pilots Who Died in WWII* (independently published, 2016), 46–47.

226   *Their safety:* Keil, *Those Wonderful Women*, 383–84.

227   *"watch a spectacular":* Ibid., 280–81.

228   *As a result, by the end:* Ibid., 281.

230   CAA SAYS: James Wright, "CAA Says WASPs Take Jobs from Able Men Fliers," *Buffalo Evening News*, March 31, 1944.

230   ARMY PASSES: "Army Passes Up Jobless Pilots to Train WASPs," *Chicago Tribune*, February 12, 1944.

231   *"I guess":* Ibid.

231   *"The fact is":* Drew Pearson, "Washington Merry-Go-Round," *Kingsport Times*, August 6, 1944.

231   *"WASP Training":* Nat Finney, "Fight Rages over WASPs," *Des Moines Tribune*, May 13, 1944.

231   *"While lack of men":* Hazel Taylor, "Letter from Hazel Taylor, Director Women's Interest, AAF, WASP Public Relations, Air WAC Liaison Air Forces Group to Mr. S. Ralph Cohen, Associate Editor, National Aeronautics, Washington, DC," January 21, 1944, Jacqueline Cochran and the Women's Airforce Service Pilots (WASPs), Dwight D. Eisenhower Presidential Library, Digital Collection.

232   *"Young American women":* Ibid.

234   *"make it evident":* "Memo from General H.H. Arnold, Commanding General, Army Air Forces to Director of Women Pilots Re: Deactivation of Women Pilots," October 1, 1944, Jacqueline Cochran and the Women's Airforce Service Pilots (WASPs), Dwight D. Eisenhower Presidential Library, Digital Collection.

234   *"I felt sure":* Jacqueline Cochran, "Letter from Jacqueline Cochran to Members of the 43-W-3 Class," October 12, 1944, Jacqueline Cochran and the Women's Airforce Service Pilots (WASPs), Dwight D. Eisenhower Presidential Library, Digital Collection.

234   *"To have":* Carl, *WASP Among Eagles*, 111.

234   *"They taught us":* Keil, *Those Wonderful Women*, 329.

235   *"It will take":* Miller, *To Live and Die a WASP*, 7.

236   *"I was alone":* Carl, *WASP Among Eagles*, 101.

236   *"the step":* Ibid., 102.

## 22: "WACS ARE GOING PLACES!"

237 *Katherine Keene:* The stories that follow about Katherine Keene's experience in Europe are drawn primarily from her personal papers, including her diaries and letters while posted abroad. See Keene, "Memoir of Service in WAAC or WAC."

241 *By one estimate:* Craven and Cate, *Army Air Forces,* 350.

241 *The American Eighth:* Millett, Maslowski, and Feis, *For the Common Defense,* 413; Millett and Murray, *Military Effectiveness,* 61.

242 *"where a particular":* Keene, "Memoir of Service in WAAC or WAC," 16.

242 *"on this day":* Ibid.

245 *"if the Germans":* Millett, Maslowski, and Feis, *For the Common Defense,* 421.

245 *"air attacks":* Ibid.

245 *The Bronx:* The details that follow about Gertrude Pearson's experience in Europe are drawn primarily from an oral history of her time in the service. For more, see Gertrude Pearson Cassetta Collection (AFC/2001/001/24117), Veterans History Project, American Folklife Center, Library of Congress.

248 *"networks of wire":* George Raynor Thompson and Dixie R. Harris, *The Signal Corps: The Outcome,* CMH Pub 10–18 (Washington, D.C.: US Army Center of Military History, 1966), 15.

249 *According to a 1944:* Treadwell, *Women's Army Corps,* 318.

249 *Over sixty percent:* Ibid.

250 *Dismayingly, Eisenhower found:* Millett and Murray, *Military Effectiveness,* 426.

## 23: "I'D RATHER BE WITH THEM—THAN WAITING"

251 *they took intrepid women:* The details that follow are based primarily on Zahn's letters and recollections from the time and interviews with her family members. Kathy Gonzales, Interview with Author; personal papers of Evelyn Zahn, privately held.

257 *Charity Adams boarded:* Earley, *One Woman's Army,* 104.

258 *"I had been involved":* Ibid., 122.

259 *In a single month:* "Letter Mail Handled During October 1943," n.d., RG 160, Entry NM-25 21, Army Service Forces, Director of

Administration, Decimal Correspondence File, 1942–43, 333–383.6, Box 2, National Archives and Records Administration, College Park.

260  *"the unit broke":* Earley, *One Woman's Army*, 151.

260  *"output of work":* General Board, "Study of the Women's Army Corps in the European Theater of Operations," Study No. 11, 1946, Appendix 10.

261  *"If our girls":* Earley, *One Woman's Army*, 160–62.

262  *"They were proud":* Ibid., 183.

263  *"This is a solemn":* Harry Truman, "Announcing the Surrender of Germany," May 8, 1945, Miller Center, University of Virginia, https://millercenter.org/the-presidency/presidential-speeches/may-8-1945-announcing-surrender-germany.

263  *In Barracks 438:* Aileen Kilgore Henderson, *Stateside Soldier: Life in the Women's Army Corps, 1944–1945* (Columbia: University of South Carolina Press, 2001), 173.

264  *"Everybody sits":* Ibid., 176.

## 24: "BLUEPRINT FOR VICTORY"

267  *Twenty years before:* The information that follows on Mary Sears is drawn primarily from interviews with close personal friends. See Nan Denton, Interview with Author, Phone, October 5, 2021; For more, see Catherine Musemeche, "Mary Sears' Pioneering Ocean Research Saved Countless Lives in WWII," *Smithsonian*, August 2022.

268  *"to afford the":* "Office of the Chief of Naval Operations: Hydrographic Office" (Washington, D.C.: Historical Section, Hydrographic Office, n.d.), US Naval Administrative Histories of World War II, Navy Department Library, Naval History and Heritage Command, 20.

268  *By the time Sears:* Ibid., 128.

269  *Most Hydro sections:* Ibid., 172.

269  *They began requesting:* Ibid., 137.

269  *Instead, the Navy:* Ibid., 141.

269  *"I'm not allowed":* Karen Berkey Huntsberger, *I'll Be Seeing You: Letters Home from a Navy Girl* (Eugene, Ore.: Luminare Press, 2018), 84.

270  *"In view of the probability":* "Office of the Chief of Naval Operations: Hydrographic Office," 196.

270  *"ocean currents":* Williams, *Improbable Warriors*, 50.

270  *Sears's first:* Catherine Musemeche, "Mary Sears' Pioneering Ocean Research Saved Countless Lives in WWII," *Smithsonian.*

271  *By 1944, Hydro:* Williams, *Improbable Warriors*, 56.

271  *These quick-turn taskings:* Musemeche, "Mary Sears' Pioneering Ocean Research."

271  *"It does feel good":* Huntsberger, *I'll Be Seeing You*, 97.

## 25: "TO MAKE MEN FREE"

272  *In 1943 alone:* Matloff, *Strategic Planning*, 398.

272  *By 1945, the Navy:* "US Navy Personnel in World War II: Service and Casualty Statistics," Naval History and Heritage Command Online Reading Room, Navy Department Library, https://www .history.navy.mil/research/library/online-reading-room/title-list -alphabetically/u/us-navy-personnel-in-world-war-ii-service-and -casualty-statistics.html, accessed April 18, 2022.

272  *"protecting womanhood":* McAfee, Transcript of Oral History Interview of Mrs. Horton by John T. Mason Jr., 99.

272  *"control the situation":* Ibid.

273  *"members of the":* "History of the Women's Reserve," 161.

273  *"The girls were simply":* McAfee, Transcript of Oral History Interview of Mrs. Horton by John T. Mason Jr., 99.

274  *"demonstrated maturity":* Hancock, *Lady in the Navy*, 199.

274  *"Be it Maryland":* Ibid., 205.

275  *"I shall":* "M'Arthur Renews Philippines Pledge," *New York Times*, March 18, 1944.

276  *"I know well":* MacArthur, *Reminiscences*, 215–18; "The Story Behind the Photo—An Excerpt [from] MacArthur at War," Medium, May 10, 2016, https://medium.com/@littlebrown/the-story-behind -the-photo-an-excerpt-form-macarthur-at-war-dcd71cb57cb8.

277  *"the war in the":* Millett, Maslowski, and Feis, *For the Common Defense*, 420.

277  *The Army alone:* Ibid., 434.

278  *"Japanese defenders":* Williamson Murray and Allan R. Millett, *A War to Be Won: Fighting the Second World War*, 3rd ed. (Cambridge: Belknap Press: An Imprint of Harvard University Press, 2001), 511.

278  *"One night":* Danner, *What a Way to Spend a War*, 282–92.

279  *transferred Still:* Unless otherwise noted, details about Still's rescue are

drawn primarily from her memoir of her captivity. See Danner, *What a Way to Spend a War*, 281–94.

280    *"little princess"*: Ibid., 284.

282    *In nearly three:* Murray and Millett, *War to Be Won*, 514.

283    *"the light"*: Carl, *WASP Among Eagles*, 17.

### EPILOGUE: "GOOD SOLDIER"

285    *"If there was mention"*: "Letter to the Editor," May 19, 1995, MSF 366 Dorothy Stratton Papers, Box 1, Folder 15, Purdue University Archives and Special Collections, Purdue University Libraries.

287    *"I was opposed"*: Cochran, *Stars at Noon*, 223.

289    *With some notable exceptions:* Tanya L. Roth, *Her Cold War: Women in the U.S. Military, 1945–1980* (Chapel Hill: University of North Carolina Press, 2021).

290    *"When this project"*: "Hearings Before Committee on Armed Services of the House of Representatives on Sundry Legislation Affecting the Naval and Military Establishments," 80th Cong., 2nd Sess., (Washington, D.C.: US Government Printing Office, 1948), 5563.

294    *"Like most of you"*: *USCGC Stratton Commissioning*, YouTube, 2012, https://www.youtube.com/watch?v=5R5EgOdoMLw.

# INDEX

Note: Page numbers in *italics* indicate illustrations